Praise for *Verified*

"*Verified* is the book and mindset that society needs course, assuming that you want society to survive."
GUY KAWASAKI, Host of "Remarkable People" and *Mindset*

"The internet accelerated the spread of misinformation but has also given us veritable superpowers for vetting the information that we encounter. This is the genius of Caulfield and Wineburg's approach. We don't have to be passive dupes of online misinformation. We can use the wonders of an online world to become better information consumers than ever before."
CARL BERGSTROM, coauthor, *Calling Bullshit: The Art of Skepticism in a Data-Driven World*

"*Verified* is a sorely needed intervention into today's chaotic, often deceitful, information environment of influencers, ChatGPT, deepfakes, viral videos, and distrust. Offering ways to combat the mindset of knee-jerk cynicism, it responds to a world in which political power, not truth-seeking, has too often become the ultimate arbiter of truth. *Verified* will be a treasured resource for debunking internet disinformation to instructors, students, and for you (to hand to parents and skeptics)."
ANDRé BROCK, author of *Distributed Blackness: African American Cybercultures*

"*Verified* is a lifeline. With research-verified and surprisingly simple techniques, the authors show us, step-by-step, how to sift the real, useful, true information from the tsunami of online bogosity. Read it, give it to parents and their high school-age children, give it as high school graduation gifts, and please teach it at colleges and universities."
HOWARD RHEINGOLD, internet futurist and author of *Net Smart: How to Thrive Online*

"Anyone who wants to avoid being duped by all the fake news, distorted videos, and stealth ads that populate today's online universe needs this book. *Verified* offers a multitude of user-friendly tools for navigating our digital new world in which we cannot always trust the seemingly trustworthy sources we encounter."

GERALD GRAFF AND CATHY BIRKENSTEIN, authors of *They Say, I Say*

"*Verified* does more than preach against the dangers of misinformation and online mischief, it provides clear, focused strategies for navigating and researching online that should become part of every literate person's repertoire of skills. Every educator whose students touch the web—which is to say all of us—needs this book."

ELYSE EIDMAN-AADAHL, Executive Director, National Writing Project

"*Verified* offers an ethos that can help all of us understand and confidently use what we find online. This book belongs in every backpack, classroom, library, workplace, and home."

PHILLIP JONES, Grinnell College Libraries

"Caulfield and Wineburg have gone remarkably deep into how our children—and all the rest of us in America—think and learn. At the moment we are losing the battle against ignorance and misplaced assumptions, but this wonderfully written book could save us. Among many wise pieces of advice, they recommend we not only be critical thinkers, but savvy critical IGNORERS. That means learning how to detect crappy sources of information quickly and efficiently. We all need to read this."

JAY MATHEWS, education journalist

"*Verified* will help librarians, students, and anyone else move beyond well-meaning but oversimplified checklists to be better at sifting the wheat from the chaff when looking for good information online."

BRAD SIETZ, Director LOEX

"Under a deluge of disinformation and conspiracism, our modern world faces an epistemological crisis—an inability to parse reality from fiction, truth from lies. *Verified* offers readers the invaluable tools they need to navigate the flood; to regain clarity and attachment to the real world of facts, logic, and reason; and to restore the foundations of democratic discourse. It's essential reading for our chaotic times."

DAVID NEIWERT, author of *The Age of Insurrection: The Radical Right's Assault on American Democracy*

"As the value of information literacy becomes increasingly clear to society at large, *Verified* offers timely, research-based solutions to the ever-present and often elusive problem of misinformation run amok."

ROB DETMERING AND AMBER WILLENBORG, University of Louisville

"With humor, clarity, and real-world examples, the authors illustrate both simple and nuanced strategies for making sense of an increasingly complex digital realm. Students, everyday citizens, and educators at all levels will find their varied examples relevant and applicable."

ANDREA BAER AND DANIEL KIPNIS, Librarians at Rowan University

VERIFIED

HOW TO THINK STRAIGHT,
GET DUPED LESS, AND MAKE BETTER DECISIONS
ABOUT WHAT TO BELIEVE ONLINE

Mike Caulfield and Sam Wineburg

THE UNIVERSITY OF CHICAGO PRESS

Chicago and London

The University of Chicago Press, Chicago 60637
The University of Chicago Press, Ltd., London
© 2023 by Mike Caulfield and Sam Wineburg
All rights reserved. No part of this book may be used or reproduced in any
manner whatsoever without written permission, except in the case of brief
quotations in critical articles and reviews. For more information, contact
the University of Chicago Press, 1427 E. 60th St., Chicago, IL 60637.
Published 2023
Printed in Canada

32 31 30 29 28 27 26 25 24   2 3 4 5

ISBN-13: 978-0-226-82983-8 (cloth)
ISBN-13: 978-0-226-82206-8 (paper)
ISBN-13: 978-0-226-82984-5 (e-book)
DOI: https://doi.org/10.7208/chicago/9780226829845.001.0001

Library of Congress Cataloging-in-Publication Data

Names: Caulfield, Mike, author. | Wineburg, Samuel S., author.
Title: Verified : how to think straight, get duped less, and make better
    decisions about what to believe online / Mike Caulfield and Sam Wineburg.
Description: Chicago : The University of Chicago Press, 2023. | Includes
    bibliographical references and index.
Identifiers: LCCN 2023012190 | ISBN 9780226829838 (cloth) |
    ISBN 9780226822068 (paperback) | ISBN 9780226829845 (ebook)
Subjects: LCSH: Internet literacy. | Internet searching. | Information
    literacy. | Verification (Empiricism)
Classification: LCC ZA4235 .C38 2023 | DDC 025.042—dc23/eng/20230421
LC record available at https://lccn.loc.gov/2023012190

♾ This paper meets the requirements of
ANSI/NISO Z39.48-1992 (Permanence of Paper).

CONTENTS

Introduction

The video is shocking. Two women approach a historic painting in London's National Gallery and seemingly destroy it. As orange goop streaks down the painting, they read a statement about climate change and glue themselves to the gallery wall. Tweeting the video to his eighteen thousand followers, British journalist Damien Gayle reveals that the activists "have thrown tomato soup"[1] on Van Gogh's beloved *Sunflowers*, an artwork reproduced on innumerable refrigerator magnets and valued at an estimated eighty-four million dollars. By the next morning, Gayle's tweet had spread far and wide, with over forty thousand retweets and twenty thousand replies. Within twenty-four hours, the video racked up forty million views.

Reaction was swift. For a rare moment, the political left and the political right found common cause. Destruction of art, as one tweeter summarized, "represents a repudiation of civilisation and the achievements of humanity."[2] The sentiment received over ten thousand retweets. Replies and retweets advocated long prison sentences for the women or, Van Gogh–like, cutting off their ears. Others argued for compassion but mourned the loss of one of the world's great works of art.

All this outrage and concern missed a crucial fact: *Sunflowers* was behind glass.

Apart from minimal damage to the frame, the painting emerged unscathed. The soup had splashed harmlessly on the painting's protective case—a fact the protesters knew, many bystanders knew, and the gallery knew. A counterproductive and senseless act? Opinions vary. Art crime of the century? Decidedly not.

Welcome to the 2020s, where each morning provides fresh outrage only to be debunked by evening. By then, the mob has moved on to the next shiny thing, with corrections garnering a fraction of the attention the earlier confusion received.

It used to be much simpler. When Mike and Sam, the authors of this book, grew up, there were only three TV networks. The information they consumed had already passed through society's gatekeepers: subject matter experts, TV producers, newspaper editors, librarians, and a host of others. Mistakes crept in, even then. But there were widely accepted mechanisms for separating fact from fiction. The consequences of getting things wrong ranged from a ding on one's reputation for minor indiscretions to outright dismissals for mangling the truth.

Yet that age had its own problems. Three news stations often presented just two points of view, if that. Wide swaths of lived experience were ignored. Niche information was often not available at all.

The internet was supposed to solve all that. It promised an information superhighway that would put us in the driver's seat.

So how come it feels like the internet is driving *us*?

Think of this book as the internet driver's manual you never got. We can't guarantee an accident-free existence as a result of the techniques you'll learn here. However, they will allow you to do the following:

- Verify news stories and other events in as little as thirty seconds (seriously)
- Determine if the article you're citing is by a reputable scholar or a quack
- Detect the slippery tactics scammers use to make their sites look credible
- Decide in a minute if that shocking video is truly shocking or something ripped out of context
- Deduce who's behind a site—even when its ownership is cleverly disguised
- Uncover if that feature story is actually a puff piece planted by a foreign government
- Use Wikipedia wisely to gain a foothold on new topics and provide leads for digging deeper

Instead of being driven by emotion and outrage, you'll come to see your gut reactions as precious gifts that signal you to pause, take a breath, and ask a basic question: Is what I'm looking at even what I think it is? As the strategies in this book become second nature, you'll gain confidence and develop clarity in understanding how the internet works.

This book lays out a problem and proposes a series of solutions. The problem is that we left the three-channel-TV-world years ago, but the skills many people learn today remain stuck there. This is true even for those of you who have grown up in the new networked environment. You may have been born in 2003, but you've likely been taught a media literacy approach from 1978.

We are set up to fail when we apply analog concepts to a digital medium. Instead of being in the driver's seat, we end up being taken for a ride. Age-old intuitions about how to sort truth from falsehood steer us wrong. Viewing orange goop slithering down yellow sunflowers, we still act like we are in that old world, having seen something on TV or heard it from a friend. As you'll see later in this book, the average person (wrongly) falls back on their own sense of *plausibility*, attempting to answer whether something is true by asking whether it *seems* true, *looks* credible, or *feels* authoritative.

Our solution to this problem? We need a new way of approaching the web—a way that makes quick work of clickbait and sets up deeper investigations for better success.

Take that Van Gogh video. The people who asked whether such a destruction was plausible were duped. There was a video, after all. It was described by someone who is "verified" by Twitter. It didn't appear altered. It felt possible. Old, preinternet thinking would take these elements into account and render judgment. The internet, however, provides better options—instantly. For one, you could visit the National Gallery's Twitter account, where you'd find a statement, very soon after the event, that the painting was unharmed. If you were waking up to the controversy, you could check the *Sunflower*'s Wikipedia page, freshly updated with the important context about the glass screen. Up a bit earlier? A Google search would show an article with the crucial information.[3]

While this book is relatively compact, it represents years of work in figuring out which information literacy skills matter most. Mike's work began in 2010 at a small public college, as he puzzled over why students taught traditional media literacy skills remained "bad at the web." He set out to build a new domain of "civic digital literacy." Sam's work began in 2015, when he and his colleagues at Stanford University discovered the crucial differences between how professional fact-checkers and others determined credibility and plausibility on the web.[4]

What we learned from our work was both shocking and hopeful. We documented how professional fact-checkers cut through layers of hype to arrive at reliable information, leaving many others, including intelligent academics, in the dust. Examining an unfamiliar website, these professionals didn't dwell on whether it was a dot-org or a dot-com. They knew that this distinction, last relevant during the internet's Paleolithic era, means little today. Fact-checkers momentarily glanced at—or ignored entirely—a site's "About" page, the web's version of a curated Instagram profile. They knew that spiffy-looking graphics and a fancy interface indicated little more than a well-spent budget. They understood how frequently first impressions mislead.

Instead of reading a website like a static piece of print, fact-checkers saw it as part of a vast, electronically linked, *webbed* network. Here is what's hopeful from what we learned: The way to understand an element in a network is to see how it connects to and forms a pattern with other elements—a change in perspective you can learn. To use the web effectively, you need to exploit its web-like features. You need to use the web to *check* the web.

Print-based conceptions of critical thinking don't cut it. Skillfully navigating the internet requires conceptions of critical thinking tailored to a digital environment. We set out to distill a small set of flexible techniques that would allow users to resolve easy questions quickly and inform difficult ones in not much more time. And we committed to testing our ideas in rigorous studies with people from all walks of life.

Along with teams of fellow researchers, we field-tested our approach with students in middle school, high school, and college, as well as with adults in the United States, Canada, Sweden, and the United Kingdom. To date, thirteen separate studies involving nearly ten thousand participants have shown the effectiveness of our approach in helping people make better choices online.[5] And in one of the most recent studies, students showed a sixfold increase in use of fact-checking techniques and a fivefold increase in citations of appropriate context after only seven hours of instruction.[6] Today, Mike's SIFT methods (discussed in chapter 1) have become a mainstay of information literacy workshops, while the Civic Online Reasoning curriculum developed by Sam's team at Stanford is used in high schools all over the country.[7] Together, our methods appear on hundreds of high school, college, and university websites.

We can't promise that if you follow the advice in these pages, you'll never again forward a celebrity death hoax or cite a sketchy publication in your health policy paper. What we can guarantee is that those errors will be fewer and farther between. Just as important, you'll become more confident sharing things that matter to you. When you forward a striking story on something you're passionate about, your answer to the question of how you know this is real won't be "Well, uh . . . I'm not sure" but rather "It's real and here's how I know."

Whatever your politics or values, we hope you agree that when reading online, you should take at least minimal action to evaluate the sources and claims that flash across your screen. This book shows you how to do that—quickly—using methods employed by the most competent web searchers. Along the way, you'll become more accurate in your assessments and waste less time reading nonsense.

Let's get started.

Get Quick Context

IT CAN TAKE AS LITTLE AS
THIRTY SECONDS—SERIOUSLY!

We're going to start off this book a bit morbidly. We're going to talk about death hoaxes.

One of the most persistent genres of hoaxes on the internet has been the death hoax.[1] Britney Spears has been dying since at least 2001.[2] Assorted YouTube personalities "die" occasionally as well. Even Keanu Reeves, action star and generally decent human, is sometimes reported as dead. Although the path to internet death varies, it tends to follow some broad patterns. A 2014 analysis found 16 percent of internet death hoaxes involved supposed snowboarding accidents. A full 20 percent involved "falls from cliffs."[3]

To some extent, this isn't new. When Mike was a kid, ages ago, the story was that "Mikey" (a kid made famous by a 1972 cereal commercial) had died eating Pop Rocks (a candy that crackled when you ate it). The story was passed around in hushed tones on the playground: "You heard about Mikey, right? He ate Pop Rocks while drinking Pepsi and they expanded so fast they ruptured his stomach!"

Back then, before the internet, your options were limited if you wanted to figure out if such a story was true. Really, your only option was to dig into the plausibility of the story. Could a crackling candy combined with a popular soda generate enough force to burst a stomach (children of the twenty-first century: think Mentos and soda if it helps)? What if normally no, but Mikey had a genetic defect? On the other side of the equation, if Pop Rocks were really that dangerous, wouldn't you have heard about that?

Such analysis may have made us feel smarter about the stories we chose to believe, but that intelligence was mostly an illusion.[4] Mike (the coauthor of this book, not the child star) was firmly in the Mikey-didn't-die camp, based on his belief that Pop Rocks couldn't have ruptured anything. This belief was grounded in—well, the assumptions of a fourth grader about human anatomy and obscure chemical reactions. Others pointed to compelling evidence for death—if that kid from the commercial was still alive, why hadn't we seen him recently? Pretty suspicious, right?

Fast forward to today. You'd think we'd have this problem licked. In the era before the web, all we had was speculation. But today, if you are told someone died, checking whether that's true takes seconds. The steps would be:

1 Do a news search looking for reports of that person's death.
2 That's it.

The Keanu Reeves Rule is simple: If Keanu Reeves were to die, there would likely be a bunch of publications covering it. If you search and find there's no one covering it except an anonymous Facebook poster or Instagram account, then Keanu Reeves is probably still alive.[5]

What would be a bad way to figure out if a celebrity died? Well, it would look like that 1970s playground method. Keanu Reeves died while snowboarding, you say? Did Keanu Reeves seem like a winter sports person? Was the weather good for snowboarding today? What's the relative frequency of people in their 50s dying in such accidents?

All of the above questions may *feel* like analysis. But it's ridiculous to approach the problem this way in a world where the answer to the question we actually care about—whether the celebrity died—is readily available. And, as we'll see, it's also potentially harmful to use this playground method when approaching questions of significant social or personal import.

The Three Contexts

Over the past decade, we've looked at how students and the general public judge information that reaches them through the web. Our first finding will not surprise you, given both the state of the world and your social media feeds: on the internet, people reason quite poorly.[6]

The second finding is more surprising. Many so-called experts assumed that the mistakes people made on the web resulted from a lack of critical thinking, at least as critical thinking has been traditionally defined. It certainly looked that way to high school teachers. Presented with web information of unknown origin and veracity, students were unsure about which sources to trust and what evidence to believe. When asked to explain their judgments, students engaged in ungrounded speculation, doubled down on first impressions, and leaned into bias. But when we looked at why people got confused, we found it wasn't their thinking that malfunctioned. In fact, people were thinking quite hard. But their thinking was like the playground logic of Mikey and the Pop Rocks. Confronted with a question, they immediately raced toward those other questions: Does this seem plausible? Does this match how I think the world works?

Those are not bad questions. However, in areas where people have little expertise, or lack direct experience, asking such questions isn't the first order of business. The first task when confronted with the unfamiliar is not analysis. It is the gathering of context. Let's consider three crucial contexts that ground reasoning on the web and elsewhere:

- The context of the *source*. What's the reputation of the source of information that you arrive at, whether through a social feed, a shared link, or a Google search result?
- The context of the *claim*. What have others said about the claim? If it's a story, what's the larger story? If a statistic, what's the larger context?
- Finally, the context of *you*. What is your level of expertise in the area? What is your interest in the claim? What makes such a claim or source compelling to you, and what could change that?[7]

We found when students attended to these contexts, spending as little as thirty seconds reflecting and seeking basic information on the web, something happened. Something *stunning* happened. Supposedly weak "critical thinkers" became strong critical thinkers, without any additional training in logic or analysis. They made better decisions, leaned less on faulty presuppositions, and were fooled less by deceptive appearances and dirty tricks. They often showed greater nuance and stronger logical argument.

How could thirty seconds of simple web techniques, applied consistently, result in such transformation? While the death-hoax example is relatively simple, it illustrates how important gaining a quick context can be. People who don't seek context find themselves devoting a lot of thought to the issue. Their thinking, however, is not a whole lot more advanced than mere playground speculation. People who aren't experts in snowboarding or the state of Keanu Reeves's health will find themselves trying to apply logic to a lack of facts, essentially multiplying by zero. Lacking knowledge of whether the source of the information is a close friend of Reeves's or an internet rando, they judge it by its look and feel, or maybe simply by whether it agrees with their intuitions.

If you remember the *Sunflowers* story from this book's introduction, you'll recognize this behavior. While mistakes initially appear to be related to a deficit of thinking, they are much more related to *doing*. Once students engaged in context-seeking, the thinking often sorted itself out. With a dose of context, they were able to solve simple problems (such as a death hoax) quickly, and they grounded deeper investigations in better sources, assumptions, and data.

The death hoax is a simple example, but simple examples can be instructive. Note the difference between trying to reconstruct probabilities of death by snowboarding for specific celebrities versus attending to a small set of initial concerns.

"Do I Know What I'm Looking At?"

Let's jump into context-building. First, begin with the "context of you"—in this case, realizing that you are unlikely to have any useful knowledge to bring to this subject. Looking at the post, text, or update you have received, you ask the most important initial question. That question is not "Is this true?" but rather "Do I know what I'm looking at here?" *Do I recognize the source? Have I heard this elsewhere from reputable sources?* If there's evidence—a screenshot of a headline: *Do I know that it is not a photoshopped image, or am I merely guessing?*

Assuming the answers there are "no," "no," and "yes, you caught me, I'm guessing," there are two pieces of context that could help support the claim (in this instance, the idea the celebrity has died).

- The person you hear it from knows the celebrity well (e.g., is a good friend, spouse, or family member).
- When you search for reporting on it, a number of reputable publications say the person has died.

If one of those things is true, all your dorm-room speculation doesn't matter. The news is likely credible. If both of those things are false, it's unlikely to be a real story.

Of course, this is a simple example. Outside zombie cinema, there's not that much middle ground between alive and dead. But by making such context-seeking a habit—and by seeking context before engaging in analysis—you can get further faster on a wide variety of issues. And these two aspects—thinking about the authority of the source you heard it from and seeing what others say—will be central.

Introducing SIFT

It's one thing to know the context you need. It's another to build a habit of seeking it out. In our scholarly work, we've often pretested participants on examples, telling them that they should assess the credibility of a claim by whatever means might help, including leaving a site and searching the web. We get a variety of responses. Some participants remained glued to the original website, descending into "plausibility analysis"—that is, given what I know, do I think this thing is likely to have happened? Does it "sound" right? Never mind that the issue at hand is about cell biology and one's experience consists solely of having watched the TV show *House, M.D.*

More perplexing is the response of a smaller number of participants, often formulated as "I'd have to know." For example, a student might say, "To know if this was credible, I'd have to know more about the author." That's true, of course, but misses the bigger question: What's stopping the student from finding out more? It's a simple act of opening another tab and starting the search. Still, for some students, the gap between thought and action proves to be too large.

For this reason, the main tool we give students is formulated not as a set of questions to ask but as a set of *things to do* before they start reasoning about a specific piece of content that reaches them through the web. Here's a brief definition of these "things to do," which we'll return to throughout the book. We've put them in an easy-to-remember acronym: SIFT.

- *Stop.* Ask yourself what you really know about the claim and the source that's sharing it. For the moment, forget about questions of truth or falsehood. Do you really know what you're looking at? Are you sure? If you find it upsetting or surprising, why?
- *Investigate the source.* Do a quick check to see if the source is trustworthy for this purpose. In a lot of cases, for simple claims, you can stop here if the source is good.
- *Find other coverage.* Whether you are looking at a news report or a research claim, take a second to zoom out and see what other sources say. If the story or claim is not being picked up by other reputable sources, proceed cautiously.
- *Trace the claim, quote, or media to the original context.* Sometimes the first source you encountered isn't great, but it links to where it got its information. Go to that original source and judge (a) whether it's reputable, and (b) whether it actually supports the assertion.

Let's look at a few quick examples, including some where rather smart people got spun around in circles.

Stop! (Or, How to Fail at Source-Checking
Even If You're the *New York Times*)

On March 7, 2018, an interesting Editors' Note ran under a column by Bari Weiss, at that time a *New York Times* columnist: "An earlier version of this essay cited criticism of the commentator Dave Rubin as an example of left-leaning attacks on liberals in the public sphere, and linked to tweets that described him as a fascist. Those tweets came from an account that has been reported to be fake. Therefore the example and the links have been removed." Weiss's column was titled "We're All Fascists Now." She complained that the far left had been attacking even centrists as fascists. Her point? Antifascism had gone so far that it was doing damage to even progressive causes.

Central to the column was the (soon-to-be-removed) example of Dave Rubin, a political commentator with a popular podcast, who, Bari Weiss pointed out, had been attacked by the antifascist left: "Dave Rubin, a liberal commentator who favors abortion rights, opposes the death penalty and is married to a man, yet is denounced as an 'Anti-L.G.B.T. fascist' and a 'fascist lieutenant' for criticizing identity politics."

Wow. As they say, *big if true*. The left criticizing a gay man as being an anti-LGBT fascist? Clearly an example of political correctness run amok. And Weiss initially provided receipts of sorts, linking the two quoted terms here ("Anti-L.G.B.T. fascist" and "fascist lieutenant") to comments by an antifascist group, with a significant following, making exactly these sorts of charges. The group was apparently even plotting to shut down ("deplatform") Rubin's event![8]

This is one of the simplest sorts of claims. When we look at this "Official Antifa" account, we don't have to ask about expertise. No matter whether those running the account are right or wrong in what

Official Antifa
@OfficialAntifa

Looks like the Fascist Lieutenant @RubinReport is speaking at an Alt-Right event today. You know what to do, comrades. #Antifa #NoPlatform

Dave Rubin ✔ @RubinReport
Speaking at the @sfliberty event later today. As you can see it's some pretty far right craziness going on over here.

10:12 AM 29 - Apr 2017

FIGURE 1.1 One of two @OfficialAntifa tweets cited by Weiss (https://twitter.com/official antifa/status/858368322039164928)

they believe, they are an authoritative source on their own publicly expressed beliefs. The one real question here is, "Do they represent the left?" as alleged by Weiss.

Ah, says someone from the back of the class, "What does it mean to represent the left, and can any single organization truly claim to . . ."

OK, stop. Just *stop*. Those are good insights. And we can talk about them later. But that's not what we're talking about at the moment. Before we get all Philosophy 101 here, let's answer the simple question: Who runs the @OfficialAntifa account? In other words, do we even know what we're looking at? Is this what I think it is?

So let's *investigate the source*. Ready? You've packed a lunch and cleared out your calendar? All set to spend the day investigating? Let's start by throwing the account name into Google and seeing how reliable sources have described it.[9]

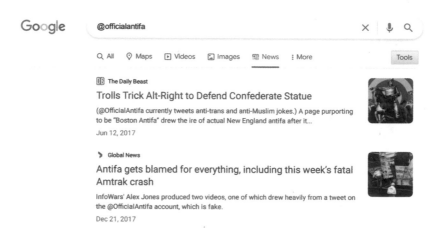

FIGURE 1.2 Search results of news articles available in early March 2018 mentioning the @OfficialAntifa Twitter account. (Google and the Google logo are trademarks of Google LLC.)

OK, forget about that packed lunch. We're done, actually. As you can see from these results, available the day that Weiss ran her column, the account is a known fake account.[10] It's not related to the left at all. It's as much an antifa account as *The Onion* or Clickhole is a news site. Maybe even less so, as the examples cited here of its past behavior seem to indicate it exists not for the purpose of humor but to fool right-wing people into believing it is real, while making outrageous proclamations. Just as they fooled Bari Weiss.

Please notice what we're *not* doing here: We're *not* asking, "Does this sound like antifa?" We're not playing the "is it possible to die from Pop Rocks" playground game. We're *not* going into long-winded philosophical questions about the relative representativeness of various sectors of liberalism. We're simply opening another tab and taking a few seconds to make sure we understand what we're looking at. And we're doing that *before* we start thinking about it.

FIGURE 1.3 Tweet from a few weeks before COVID-19 was declared a pandemic (https://twitter.com/RSantosTV/status/1230933950249369605)

Investigate the Source

Sometimes a source check can be as simple as hovering over a profile. Really. It can be that simple. Take this example from February 2020, where a person states that the first COVID-19 case in Sacramento, California, has been discovered.

We note that the account has a blue checkmark, but checkmarks do not mean that the person is reliable. Who is she, exactly? We'll "hover," putting our mouse over her photo, until her brief Twitter bio pops up.[11]

When we do that, we find two things we like to see in sources. First, Renee Santos is in a particular "position to know" here: this is a claim about a COVID-19 case in Sacramento, and Santos is a local

Renee Santos ✓
@RSantosTV

Follow ∨

Follow

Sacramento County has confirmed Coronavirus amento

Renee Santos ✓
@RSantosTV

amento, CA

Emmy Award-winning reporter @CBSSacramento. **Diehard** @Lakers @Raiders @Dodgers **fan. Opinions are my own.** @Fresno_State **alumna.**

1,122 Following   **3,016** Followers

FIGURE 1.4   Hovering over a name on Twitter to reveal profile information, February 2020 (https://twitter.com/RSantosTV/status/1230933950249369605)

Sacramento reporter. Second, her position, reporter, puts her in a class of people that have reputational incentives to get things right. That doesn't mean she's always right. But she's likely to be more careful with the truth than your average opinion columnist or political activist, because getting things wrong in her profession has more significant professional repercussions.

Compare Renee Santos's tweet to this next example, again, from February 2020. It's an article about how various government reactions to the pandemic were supposedly power grabs by the "New World Order," an underground government with plans to take over the world.

Maybe there is a grain of truth to this, maybe not. Just looking at it, it's hard to say, at least at first. It's certainly the case that history provides examples of some groups using crises to take power, and we'd be foolish to think such actions are impossible.

But, just as we saw with Bari Weiss's "antifa" example, this question— whether such a thing is plausible—shouldn't be our *first* question.

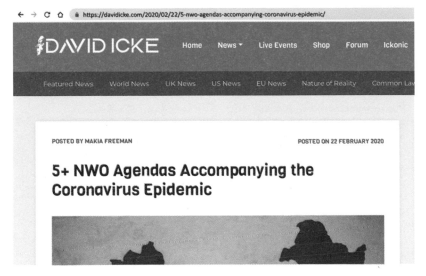

FIGURE 1.5 Article from DavidIcke.com (https://davidicke.com/2020/02/22/5-nwo
-agendas-accompanying-coronavirus-epidemic/)

Our first question is always, *Do we know what we're looking at?* Let's
take a look.

To this point we've used a couple of simple and straightforward
techniques. In the Bari Weiss example, we opened a tab and did a
search. In the reporter from Sacramento example, we hovered. This
next technique is the *tiniest* bit more complex, but it is one of the
most useful techniques for looking into organizations and publications with which you are not familiar. We call it "Just Add Wikipedia."

Yes, we know, you're probably wondering why a book on finding truth on the internet is bringing up Wikipedia at all. Isn't Wikipedia bad?

In a word, no. Later on, you'll read a whole chapter where we explain why. For now, let's just say that when you want to get a quick
read on an organization or publication, Wikipedia remains one of the

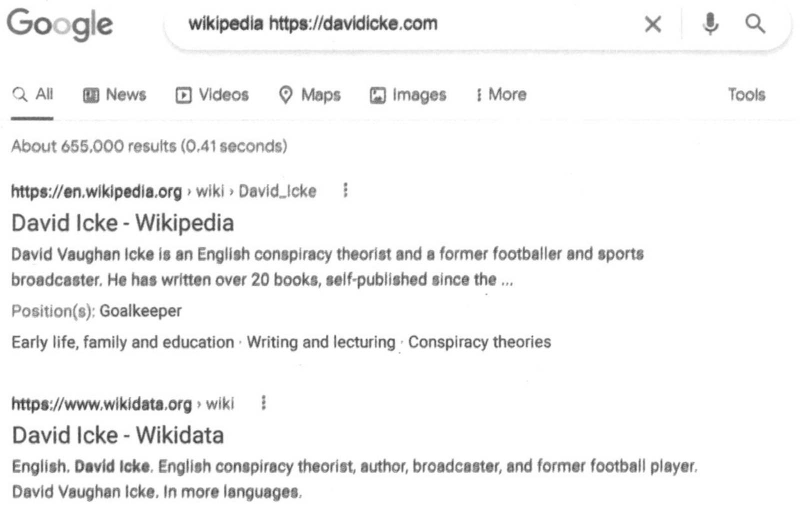

FIGURE 1.6 Quick search to surface Wikipedia pages related to websites. (Google and the Google logo are trademarks of Google LLC.)

best resources out there. It is often the most frequent first stop of fact-checkers the world over.[12]

But we didn't come here to fight—we'll have a lot more to say about Wikipedia. For now, we just want to show you how to use it on a relatively simple source check.

Back to our "NWO agendas" article. It's on a site run by David Icke called DavidIcke.com. We're going to put that domain (davidicke.com) into a search engine, along with the term "Wikipedia" and hit enter. There's nothing magic about this search, by the way. It's just a quick way to find a relevant Wikipedia article. And, in this case, it works, floating an article on Icke to the top of the results.

Even before we click into the article, we sense trouble. Do you see

David Icke   ⊕ 🔒

From Wikipedia, the free encyclopedia

David Vaughan Icke (/ˈdeɪvɪd vɔːn aɪk/; born 29 April 1952) is an English conspiracy theorist and a former footballer and sports broadcaster.[1][3][4][5][6] He has written over 20 books, self-published since the mid-1990s, and spoken in more than 25 countries.[7][8][9]

In 1990, he visited a psychic who told him he was on Earth for a purpose and would receive messages from the spirit world.[10] This led him to state in 1991 he was a "Son of the Godhead"[6] and that the world would soon be devastated by tidal waves and earthquakes, predictions he repeated on the BBC show *Wogan*.[11][12] His appearance led to public ridicule.[13] The books Icke wrote over the next 11 years developed his world view of New Age conspiracism.[14] His endorsement of an antisemitic forgery, *The Protocols of the Elders of Zion*, in *The Robots' Rebellion* (1994) and *And the Truth Shall Set You Free* (1995) led his publisher to stop handling his books, which have been self-published since then.[9]

David Icke

Icke in 2013

Born	David Vaughan Icke
	29 April 1952 (age 70)
	Leicester, England

FIGURE 1.7 Wikipedia page for David Icke with the part that jumps out at us highlighted (https://en.wikipedia.org/wiki/David_Icke)

the brief description pulled from Wikipedia? It reads, "David Vaughan Icke is an English conspiracy theorist and former footballer."

So, OK, a conspiracy theorist. How bad can it be? Let's click in and find out.

Note that the claim that Icke is a conspiracy theorist is not made lightly. There are no less than five footnotes supporting it. In fact, his only other real claims to fame seem to be as a soccer player and sportscaster.

Now, if you still are worried that this charge is being thrown around lightly, you can click through Wikipedia's footnotes and take a look. Let's look behind footnote 3.

Um . . . yeah. We're as open minded as the rest, but we prefer to get our health policy analysis from the set of people who *don't* think the world is ruled by a secret race of lizard overlords.

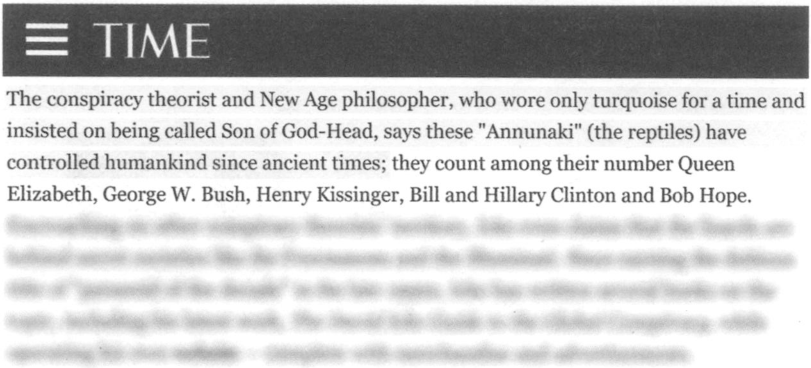

☰ TIME

The conspiracy theorist and New Age philosopher, who wore only turquoise for a time and insisted on being called Son of God-Head, says these "Annunaki" (the reptiles) have controlled humankind since ancient times; they count among their number Queen Elizabeth, George W. Bush, Henry Kissinger, Bill and Hillary Clinton and Bob Hope.

FIGURE 1.8 Linked *Time* article noting interesting beliefs of Icke, highlighted here (https://content.time.com/time/specials/packages/article/0,28804,1860871_1860876_1861029,00.html)

Find Better Coverage

Back to our death-hoax example. Did Keanu Reeves really die in a snowboarding accident?

OK, well, hindsight is twenty-twenty. It's fairly obvious that the actor who has since 2012 starred in a bunch of *John Wick* films and a *Bill & Ted's Excellent Adventure* sequel did not die in a snowboarding accident in 2012. But it wasn't obvious at the time, which is why quite a few people fell for it.

We come back to this case because it's a good example of how a lot of what people have been taught to look for in a source fails—or, rather, makes them *worse* at the web than had no one taught them anything at all!

We've already talked about how competent web readers would approach this sort of question. They'd learn it was fake (or at least *misinformed*) in maybe ten seconds, tops.

A short search here reveals top stories about Reeves, including a

Actor Keanu Reeves Dies In Snowboard Accident

Actor Keanu Reeves is reported to have died shortly after a snowboard accident earlier today - January 9, 2011.

The actor & novice snowboarder was vacationing at the Zermatt ski resort in Zermatt, Switzerland with family and friends. Witnesses indicate that Keanu Reeves lost control of his snowboard and struck a tree at a high rate of speed.

Keanu Reeves was air lifted by ski patrol teams to a local hospital, however, it is believed that the actor died instantly from the impact of the crash. The actor was wearing a helmet at the time of the accident and drugs and alcohol do not appear to have played any part in his death.

FIGURE 1.9 Story about Keanu Reeves "dying," January 2011 (http://keanu.reeves .mediafetcher.com/news/top_stories/actor_skiing.php)

Google | keanu reeves | × ⬤ Q

Q All 📰 News 🖼 Images ▶ Videos 📖 Books ⋮ More   Tools

Recent ▾ Sorted by date ▾ Hide Duplicates ▾ Clear

Ⓜ MovieWeb

5 Ways Speed 3 Can Be Saved From Box Office Failure

Keanu Reeves has starred in cult classic movies, from Bill & Ted's Excellent Adventure to The Matrix. He is also no stranger to sequels, with his most...

10 hours ago

Metro

Keanu Reeves and girlfriend Alexandra Grant look relaxed at JFK

Hollywood star Keanu Reeves and girlfriend Alexandra Grant looked relaxed as they made their way through JFK airport at the weekend.

11 hours ago

The Independent Singapore News

Keanu Reeves makes a young fan's day at airport

In a now-viral thread on Twitter, TV producer Andrew Kimmel who was on the same flight as Reeves said the actor was at the airport luggage claim area when...

FIGURE 1.10 News search results for Keanu Reeves. (Google and the Google logo are trademarks of Google LLC.)

Mike Caulfield
5m

•••

Um, this is not the "cool nature" story I was looking for

LIVESCIENCE.COM

Millions of palm-sized, flying spiders could invade the east coast, scientists say
Scientists believe that Joro spiders arrived in the U.S. as stowaways in a shipping container.

FIGURE 1.11 Mock-up of a *Live Science* story card, April 2022. (Photo by Christine Butler, licensed under Creative Commons Attribution 2.0.)

viral video where Reeves graciously answers a string of questions from a young fan at the airport, a behavior usually seen as incompatible with being dead. No stories about Keanu Reeves's funeral. Had Reeves suffered a fatal accident, we would expect to see multiple stories about it, and fewer stories about heartwarming airport interactions. So, we can rule this out.

These quick checks are not just about *debunking*. In fact, one of the most common experiences we've had in this work is realizing that some sensational story that we had initially dismissed as false was actually true. Or at least somewhat true. Take this story about palm-sized spiders, flitting across Facebook in March 2022.[13]

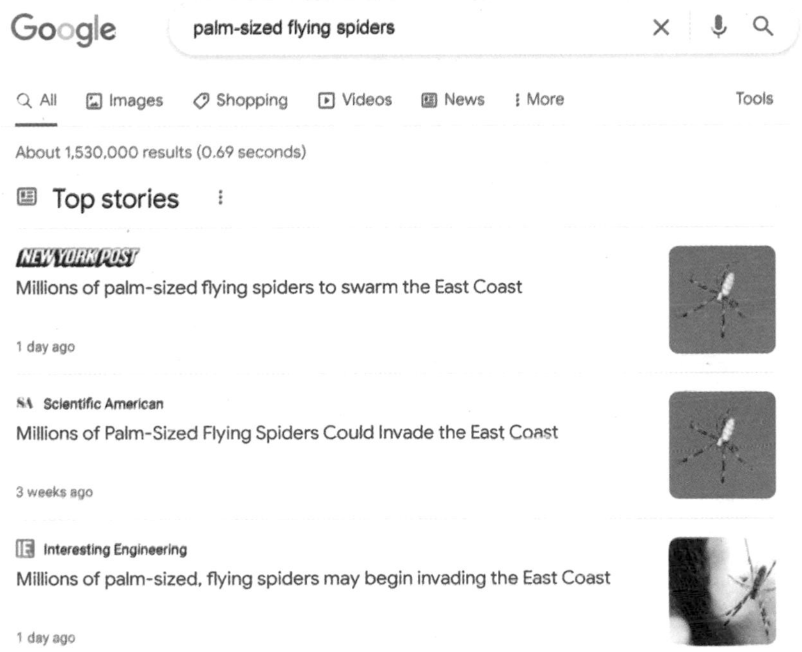

FIGURE 1.12 Search results for "palm-sized flying spiders" shortly after the first article was discovered, March 2022. (Google and the Google logo are trademarks of Google LLC.)

This can't be true, right? Palm-sized, flying spiders? We apply our "find" move and get the results in figure 1.12.

While the first result may not be the best source of science information, the second result and many subsequent results not shown are from reliable publications. This spidery thing, whatever it is, looks like it may be happening.

Now note that when you get a result like this, you don't stop here. If you are truly alarmed by palm-sized flying spiders, you want to click into the better articles and get the relevant context. Given that they are, well, *palm-sized flying spiders*, we thought this might be worth a few more minutes of our time, and so we clicked through the links. In this case, the story is a bit mixed. If you're living in the American Northeast, it does look like you may soon be acquainted with this monster arachnid. That said, clicking into the actual article may allay some of your fears. As the *Scientific American* article notes, "True to its mythical reputation, the Joro spider is stunning to look at, with a large, round, jet-black body cut across with bright yellow stripes, and flecked on its underside with intense red markings. But despite its threatening appearance and its fearsome standing in folklore, the Joro spider's bite is rarely strong enough to break through the skin, and its venom poses no threat to humans, dogs or cats unless they are allergic."[14] Joro may even help reduce some other pests, such as mosquitos. So, is this post "true"? For something like this, that's a limiting question. Rather, in our case, it might be more productive to say that we initially dismissed it as false, were slightly terrified to find out it might be true, then relieved to find out that it was not true in the way that we most feared. At each step of the way, we gathered the context around the claim (what do others say?), which helped to refine and improve our reaction to the story in a way that simply speculating on whether such spiders exist could never do.[15]

Trace Claims, Quotes, and Media to Their Original Context

So far, we have ourselves a tidy little model. There are three contexts (source, claim, and you). There are the first three moves of SIFT (stop, investigate, and find). The contexts more or less match the moves. For the first context, the context of the source (and it's almost too easy a match here), you *investigate the source*. For the second context, the context of the claim, you *find better coverage*. For the third context, the context of you, you ponder your own strengths and limitations. You ask yourself what you think you're looking at and how sure you are about it: you "stop." (OK, our order is a bit off here, but they match).

Three contexts. Three moves. So why do we want to go mucking it up with a fourth item? Are we asymmetrical sadists?

The answer, as we're sure you're tired of hearing by now, lies in what we've learned in teaching these skills over the last five years. Take our flying spider example.

In that example there were two sources to consider. The first was the *sharing source*. In that mock-up, we made Mike the sharing source—that is, the source who passed the information on to friends and family.

If it were an article on web credibility that Mike was sharing, maybe the sharing source would have been enough (as it was for us in the earlier example where a Sacramento reporter posted about COVID-19 in Sacramento). Sometimes the person sharing something with you knows a lot about the subject. If they say the article is legit, you pretty much take their word for it.

Other times it's more complex. If the person sharing isn't known to have extensive knowledge of that field but is sharing a story from a news outlet, the authority of the claim being made is derived from the *reporting source*, the news outlet where the person sharing found the item.

This seems like an obvious point, but we've found that some people struggle with it. Presented with a TikTok Crocs influencer sharing an article from the *New York Times*, we sometimes see students say something to the effect of "I checked out the source, and this is not a spider expert. They sell Crocs!" Or maybe, in our example, "He works in media literacy!" Nice try, nerd!

In any case, in this example, the authority for the claim came from the *reporting source*, and that's where we had to go to evaluate the claim.

A headline can be deceiving, and in this case, it was. When we clicked through to obtain some much-needed context about these spiders (which, need we remind you, can fly nearly *one hundred miles*), we found an authoritative source, *Scientific American*, a science magazine that's been around for 176 years, that presented a far different story than the headline.

When we encourage you to *trace claims, quotes, and media to the original context*, we don't intend for you to have to find your way to some original spreadsheet from Spider Labs, Incorporated. We don't want you to have to become an arachnologist just to figure out whether spiders are likely to ruin your spring break. But as information travels on the web and makes its way from researcher to newspaper article to blog entry and ends up on your Aunt Velma's Facebook page, context is the first casualty. Seeing evidence in its original context can prevent you from selling your New England house in a panic just because a headline writer at *Live Science* was feeling saucy.

And there you have it—SIFT. We stopped. We investigated the source. We found other coverage. We did a very rudimentary tracing of the claim to the original context (OK, we clicked a link). Sometimes the source we found was good enough to stop there. Sometimes the story was true, but we needed a better version. In most cases, we were able to verify the original source in under a minute. When things got a bit more complex, we dug a little deeper to find better context. Unlike the playground children of the 1970s, we didn't sit on a mountaintop meditating on the question whether a crackling candy really ruptured someone's stomach. Which we should come back to here: Did that kid from the Life Cereal commercials really die? Are Pop Rocks dangerous? Are stomachs really so fragile?

We've come this far. Now you have the skills. So maybe we'll leave this one for you to investigate yourself.

It will take as little as thirty seconds—seriously!

Takeaways

▷ When we encounter something online, our first question shouldn't be "Is this true?" but rather "Do we know what we're looking at?"

▷ Knowing what we're looking at requires getting quick context. What do we know about the source? What have others said about the claim? We don't need to make a production of it. Focus on getting basic context first.

▷ SIFT (Stop, Investigate the Source, Find Other Coverage, Trace the Claim to the Original Context) is a way to help you get the sort of quick context that is essential to knowing what you're looking at.

▷ Practicing the moves of SIFT can help you answer simple questions quickly and ground your understanding before moving on to more nuanced investigations.

Cheap Signals

OR, HOW NOT TO GET DUPED

The guides for teaching media literacy go by a dizzying variety of acronyms—RADCAB, ABC, CARS, and the most popular, CRAAP, which stands for *currency, relevance, authority, accuracy,* and *purpose.*[1] These guides list questions to determine a website's credibility. In the version that appears in figure 2.1, each question gets a score, and if the score is high, you can assume the site is trustworthy. Let's try it out.

You're researching the health issues connected to sugar. How much is too much? Is sugar linked to obesity, or is the culprit a sedentary lifestyle?

One of the first sites to come up is the International Life Sciences Institute, ilsi.org. It looks professional. Its home page features pictures of succulent fruit and healthy whole grains. Plus, it's a dot-org.

Just to be safe, you grab your checklist.

- *When was the information published or posted?* Recently—the home page lists a 2022 update.
- *Has the information been reviewed, revised, or updated?* Not sure, but

CRAAP Test for Evaluating Sources SCORE CARD

Use the questions below to help you evaluate your sources. This can be used for print and online sources. Answer the questions then score each section from **1 – 10** (**1** = unreliable, **10** = excellent). Add up the scores to help you decide whether you should use that particular source for your assignment.

Currency .... ☐

YES NO

When was the information published/posted? _____

Has the information been updated? ☐ ☐

Does the information need to be current for your needs? ☐ ☐

Relevance .... ☐

Does the information you found match the topic for your assignment? ☐ ☐

Have you looked at other sources before selecting this one? ☐ ☐

Are your questions answered by this source? ☐ ☐

Authority .... ☐

Who is the author or publisher of the information? _____

Can you find and verify the author or publisher's credentials? ☐ ☐

Does the URL help you determine the source? (.edu; .com; .gov) ☐ ☐

Accuracy .... ☐

Can you verify this information in another source? ☐ ☐

Did the author back up his/her statements with evidence and list sources? ☐ ☐

Are there lots of spelling or grammar errors or typos? ☐ ☐

Purpose .... ☐

What is the purpose of the information? Does it aim to teach, entertain, sell, etc.? _____

Is the information unbiased; does the author or publisher seem impartial? ☐ ☐

Are there political, religious, cultural or other biases present?. ☐ ☐

Scoring: **TOTAL SCORE** ☐
45-50 Excellent • 40-44 Good • 35-39 Average
30-34 May or may not be Acceptable
Below 30 Not an acceptable source

The Score Card is adapted from the CRAAP test created at the Meriam Library at California State University Chico.

FIGURE 2.1 Example of a CRAAP test checklist. (Source: Pikes Peak State College, https://libguides.ppcc.edu/c.php?g=16624&p=3509587.)

FIGURE 2.2 Website of the International Life Sciences Institute (www.ilsi.org), January 2022

the site displays something called the "Gold Transparency Rating" from 2021.

- *Are the links functional and up to date?* All of them.
- *Does the information relate to your topic or answer the question?* There are sixty-one different entries about sugar: articles, webinars, and scholarly papers—and not just from the United States.
- *Who is the author/publisher/sponsor?* The International Life Sciences Institute is a "non-profit, charitable organization organized under Section 501(c)(3) of the U.S. Internal Revenue Code." The organization follows "a strict code of ethics" and believes "that good science can have a positive impact on public health." It also publishes a scientific journal, *Nutrition Reviews*, and organizes scientific conferences around the world.
- *Are there spelling, grammatical, or typographical errors?* The site is impeccably prepared.
- *What is the purpose of the information? Is it to inform, teach, sell, entertain, or persuade?* The organization is a nonprofit whose purpose is to conduct work that "improves human health and well-being and

safeguards the environment." It does not "lobby, conduct lobbying activities, or make policy recommendations."

- *Is the author qualified to write on the topic?* The leadership and board of directors includes scientists and university professors, including one who directs the University of Georgia's Center for Food Safety.

Studying the site carefully, you can answer all the checklist's questions. The only one you can't is whether the information can be verified "in another source." You make a brief detour to the University of Georgia's website to confirm that (a) there's something called the "Center for Food Safety," and (b) the guy from the board of directors appears there. Checks out.

Bottom Line: The site's trustworthy.

This is where the trouble begins.

Easily Fakeable Questions

The International Life Sciences Institute is an industry-supported interest group founded in 1980 by a former Coca-Cola vice president. The group has embraced everything from minimizing the harmful effects of tobacco to casting doubt on dietary guidelines that tell people to consume less sugar.[2] A *New York Times* report described the organization as "little more than a front group advancing the interests of the 400 corporate members that provide its $17 million budget."[3] Although the group claims it doesn't lobby, memos obtained through the Freedom of Information Act tell a different story. The organization's founder, Alex Malaspina, wrote his board of trustees asking for advice about how to get the head of the World Health Organization to soften her stance on sugar: "We must find a way to start a dialogue. . . . If not, she will continue to blast us with significant negative consequences on a global basis. This threat to our business is serious."[4] The "business" of the International Life Sciences Institute, it sure seems, is to protect the interests of the sugar industry.

Gameable Signals of Credibility

How did a website that aced a credibility test turn out to be a wolf in sheep's clothing? Pretty simple. It manipulated a series of *cheap signals* that lent it a patina of credibility. On today's internet, these signals are ludicrously easy to game.

What's a cheap signal? Let's start with an even more basic question: What do we even *mean* by a signal?

A signal is any observable element that we use to make judgments about something we can't see. This sounds complicated, but we use signals all the time. You go to a job interview and you're trying to get a sense of whether the company is an established entity or a fly-by-night operation. You might notice the building it's housed in. Or where the interview takes place. You might recall where you initially saw the advertisement. An ad in a trade journal feels a bit more credible than one stapled to a telephone pole.

We shouldn't dismiss a site because of a single signal. Instead, we should ask whether the signals we see align with the story the source is telling us. An ad for a dogwalker on a telephone pole makes sense. An ad promising a five-thousand-dollar monthly income stapled to a telephone pole feels a bit dodgy.

It works the same way with people. A date claiming to be a middle school social studies teacher shows up in a 2015 Prius? That tracks. On the other hand, a date who claims to be super generous but who leaves a server a 5 percent tip raises suspicion. These signals aren't foolproof. But each signal allows us to ask whether the stories these people tell about themselves match the signals we see.[5]

Many of the questions on the CRAAP test reflect an understanding that, like it or not, we rely on signals. Almost always. At least on the surface, the test's questions make sense. We expect that a scholarly source would have an editing process that avoids spelling errors or that a major institute would be able to keep its website updated and free of linkrot.

The problem is that these signals are *cheap* and *purchasable*. We're not saying you shouldn't slow down and rethink an academic article that's full of typos. Of course you should. But think about it: is good spelling and proper grammar *that* hard to pull off in an era of spellcheck and Grammarly? In the web's early days, a professional website cost wads of money. But even back then, a well-designed site didn't necessarily mean the organization was trustworthy. It did mean that the company behind it might at least be as big and influential as it claimed. Not anymore. Now, a slick-looking web template can be had for lunch money.

Taking at face value how an organization describes itself is like scrolling through someone's Instagram feed and assuming they lead a charmed life. But it's easy to look good when you control the camera angle and the filters are free. No one needs to explain that Instagram is all about image. Why would we expect anything different from an organization trying to cast itself as something it's not? Would you expect the International Life Sciences Institute to come right out and give you the following warnings?

> You should know that we receive major contributions from PepsiCo, General Foods, Hershey's, Kellogg's, and other giants in the food and beverage industry.[6]

> To *draw* you in, we "exploit the credibility of scientists and academics to bolster industry positions and promote industry-devised content."[7]

> Former clients, like Mars Inc., makers of M&Ms and Skittles, have cut ties to us because they don't "want to be involved in advocacy-led

studies that so often, and mostly for the right reasons, have been criticized."[8]

Sites like ilsi.org count on the fact that they can use a slick appearance, scientific language, and a whole array of cheap signals to achieve their ends. However, if we're aware of these ruses, we'll get fooled less often. Let's review some of the most common.

First Impressions Matter . . . Except When They Don't

First impressions matter. You land on a website with pictures of snow-capped mountains, lush green forests, and cloudless skies with a headline, "Safeguarding the Planet for You and Future Generations." You conclude it's from some environmental group. Only the congenitally suspicious among us will automatically assume that it's a logging-industry site scamming us while ravaging the landscape.

Welcome to how public policy plays out on the internet, where a little dose of suspicion isn't such a bad thing.

On nearly every issue—climate change, food regulation, charter schools, private prisons, mass transit, minimum wage, immigration, public transportation, *you name it*—myriad forces work overtime to sway our minds and gain our vote. For each of these issues, millions of dollars hang in the balance. With so much at stake, coming up with a slick website with high-definition images and multicolored graphics is child's play.

First impressions can steer us wrong in the other direction too. You land on a site that looks like it was designed in the early 2000s, back when MySpace was the internet's cool place to be. But a bare-bones website doesn't necessarily mean there's a problem with the organization behind it.

Take the website of the Against Malaria Foundation. Not only does

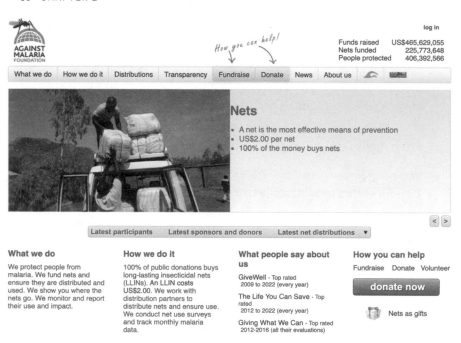

FIGURE 2.3 Landing page for the Against Malaria Foundation (www.againstmalaria.com)

it look like it's in need of a makeover—it's a dot-com to boot (we'll talk about dot-coms a bit later). Turns out that the Against Malaria Foundation is a philanthropic organization that has won awards for its work eradicating malaria in Africa. For whatever reason, the organization has decided that buying more mosquito nets takes priority over upgrading its website.

URLs Matter . . . Except When They Don't

For as long as there's been a web, teachers have been telling us to examine the URL.

Generally good advice. You press on a link and think you're headed in one direction, but because you didn't look at the URL, you end up

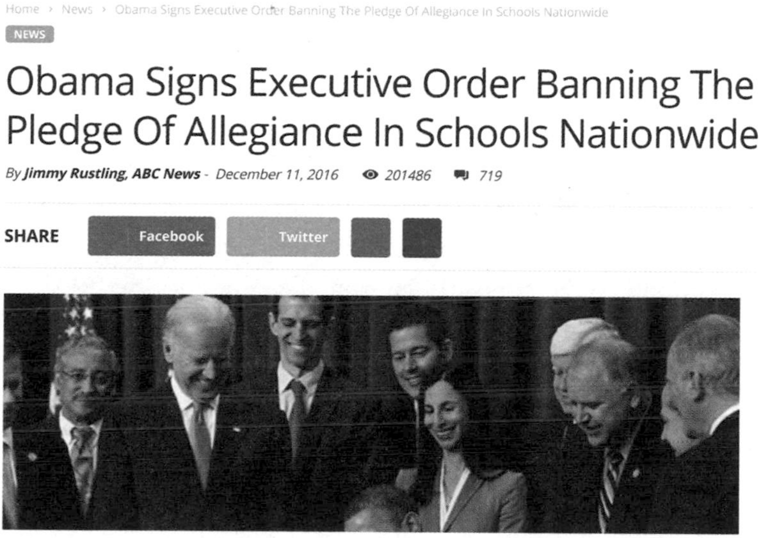
Home › News › Obama Signs Executive Order Banning The Pledge Of Allegiance In Schools Nationwide

NEWS

Obama Signs Executive Order Banning The Pledge Of Allegiance In Schools Nationwide

By *Jimmy Rustling, ABC News* - *December 11, 2016* 201486 719

SHARE Facebook Twitter

FIGURE 2.4 Fake news from the now defunct website abc.com.co

sliding into disinformation oblivion. Consider a story that made the rounds a few years ago: President Obama signed an executive order banning the Pledge of Allegiance in public schools. Utter and complete nonsense. Yet many of the thousands of people who shared it thought they were on the site of ABC News (abcnews.com). Instead, they were taken to a crafty look-alike site, abcnews.com.co. So, it's never a bad idea to take a quick look at the URL.

On the other hand, the imperative to "examine the URL" gets us into trouble when we think we can get away with judging a site's credibility by glancing at the three letters of the top-level domain (e.g., .com, .org, .edu, .mil, .gov, .net). One of the most entrenched beliefs we've run into is the idea that dot-org sites are inherently more trustworthy than dot-coms. The reasoning goes something like this: Dot-orgs are nonprofit organizations that serve the common good. Dot-coms, on the other hand, are just out to make a buck.

Perhaps you've heard that dot-orgs go through a special approval process before getting to display those three letters. Lots of people—half of all Americans and higher percentages in France, India, and Brazil, according to one survey—believed that an organization had to "meet criteria" to register a dot-org URL.[9] Universities like Penn State, Boston College, Harvard, and many others teach students that dot-orgs are synonymous with nonprofit, "tax exempt" organizations, a designation granted by the US Internal Revenue Service (IRS).[10]

We have some news.

Want to have your own dot-org site? Like right now? For yourself? Heck, even for your goldfish? You (and they) can! The entire process of registering *my-goldfish-are-the-bomb.org* will take about five minutes and about fifteen dollars. The process will not verify whether you are a nonprofit. It will not verify whether you act on behalf of the public good. It will not verify whether you are a person or a goldfish. It will verify whether you (a) have an email address, and (b) have fifteen dollars.

Mind you, thousands of legitimate, socially beneficial groups carry the dot-org domain—the Red Cross, American Association of Retired People, Save the Children, the National Geographic Society, and many, many others. But so do lobbyists, political action committees, and front groups for corporate interests. Hate groups too. Stormfront.org, a notorious neo-Nazi site, proudly displays the dot-org flag. In fact, 49 percent of organizations designated as hate groups by the Southern Poverty Law Center carry the dot-org domain.[11]

What about Dot-Coms?

Yes, the dot-com domain was originally intended for commercial sites. However, if your knee-jerk reaction is to reject a site because of those three letters, you'll be rejecting every news site on the planet, whether liberal (the *New York Times*) or conservative (the *Wall Street Journal*) and everything in between (*Vice*, ABC, NBC, CBS, Fox, MSNBC). And you can forget about news magazines (*Slate*, *Scientific American*, *Time*, etc.) too. Although it's true that most dot-com sites *are* businesses, not all are. Remember the Against Malaria Foundation website, againstmalaria.com? Sometimes a charitable organization will register as a dot-com if another group with a similar name has already registered as a dot-org. It goes in the other direction too. Craigslist, the for-profit classified advertising site, is craigslist.org.

The most ridiculous example of rejecting a dot-com site occurred in a workshop for *faculty* that Mike conducted on digital skills. He showed an article from the website for the *British Medical Journal*, one of the world's premier medical journals. Impact factor, if you're into that sort of thing, of *thirty*.[12] Mike asked the faculty members if they trusted the site. Their conclusion? Complete trash! Why? Because the URL was bmj.com, after all, and "you can't trust dot-coms." Plus, the all-lower-case logo on its cover seemed "fake" and "not academic, like a scammy site."

The BMJ

文A 29 languages ∨

Article   Talk   Read   Edit   Edit source   View history   ☆   Tools ∨

From Wikipedia, the free encyclopedia

"BMJ" redirects here. For other uses, see BMJ (disambiguation).

The BMJ is a weekly peer-reviewed medical trade journal, published by the trade union the British Medical Association (BMA). *The BMJ* has editorial freedom from the BMA.[1] It is one of the world's oldest general medical journals. Originally called the **British Medical Journal**, the title was officially shortened to *BMJ* in 1988, and then changed to *The BMJ* in 2014.[2] The journal is published by BMJ Publishing Group Ltd, a subsidiary of the British Medical Association (BMA). The

The BMJ

FIGURE 2.5 Wikipedia entry for the *British Medical Journal* (https://en.wikipedia.org/wiki/The_BMJ)

GOING DEEPER

The "Org" of Dot-Org Is Big Business

Despite dot-org's status as a domain open to anyone, its last three letters shine a light that blinds many people's mental faculties. In 2019, Sam's research group surveyed 3,446 high school students and asked them to evaluate a climate-change-denial website. A quick search reveals the group's past ties to the fossil fuel industry. Yet, 96 percent of students never uncovered the connection. Often their evaluations began and abruptly ended at three letters: "This page is a reliable source to obtain information from," one student wrote. "You see in the URL that it ends in .org as opposed to .com."[13] Since no human is born thinking that a dot-org is better than a dot-com, how did this belief take root? Two words: big money. The dot-org domain is controlled by an organization called the Public Interest Registry (PIR). In 2018 alone, registration fees generated ninety-two million dollars in revenue for the group. Much of PIR's success has to do with crafty marketing that plays up the supposed difference between its brand and the "inferior" dot-com. For example, in 2019 PIR unveiled a new logo painted in "deep royal blue," a shade it touted as conveying "feelings of trust, security and reliability." Its marketing campaign promised new registrants that they could expect a jump in "donations, and trust for donors" once they signed up for the "domain of trust."[14] We would like to offer a modest suggestion to the Public Interest Registry: if it truly wants to act on behalf of the "public interest," we encourage it to add a deep-red asterisk to its royal-blue logo: "Dot-org implies absolutely nothing about an organization's intent. *Buyer Beware.*"

Nonprofit Status: "Nearly Anything Goes"

You'll often find claims that dot-org is equivalent to nonprofit status. Let's take a moment to clear that up. It's wrong. Some dot-orgs have nonprofit status. Some don't. While we're at it, let's clear up another issue. By itself, nonprofit status is not proof that a group can be trusted.

To be designated as a nonprofit organization in the United States, a group must file paperwork with the IRS. If approved, it earns the official IRS designation as a 501(c)(3) "tax deductible" organization. When many people see 501(c)(3) status on a website, they automatically assume they're in good hands. Bad move.

With cutbacks at the IRS and the mountain of nonprofit applications it needs to process, obtaining 501(c)(3) status is just a tad more difficult than renewing your driver's license. In 2015 alone, the IRS reviewed 101,962 applications, nearly double the number of applications it processed in 1998. Of these, 94 percent, or 95,372, were approved.[15] Odds we would love at Las Vegas slot machines. Hundreds of trade associations and shadowy lobby groups carry the nonprofit designation. A report by the Stanford Center on Philanthropy and Civil Society found that, in a single year, groups like the International Society of Talking Clock Collectors, which "appears to be the private collection" of a single collector held in his home; the Metempyrion Foundation, where "people with intuitive and telepathic potential will be given an opportunity to enhance their skills"; and Planet Jelly Donut, whose goal is to spread "the common belief that the core essence of the human spirit is goodness," all received approval.[16] It's no exaggeration, the report concluded, that when it comes to obtaining nonprofit status, "nearly anything goes."

Numbers That Bamboozle

When you think of cheap signals, numbers and statistics don't immediately come to mind. Numbers are the hard evidence that back up a claim, right? But if you have no idea where the numbers come from or how they were generated, they're as useful as a bikini on an excursion to the Antarctic.

Take this story from *The Defender*, the online newsletter of Robert F. Kennedy Jr.'s Children's Health Defense organization. Lacking a degree in medicine but trading on his family's famous name, Kennedy has emerged as a leading spokesman for the antivaccine movement. His website recycles debunked claims tying vaccines to autism.[17] As the pandemic surged, his antivaccine mission saw its site's gross revenue swell from $1.1 million in 2018 to $6.8 million in 2020.[18] The site broadcasts bone-chilling numbers, as seen in this headline:

06/04/21 · BIG PHARMA › NEWS

Latest VAERS Data Show: 5,165 Deaths Reported Following COVID Vaccines

VAERS data released today showed 294,801 reports of adverse events following COVID vaccines, including 5,165 deaths and 25,359 serious injuries between Dec. 14, 2020 and May 28, 2021.

By Megan Redshaw   119   f y ✉ 🔗 🖨

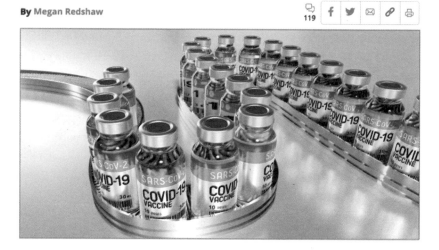

FIGURE 2.6 Misleading headline from the newsletter of Children's Health Defense (https://childrenshealthdefense.org/defender/vaers-data-deaths-reported-following -covid-vaccines/)

Thousands of deaths caused by the COVID *vaccine*? And what is "VAERS data"? Statistics provided by some science-denying, conspiracy-mongering, fear-generating website?

Actually, *no*.

VAERS (Vaccination Adverse Event Reporting System) is a US government database tracking vaccine safety. VAERS is jointly administered by the Centers for Disease Control and Prevention (CDC), the chief governmental body responsible for dispensing information about public health, and the Food and Drug Administration (FDA), the agency responsible for approving new drugs.

Doctors, nurses, and other health-care professionals can submit reports to VAERS. But so can you and your unhinged next-door neighbor. VAERS is a come-as-you-are, no-ticket-required database. Anyone and everyone can upload a report—and they do. Originally designed as an early warning system to capture adverse vaccine reactions that might have been missed during clinical trials, VAERS was created to gain insight into what ordinary people, not just health professionals, thought was happening. But ordinary people have some bizarro ideas. Take this example: Fred got vaccinated on Tuesday and struck by lightning on Wednesday. If he believed the two were related (maybe the vaccine increased his ability to conduct electricity?), he would be within his right to file an "adverse reaction" report.

The VAERS website publishes plenty of disclaimers warning people that its numbers contain "incomplete, inaccurate, coincidental or unverifiable information."[19] But that hasn't stopped groups like Kennedy's from weaponizing VAERS to their advantage. Prominent medical officials think the site has outlived its purpose and advocate shutting it down. To dramatize the site's problems, an anesthesiologist named James Laidler submitted a report after a flu vaccination saying that it caused his skin to turn green and his muscles to bulk, turning him into the Incredible Hulk.[20] Only after the CDC personally appealed did Laidler agree to remove the report. "If I had not agreed," he wrote, "the record would be there still, showing that any claim can become part of the database, no matter how outrageous or improbable."[21]

Links That Lead Astray

We're known by our friends, the saying goes. On the internet, a site is known by who links to it, and who, in turn, it links *to*. A site linking to reputable sites may seem to be following best practice. But links, like looks, can be deceptive.

Shady sites will link to authoritative sites to bask in the glow of their authority. For example, the site minimumwage.com says it's a part of a nonprofit research organization "dedicated to studying public policy issues surrounding employment growth." (We'll have more to say about the website's sponsor, the Employment Policies Institute, in the next chapter.)

Minimumwage.com features an article comparing the price of a Big Mac in Denmark, where fast-food workers make twenty dollars an hour, to the United States, where a Big Mac costs less but half of all

ALL STATES   MINIMUM WAGE 101

Denmark's Dollar Forty-One Menu

Thursday, **October 30, 2014**, 9:00 am

Proponents of raising the minimum wage often point to Scandinavian countries like Denmark as models for American labor policy. But the devil is in the details. Take this week's ***New York Times profile*** of the comparatively high Danish minimum wage, for example. The authors ask, if the Danes can do it, why can't the United States?

FIGURE 2.7   Article appearing on the site minimumwage.com, October 30, 2014 (https://minimumwage.com/2014/10/denmarks-dollar-forty-one-menu/)

fast-food workers earn so little that they qualify for public assistance. The site claims that raising the minimum wage would "lead to higher prices and fewer job opportunities." To support the claim, the site links to the *Columbia Journalism Review*, a prestigious magazine for journalists published by Columbia University's School of Journalism.

Even though there is a link to the article, minimumwage.com doesn't *really* want you to read it—or, at least, not the whole thing. Because if you did, you'd learn that the author of the *Columbia Journalism Review* article labels minimumwage.com's sponsor as a "restaurant-lobby front" posing as a neutral think tank.

Why in the world would a website link to a source that undermines its credibility? For the simple reason that its creators are betting that you'll hover over the link just long enough—and not a second longer—to see that it takes you to the *Columbia Journalism Review*. If you actually visit the site, they're counting on the journey ending with a fleeting glance. Minimumwage.com has more to gain by linking to a prestigious source than what it has to lose from the few diehards who read the linked article from beginning to end.

Takeaways

▷ Cheap signals are easy to come by and easy to manipulate. The days of thinking you can tell whether a site is trustworthy just by looking at it—or even looking at it carefully—are over.

▷ The credibility checklists we grew up with have outlived their usefulness. Checklist-type questions—Is a site free of typos? Is the language unbiased? Is there contact information? Has the site recently been updated?—can do more harm than good. Bad actors study these lists and design their sites accordingly.

▷ Even features that require government approval, like nonprofit status, can be gamed by crafty groups that have figured out how to outsmart the IRS.

▷ Bad actors will link to authoritative websites just to bask in the glow of their authority. In some cases, links may contradict the claim they are supposed to support.

▷ The chief takeaway of this chapter can be summed up in four words: *get off the page*. Instead of thinking you can suss out who's behind an unfamiliar website by scouring its "About" page or pressing all its links, save yourself time. To navigate the internet effectively, you need to draw on the web's *web-like properties*—a topic we take up in the next two chapters.

Google

THE BESTIE YOU THOUGHT YOU KNEW

Have you ever been the family googler? The person frantically searching "is Styrofoam bad for birds?" or googling for your brother "does this look sprained?" (In order: yes, and it was.)

Sometimes we search for ourselves and sometimes for others. But the challenges are the same. The phone rings, and it's your grandmother in Denver. She's been getting headaches from cataracts, a condition where the eye clouds up and the world greets you through a dirty windshield. The neighbors, as usual, have advice: try medical marijuana, legal in Colorado since 2000. It's a cataract miracle drug!

And so, it comes to pass that your nana tells you that the good folks next door are going to pick up some five-star weed down at the local dispensary. Problem solved.

Or is it? Here's the thing about medical treatments, whether pot or pills: getting the wrong treatment is always risky. Even if there's no immediate harm, people often delay needed treatment while trying alternatives. It's important to know whether Nana's neighbors know what they are talking about—or if they're just blowing smoke.

You type "cataracts marijuana" into your search engine. You're about to hit enter when you hear a voice in your head. *Stop*, it says—the first step of SIFT.

It's not that we're for or against Nana's newfound cure, especially if it alleviates suffering. But pausing here is crucial. Too often we approach Google like throwing dice: "Let's just see what comes up." But if we don't have a decent idea of what we're looking for *before* starting, it will be harder to know when we've found it.

What kinds of sources would best answer the question? A statement from a pot-industry spokesperson? A journal article on the chemical makeup of tetrahydrocannabinol (THC)? Or something short. Authoritative. Something that doesn't take hours to wade through?

Interpreting and Mining Search Results

You type "Does marijuana help cataracts?"

Here's what Google gives you (fig. 3.2). A result at the top with your exact question. It's practically begging for you to click.

Resist the urge. You can learn a whole lot about a result *before* you click. The extra seconds it takes will pay off in the time you save later.

We're going to go through a few things here that will seem rather, well, involved. Time-consuming, at least initially. But stay with us, because once you learn the process we call *result mining*, you'll not only become more efficient at searching but you'll also be able to learn more about a subject in a glance than many people learn in an hour.

First things first. A typical Google result has three main parts:

1 The web address
2 The blue title (the link you click on)

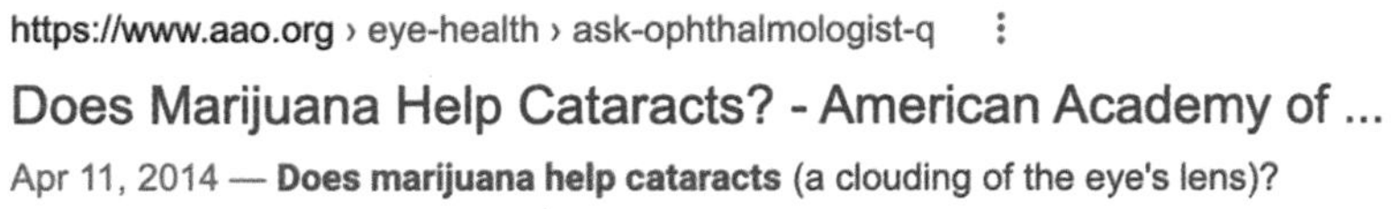

https://www.aao.org › eye-health › ask-ophthalmologist-q ⋮

Does Marijuana Help Cataracts? - American Academy of ...

Apr 11, 2014 — **Does marijuana help cataracts** (a clouding of the eye's lens)?

FIGURE 3.1 Google result for "Does marijuana help cataracts?" (Google and the Google logo are trademarks of Google LLC.)

https://www.aao.org › eye-health › ask-ophthalmologist-q ⋮ Web address

Does Marijuana Help Cataracts? - American Academy of ..^{Title}

Apr 11, 2014 — **Does marijuana help cataracts** (a clouding of the eye's lens)? Snippet

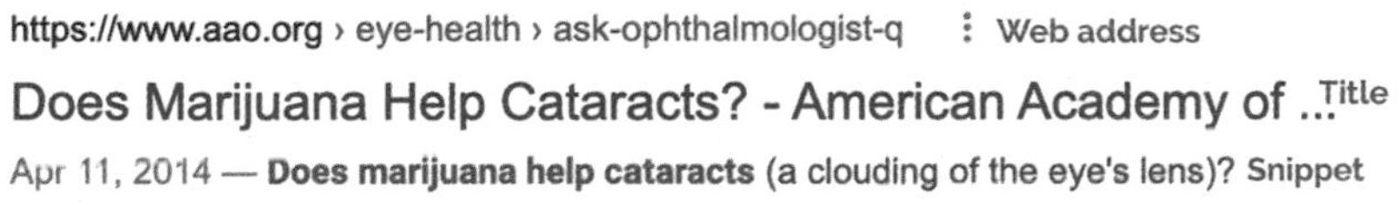

FIGURE 3.2 Elements of a Google result. (Google and the Google logo are trademarks of Google LLC.)

3 A block of text drawn from the website—Google calls this a "snippet" (in general, snippets are created when Google matches the words in your search to words in the result and then highlights them in bold)

Your search brings up aao.org. The American Academy of . . . something. You spot "ophthalmologist" after the URL; this must be a group of eye doctors. Following the dot-org domain you see these little > signs pointing to "eye-health" and then "ask-ophthalmologist-q." All this means is that there are different sections to the site, and Google is telling you where on the site the results are located. This result seems on target. Medical. Authoritative. Short. You click in.

Hmm . . . "no evidence" that marijuana helps with cataracts. (Could it be that Nana's neighbors were thinking about marijuana and glaucoma? That too looks iffy.) You could continue looking at other sites, or even search "Gary S. Hirshfield MD," the doctor who wrote the post. You could go to Wikipedia to confirm that the American Academy

Does Marijuana Help Cataracts?

APR 11, 2014

Question:
Does marijuana help cataracts (a clouding of the eye's lens)?

Answer:
There is currently no evidence to suggest that this is the case. On that note, there is a commonly held thought that marijuana does help glaucoma (a disease that increases pressure in the eye, damaging the optic nerve) by lowering intraocular pressure. However, the dosages and side effects involved to get marginal improvement make it a very poor choice for treating glaucoma.

Answered By: Gary S Hirshfield MD

Cataracts

FIGURE 3.3 The American Academy of Ophthalmology's answer about whether marijuana helps cataracts (https://www.aao.org/eye-health/ask-ophthalmologist-q/does-marijuana-help-cataracts)

of Ophthalmology, with thirty-two thousand members, is the main group of eye doctors in the United States. You could even do more research to get a better handle on this issue. For now, though, this answer suffices.

Why Seeing on the Internet Isn't Believing

A picture is worth a thousand words. But whether that picture tells the truth is another issue.

← **Tweet**

Archie McPhee ✓
@ArchieMcPhee   ···

Spider-Squirrel hybrid by dylanbaumann
buff.ly/1AvZVar

4:54 PM · Feb 26, 2015 · Buffer

19 Retweets   **12** Likes

FIGURE 3.4 Is a squirrel mated with a tarantula a *squirrelantula*? (Photo posted on Twitter by Archie McPhee, @ArchieMcPhee and attributed to Dylan Baumann; https://twitter.com/archiemcphee/status/571111017142472705.)

A squirrel mates with a tarantula to produce a . . . *squirrelantula*? A massive aquarium shatters at a Las Vegas megamall sending baby sharks circling in pools of water by Sbarro? Dolphins frolicking in Venice's canals? Crazy, right? Here's another: Australian hawks plucking embers from blazing fields and dropping them in dry grasslands to flush out prey.

FIGURE 3.5 Fire-spreading birds? (Photo posted to Reddit forum r/memes and attributed to Howie Doin.)

Decoding Google's Knowledge Panel

"Australian Birds Have Weaponized Fire" comes up on your social media feed from a source you don't recognize—the *National Post*.[1] You notice a little maple leaf poking its head out between "National" and "Post." Could this be Canada's version of *The Onion*?

Googling the *National Post* provides you with scannable intel.

Google's algorithms pull content from sources like Wikipedia, the CIA's *World Factbook*, LinkedIn, and other web sources, repackage it, and serve it all up in what Google calls the "knowledge panel": the block of text on the right. The fact that our source comes with a knowledge panel doesn't mean we can blindly trust it or that its claims are true. It just means that the *National Post* isn't some fly-by-night outfit that someone uploaded yesterday.

The knowledge panel makes no mention of satire or conspiracy

World / News

Australian birds have weaponized fire because what we really need now is something else to make us afraid

Raptors, including the whistling kite, are intentionally spreading grass fires in northern Australia, a research paper argues. The reason: to flush out prey and feast

Richard Warnica

Jan 09, 2018 • January 9, 2018 • 4 minute read • ☐ Join the conversation

Black kites (Milvus migrans) visit a grass fire in Borroloola, Northern Territory, Australia, in 2014.
PHOTO BY BOB GOSFORD

FIGURE 3.6 Article from Canada's *National Post* (https://nationalpost.com/news/world/australian-birds-have-weaponized-fire)

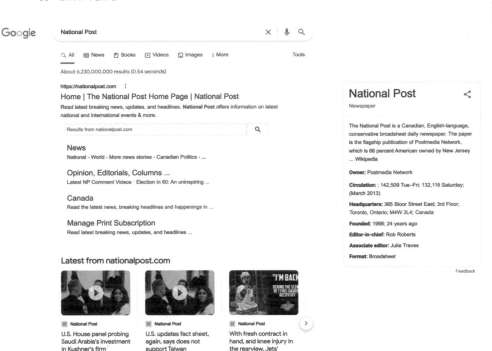

FIGURE 3.7 Google's knowledge panel for the *National Post*. (Google and the Google logo are trademarks of Google LLC.)

theories. The *National Post*, founded in 1998 and headquartered in Toronto, has a decent-sized circulation (142,509) and covers what you'd expect from a Canadian paper.

This is enough to give that story about fire-starting birds a second look. Who knew? The *National Post* story even links to a scholarly paper from something called the *Journal of Ethnobiology*: "Intentional Fire-Spreading by 'Firehawk' Raptors in Northern Australia."[2] So, watch out for brazen birds bearing embers. For squirrelantulas, watch out for Photoshop.

Different Sources, Different Purposes

Before we let those arsonist birds fly away, let's take a moment to go over the different kinds of sources we just evaluated.

- The *sharing source*. The person or group who shared the story or forwarded the meme to your social media feed.
- The *reporting source*, in this case the *National Post*. The reporting source, when it's reputable, does some basic verification on the claims.
- The *original reporting source*. Often when you click into an article, you'll find the article isn't doing any original reporting, but rather re-reporting. However, in this instance, the *National Post* appears to be doing its job and drawing on a variety of sources.
- The *research source*. Especially when science and health are involved, there's a research source as well. If you were doing a research paper, you'd want to invoke the *T* of SIFT and *trace* these arsonist birds back to the research source: the *Journal of Ethnobiology*. Is it reputable? Is it peer reviewed? (We will talk more about peer review in chapter 6.)

Why are these distinctions important? Part of the reason we're OK with quick assessments of the *reporting source* is because we're often trying to avoid moderate to really dumb errors. Sure, reporters make mistakes, even at good newspapers. But in a situation like this, a reporter who has spent a day or two getting quotes, calling sources, researching a story, and linking to a scholarly paper is more likely to get a better result than you will by spending a minute poking around Google.

But these techniques are also good starting points for deeper investigations. For a serious research project, you'll want to grapple with research sources. But when you want a quick take on something that arouses your curiosity, the original reporting source (if reliable) is probably good enough.

GOING DEEPER

What Arsonist Birds Teach Us about Different Sources

The *National Post* says that when those mischievous birds drop embers on parched grasslands, the territory becomes "a feeding frenzy" sending "small birds, lizards, insects, everything fleeing the front of the fire." This description comes from Robert Gosford, one of the authors of the research study linked to in the article. However, the words in quotation marks appear nowhere in the research article (we checked). Instead, as the *National Post* reporter wrote, Gosford provided the description to the Australian Broadcast Corporation. Using the types of sources we laid out above, this is an example of the *reporting source*, the *National Post*, quoting the *original* reporting source, Australia's national broadcasting service. At the same time, it's clear that the *National Post* journalist did his homework and went back to the *research source*, the *Journal of Ethnobiology* where these findings first appeared. That research, a collaboration between field rangers in Australia's semiarid Northern Territory and professors from Penn State and the University of Arizona, documented birds picking up "smoldering sticks" and transporting them "ahead of a fire front, successfully helping the blaze spread up a small valley." The *Journal of Ethnobiology* study provides a scientific basis to the "reality of avian fire spreading," a phenomenon already known to Aboriginal peoples, who long understood the capabilities of these flying arsonists. By itself, the *National Post* article gives you enough information and active links to feel confident forwarding it to friends and family. But if these flying arsonists inspire you to dig deeper, you'll want to go back to the original research article and read the evidence for yourself.

When Featured Snippets Get It Wrong

Back in 2014, Google started to put a descriptive search result at the top of the results page to "help people more easily discover what

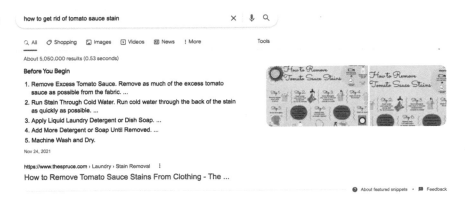

FIGURE 3.8 "How to get rid of tomato sauce stain." (Google and the Google logo are trademarks of Google LLC.)

they're seeking."[3] They called this innovation a "featured snippet" because, unlike other results, the snippet preceded the URL and page title. According to the company, you can't buy featured snippets. They're not ads. They're something Google's algorithms create from supposedly trusted sites that contain the right keywords and, in theory, quality content.

Featured snippets can be incredible time savers, especially when you're squinting at your phone. You're in a snazzy restaurant and spill puttanesca on your white shirt. What to do? Google delivers your answer in a second—0.53 seconds to be exact.

The thing is, there really isn't a whole lot of debate about how to remove a tomato stain. Yeah, someone may suggest tonic water. Someone else might stress a longer period of dabbing. People can even get a bit pushy with advice (especially if you rub instead of dab). But no one says, "What you want to do is let that stain sit as long as possible, then whatever you do, don't use detergent." There's no stain removal lobby, no stain removal culture war. (We can't promise there will *never* be a stain removal culture war. We've heard of sillier things.)

It's when things aren't so clear-cut that they get dicey.

Remember back in middle school hearing about the "shot heard round the world"? No? Here's a hint—that line is from a poem, "Concord Hymn," by Ralph Waldo Emerson.

Still not sure what the shot was? We'll remind you. It was the shot that set off hostilities in the Revolutionary War. On April 19, 1775, a ragtag band of minutemen opposed a regiment of British troops marching on their way to seize military stores at Concord. A shot rang out, and all hell broke loose. The colonists said it was the British: "Not a gun was fired by any person in our company" until they "fired on us."[4] And, you guessed it, the British responded with the eighteenth-century British equivalent of "nuh-uh." Lieutenant John Barker, a British officer, wrote in his diary that his troops advanced "keeping prepared against an attack tho' without intending to attack"

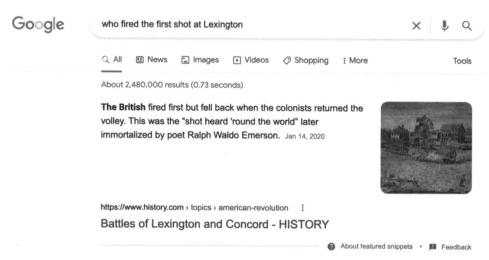

FIGURE 3.9 Google's answer for "who fired the first shot at Lexington." (Google and the Google logo are trademarks of Google LLC.)

until the colonists "fired one or two shots."[5] So, who fired the first shot? We'll never know.

Google, on the other hand, is plenty sure it's got the whole thing figured out.

If things weren't already murky, what happens when we step into one of today's raging controversies?

Take fracking. You've heard of it—it has something to do with drilling in the ground, setting off mini-explosions, and then pumping out gas and oil. You recall hearing stories about people making morning coffee and watching their mugs do a little jig on the kitchen counter. For real?

Remember what we said about researching your grandmother's cataracts? Same advice here. Before putting search terms in your browser, think about the kinds of sources that would best answer your query. Your goal is not to cram for your PhD exams in geothermal energy. You want a basic primer so you don't seem like a dunce when the topic of fracking comes up. So, is fracking safe? Google to the rescue.

We're in luck (not really—you'll see why). There's a featured snippet at the top of the page letting us know that a study from Duke University shows that wastewater from fracking is "safe."

You could stop right there. Please don't. The snippet comes from cred.org; "CRED" is an acronym that stands for "Coloradans for Responsible Energy Development."[6] Click in and you're brought to a page where a forty-two-point all-caps headline proclaims (in case you had doubts): "STUDIES SHOW FRACKING IS SAFE."

What is cred.org? The site is a dot-org (you're not impressed—you're onto the dot-org game).

To find out more, you try Wikipedia—one of SIFT's *investigate* techniques. In this case, a Google search for "Wikipedia + Coloradans for Responsible Energy Development" comes up empty. But the search

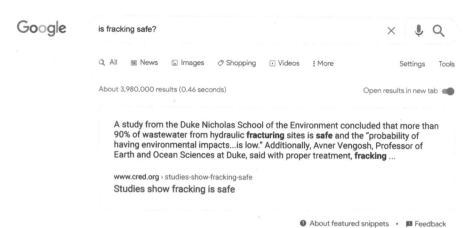

A study from the Duke Nicholas School of the Environment concluded that more than 90% of wastewater from hydraulic **fracturing** sites is **safe** and the "probability of having environmental impacts...is low." Additionally, Avner Vengosh, Professor of Earth and Ocean Sciences at Duke, said with proper treatment, **fracking** ...

www.cred.org › studies-show-fracking-safe
Studies show fracking is safe

FIGURE 3.10 Featured snippet for "is fracking safe?" search, December 2020. (Google and the Google logo are trademarks of Google LLC.)

STUDIES SHOW FRACKING IS SAFE

FIGURE 3.11 Google's featured snippet links to Coloradans for Responsible Energy Development's statement on fracking safety, November 2020 (https://www.cred.org /studies-show-fracking-safe/)

results page turns up a result from a site called Ballotpedia. Its snippet says that CRED was founded by two oil and gas companies. Can that be right?

Ballotpedia is a helpful (and reliable) resource for uncovering hidden funding. But maybe you don't recognize the site. In any event, you now have a better question. Who funds CRED? Let's add a little

FIGURE 3.12 A search result from Ballotpedia about "Coloradans for Responsible Energy Development," November 2020. (Google and the Google logo are trademarks of Google LLC.)

keyword to our search: "Coloradans for Responsible Energy Development + funding."

That pulls up an article from the *Denver Post*, Colorado's largest paper. The article unmasks the group as "a public relations front" backed by Colorado's two biggest energy firms, Anadarko Petroleum and Noble Energy. These two firms bankrolled Coloradans for Responsible Energy Development to the tune of thirty million bucks in the group's first three years.[7]

Moral of the story: Just because Google offers a featured snippet doesn't mean it provides the best answer. If your search is more complicated than removing a tomato stain, scroll through the results before clicking and look for trusted sources.

BUSINESS · ENERGY

What does $80 million buy oil and gas interests? Voter profiles, door knocking and influence at local and statewide levels

Oil and gas fights back in Colorado, pouring more than $80 million into campaigns for politicians and issues and for public relations

An oil field worker places well pipe on a rig in Weld County, Jan., 27, 2016.

RJ Sangosti, The Denver Post

By **CHRISTOPHER N. OSHER** | The Denver Post
PUBLISHED: July 16, 2017 at 12:02 a.m. | UPDATED: July 17, 2017 at 4:55 p.m.

💬 80

The oil and gas industry in the past four years has poured more than $80 million into Colorado to shape public opinion and influence campaigns and ballot initiatives, creating a political force that has had broad implications throughout the state.

Environmentalists and industry officials alike call the effort one of the best-financed operations advocating for drilling in any state. Just two months ago, that political muscle came into play when the industry successfully lobbied Republican legislators to kill legislation tightening regulation in the wake of a fatal home explosion in Firestone that investigators have blamed on a severed gas pipeline.

Energy interests also have helped elect local city council candidates more favorable to allowing drilling near housing and blunted efforts across the Front Range to restrict drilling rights. Last year, industry forces played a role in keeping the state Senate in Republican hands. They spent heavily last year to convince voters across the state to make it harder to amend the state constitution, dealing a blow to anti-fracking activists' hopes to curtail drilling through a statewide ballot initiative.

The new approach has been broad, sustained and effective in its reach, according to interviews and a review of industry documents, campaign-finance records and public remarks by an industry consultant who helped develop the strategy.

FIGURE 3.13 *Denver Post* article about Coloradans for Responsible Energy Development (https://www.denverpost.com/2017/07/16/oil-gas-industry-public-influence -campaigns/)

GOING DEEPER

Google's Three Vertical Dots Are a Great Hack for Lateral Reading

In 2021, Google rolled out three vertical dots, a new feature that puts lateral reading (something we'll discuss more in chapter 4) one click away. At the tail end of each result, you will notice three little dots. (Someone in one of our workshops christened them the "Little Snowman.") When you click on them, you receive a bounty of information. In the example about fracking, we asserted (without, we should note, providing a shred of evidence) that the Ballotpedia site was a "helpful" and "reliable" resource. Use Google's three dots to do a quick fact-check on *us*!

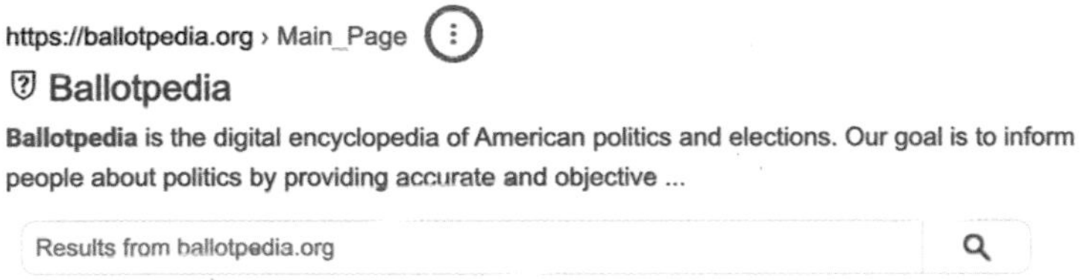

https://ballotpedia.org › Main_Page

ⓥ Ballotpedia

Ballotpedia is the digital encyclopedia of American politics and elections. Our goal is to inform people about politics by providing accurate and objective ...

Results from ballotpedia.org   Q

FIGURE 3.14 Google's three dots on the results for Ballotpedia. (Google and the Google logo are trademarks of Google LLC.)

When you press on the three dots, Google provides an instant hack for lateral reading.

You get immediate access to the Wikipedia entry. But that's just the beginning. If you press on "More about this page," you're given links that provide more information about the site. For Ballotpedia, one of links is from AllSides (allsides.com), a group that rates websites on a scale for political bias. Ballotpedia receives a "center" rating, about as fair-minded as you can get with AllSides. *(continued)*

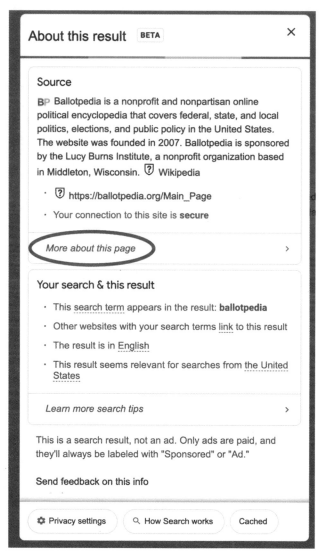

About this result BETA ✕

Source

BP Ballotpedia is a nonprofit and nonpartisan online political encyclopedia that covers federal, state, and local politics, elections, and public policy in the United States. The website was founded in 2007. Ballotpedia is sponsored by the Lucy Burns Institute, a nonprofit organization based in Middleton, Wisconsin. ⑦ Wikipedia

· ⑦ https://ballotpedia.org/Main_Page
· Your connection to this site is **secure**

More about this page >

Your search & this result

· This search term appears in the result: **ballotpedia**
· Other websites with your search terms link to this result
· The result is in English
· This result seems relevant for searches from the United States

Learn more search tips >

This is a search result, not an ad. Only ads are paid, and they'll always be labeled with "Sponsored" or "Ad."

Send feedback on this info

⚙ Privacy settings   🔍 How Search works   Cached

FIGURE 3.15 "More about this page" under the three dots. (Google and the Google logo are trademarks of Google LLC.)

Keywords and Inferred Intent: How to Think like Your Search Engine

Browse the latest tech news and you might think artificial intelligence is on the verge of replacing humans. But sometimes artificial intelligence isn't all that intelligent. And until machines can think like humans, humans sometimes have to think like machines. Put differently, in order to get the machine (or search engine) to do what you want, you have to know a bit about how it turns your request into a result.

Let's start with this: machines don't think. They seem to act like humans much of the time, and sometimes they get the same result. But what happens under the hood is quite different.

Imagine, for example, you buy a robot to fetch milk from the center shelf of the fridge. Most days, Mr. Robot works just like a human. It goes to the fridge, opens it, grabs the milk, and pours it on your Lucky Charms. One day you're being lazy when you put away the groceries, and you throw the milk in the side door and put your sriracha on the center shelf. You've reversed the positions. Guess what happens? Mr. Robot goes to the fridge, grabs the sriracha, and pours it on your cereal, causing you to discover, definitively, that not everything is improved by sriracha.

But you've also discovered something else: the robot does not "see" the way you do. When you look for the milk, you're looking at a variety of factors to determine what's milk and what's not. For you, where it's placed in the fridge doesn't have much impact. For the robot, position apparently matters much more. That knowledge is valuable to you. Now that you know how the robot "sees," you know that to avoid condiment-based disasters, you have to organize your refrigerator in a certain way. Sriracha in the side door. Milk on the center shelf.

Google can seem human-like. We ask it questions. It gives us things we might find useful to read. But like our sriracha-snatching robot, Google "sees" differently than we do. First, Google was built on a technology of *keyword searching*. Second, in more recent years, Google has devoted a lot of resources into something called "machine learning" to better determine *user intent*. Let's talk about how understanding what Google "sees" when it goes looking for things can make *you* a better searcher.

Keywords: The Underlying Architecture of Search

One of the main things Google uses to "see" is *keywords*. It works to find documents that have the specific terms you search for (or synonymous terms) in the document. Figure out the words, terms, and concepts likely to be in the document, and Google will give you what you want.[8]

We all know what happens when you haven't been specific about choosing keywords. You're researching the Montgomery bus boycott that started in December 1955. You have a vague memory that before Rosa Parks's arrest, there had been a young girl who also refused to give up her seat. But her case never achieved the iconic status that Rosa Parks's did.

You search Google: "girl arrested in Montgomery Alabama."

Recent arrest records in Montgomery, Alabama. Sriracha, not milk.

You give it another try—it's the Montgomery *bus boycott* you're interested in? You type "Who got arrested in the Montgomery bus boycott?" Still too broad; your question lands you back at Rosa Parks.

You remember it was a *teenager* who got arrested. So you put the pieces together: "Who was the teenager who got arrested in the

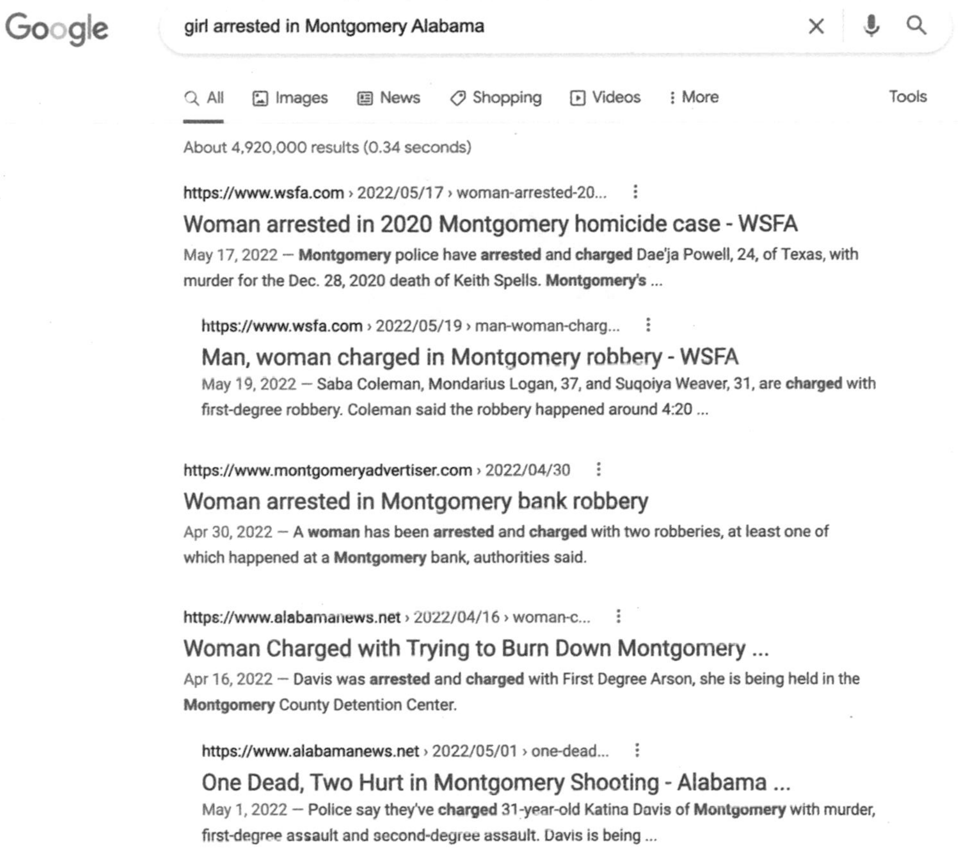

Google   girl arrested in Montgomery Alabama   ✕   🎤   🔍

🔍 All   🖼 Images   📰 News   🏷 Shopping   ▶ Videos   ⋮ More   Tools

About 4,920,000 results (0.34 seconds)

https://www.wsfa.com › 2022/05/17 › woman-arrested-20...   ⋮
Woman arrested in 2020 Montgomery homicide case - WSFA
May 17, 2022 — **Montgomery** police have **arrested** and **charged** Dae'ja Powell, 24, of Texas, with murder for the Dec. 28, 2020 death of Keith Spells. **Montgomery's** ...

https://www.wsfa.com › 2022/05/19 › man-woman-charg...   ⋮
Man, woman charged in Montgomery robbery - WSFA
May 19, 2022 — Saba Coleman, Mondarius Logan, 37, and Suqoiya Weaver, 31, are **charged** with first-degree robbery. Coleman said the robbery happened around 4:20 ...

https://www.montgomeryadvertiser.com › 2022/04/30   ⋮
Woman arrested in Montgomery bank robbery
Apr 30, 2022 — A **woman** has been **arrested** and **charged** with two robberies, at least one of which happened at a **Montgomery** bank, authorities said.

https://www.alabamanews.net › 2022/04/16 › woman-c...   ⋮
Woman Charged with Trying to Burn Down Montgomery ...
Apr 16, 2022 — Davis was **arrested** and **charged** with First Degree Arson, she is being held in the **Montgomery** County Detention Center.

https://www.alabamanews.net › 2022/05/01 › one-dead...   ⋮
One Dead, Two Hurt in Montgomery Shooting - Alabama ...
May 1, 2022 — Police say they've **charged** 31-year-old Katina Davis of **Montgomery** with murder, first-degree **assault** and second-degree assault. Davis is being ...

FIGURE 3.16 Unspecific keywords produce unspecific results. (Google and the Google logo are trademarks of Google LLC.)

Montgomery bus boycott?" Google now zooms in on "teenager + arrested + Montgomery bus boycott," as well as considering the connector "in" before the words "Montgomery bus boycott."[9] It then combs through the web looking for sources where the terms appear close together; it also compares your search sequence to that

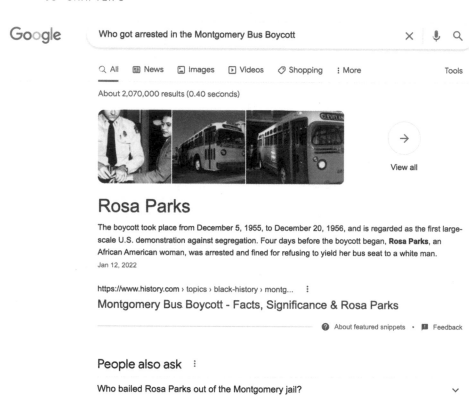

FIGURE 3.17 Keywords that are too broad. (Google and the Google logo are trademarks of Google LLC.)

of other users and the kinds of answers that satisfied them. Aided by your specificity, you now get what you're looking for: the name of Claudette Colvin, with links to sources like the *Washington Post*, the *Smithsonian* magazine, Stanford University's King Institute, NPR, and the BBC.

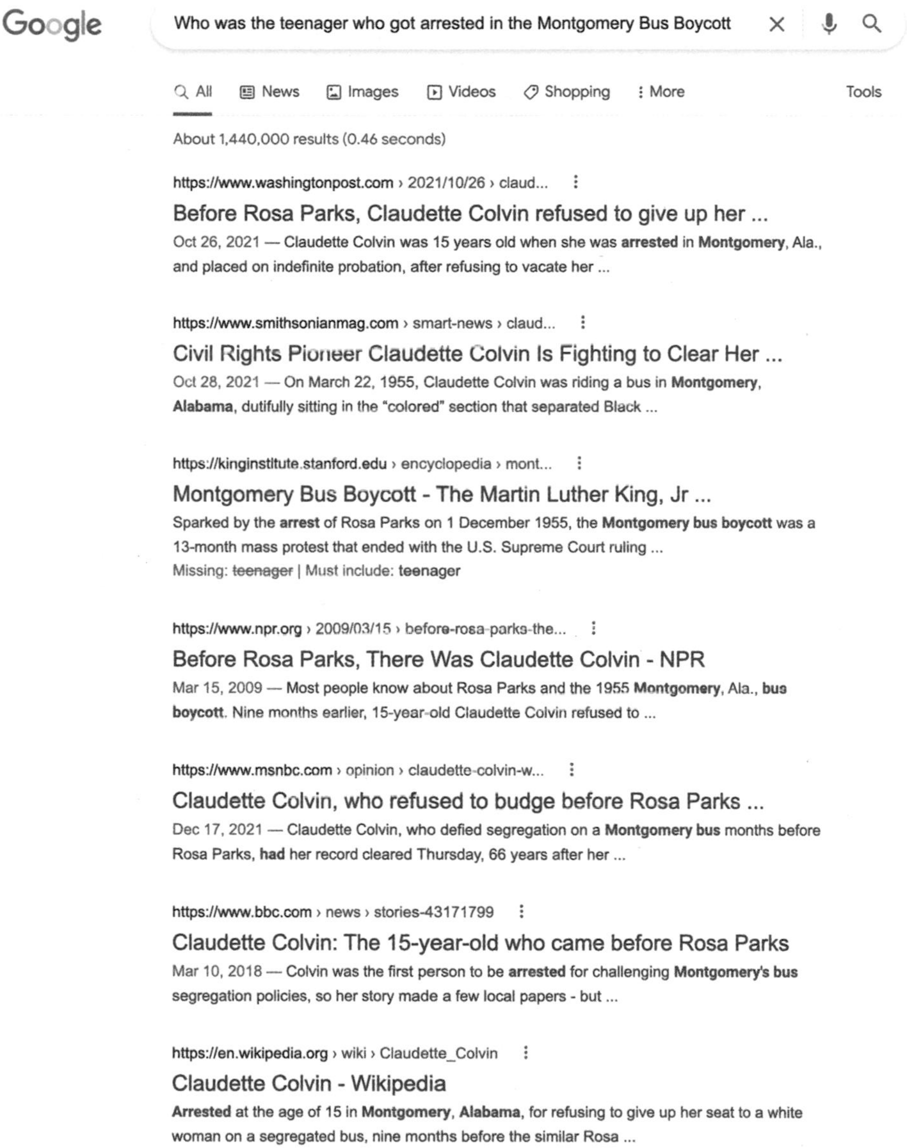

Google   Who was the teenager who got arrested in the Montgomery Bus Boycott   ✕   🎤   🔍

🔍 All   📰 News   🖼 Images   ▶ Videos   🛒 Shopping   ⋮ More   Tools

About 1,440,000 results (0.46 seconds)

https://www.washingtonpost.com › 2021/10/26 › claud... ⋮
Before Rosa Parks, Claudette Colvin refused to give up her ...
Oct 26, 2021 — Claudette Colvin was 15 years old when she was **arrested** in **Montgomery**, Ala., and placed on indefinite probation, after refusing to vacate her ...

https://www.smithsonianmag.com › smart-news › claud... ⋮
Civil Rights Pioneer Claudette Colvin Is Fighting to Clear Her ...
Oct 28, 2021 — On March 22, 1955, Claudette Colvin was riding a bus in **Montgomery**, **Alabama**, dutifully sitting in the "colored" section that separated Black ...

https://kinginstitute.stanford.edu › encyclopedia › mont... ⋮
Montgomery Bus Boycott - The Martin Luther King, Jr ...
Sparked by the **arrest** of Rosa Parks on 1 December 1955, the **Montgomery bus boycott** was a 13-month mass protest that ended with the U.S. Supreme Court ruling ...
Missing: teenager | Must include: teenager

https://www.npr.org › 2009/03/15 › before-rosa-parks-the... ⋮
Before Rosa Parks, There Was Claudette Colvin - NPR
Mar 15, 2009 — Most people know about Rosa Parks and the 1955 **Montgomery**, Ala., **bus boycott**. Nine months earlier, 15-year-old Claudette Colvin refused to ...

https://www.msnbc.com › opinion › claudette-colvin-w... ⋮
Claudette Colvin, who refused to budge before Rosa Parks ...
Dec 17, 2021 — Claudette Colvin, who defied segregation on a **Montgomery bus** months before Rosa Parks, **had** her record cleared Thursday, 66 years after her ...

https://www.bbc.com › news › stories-43171799 ⋮
Claudette Colvin: The 15-year-old who came before Rosa Parks
Mar 10, 2018 — Colvin was the first person to be **arrested** for challenging **Montgomery's bus** segregation policies, so her story made a few local papers - but ...

https://en.wikipedia.org › wiki › Claudette_Colvin ⋮
Claudette Colvin - Wikipedia
Arrested at the age of 15 in **Montgomery**, **Alabama**, for refusing to give up her seat to a white woman on a segregated bus, nine months before the similar Rosa ...

FIGURE 3.18 Search results for "Who was the teenager who got arrested in the Montgomery bus boycott." (Google and the Google logo are trademarks of Google LLC.)

Inferred Intent: Providing Google with a "Tell"

Back in 2019, an executive familiar with Google's search algorithms was interviewed for a *Wall Street Journal* exposé about how the company tweaks its algorithms. "There's this idea that the search algorithm is all neutral and goes out and combs the web and comes back and shows what it found, and that's total BS," the executive said. "Google deals with special cases all the time."[10]

It's true: Google's algorithms reflect some very real human prejudices and biases.[11] But our own responses are hardly free from bias, either. Minor variations in how we phrase a search (think of poker, where a "tell"—a seemingly imperceptible twitch of the eye, for example—gives away that we're bluffing) can produce decidedly different results. Let's see how.

You set out to research a proposed soda tax in your city. You've heard arguments for and against. On one side are people who say a soda tax lowers consumption and reduces obesity. On the other are those who say a soda tax hurts people with lower incomes because bottling companies lay people off, and where the tax has been tried, it has backfired. So, let's consider two queries, altering but a single word: "Are soda taxes a *good* idea?" and "Are soda taxes a *bad* idea?" Same question, really, that in a perfect search world would produce the same result. But that's not how Google sees things (to be more precise, that's not how Google's algorithms operate). Two ways of asking the same question give us dramatically different results. Let's start with the "good" query.

The top result, from *Time* magazine, cites a *JAMA* (*Journal of the American Medical Association*) study suggesting the taxes lead to better health. The result from Stanford University says the taxes reduce consumption. National Public Radio declares the taxes "work."

What happens when Google sees "bad"? It's just as accommodating.

https://time.com › Health › Public Health   ⋮

Soda Taxes Really Do Work, a New Study Suggests - TIME

May 14, 2019 — A new JAMA study suggests **taxing** sugary **drinks** really can make people buy fewer of them, potentially translating to **better** public health.

https://www.obesityaction.org › Article Library   ⋮

A Soda Tax — Will it Change Anything? - Obesity Action Coalition

This would reduce the number of calories from sugary beverages people drink each day, and may help with weight-loss. A **tax** of a penny-per-ounce, which is ...

https://scopeblog.stanford.edu › Latest   ⋮

Soda taxes increase prices but lower consumption, studies find

April 9, 2019 — **Taxes** encourage people to buy less **soda**, according to two new studies that find sugar-sweetened beverage **taxes** reduce local consumption.

https://www.npr.org › sections › thesalt › 2019/02/21 › u-...   ⋮

U.S. Soda Taxes Work, Studies Suggest — But Maybe Not As ...

Feb 21, 2019 — This week, the governor of Connecticut proposed a statewide **tax** on sugar-sweetened **drinks**. Several cities have already enacted such **soda** ...

https://www.taxpolicycenter.org › briefing-book › how...   ⋮

How do state and local soda taxes work? - The Policy Center

Most current **soda taxes** in the United States are based on a eligible drink's volume and not its sugar content. That is, an eight-ounce drink with two teaspoons ...

https://publichealth.berkeley.edu › research-highlights   ⋮

Do soda taxes work? - UC Berkeley Public Health

Aug 24, 2019 — Her research shows that these **taxes** significantly reduce the consumption of sugar-sweetened beverages (SSBs) — **drinks** like Coca-Cola and Pepsi, ...

FIGURE 3.19 "Are soda taxes a good idea" search results, December 2020. (Google and the Google logo are trademarks of Google LLC.)

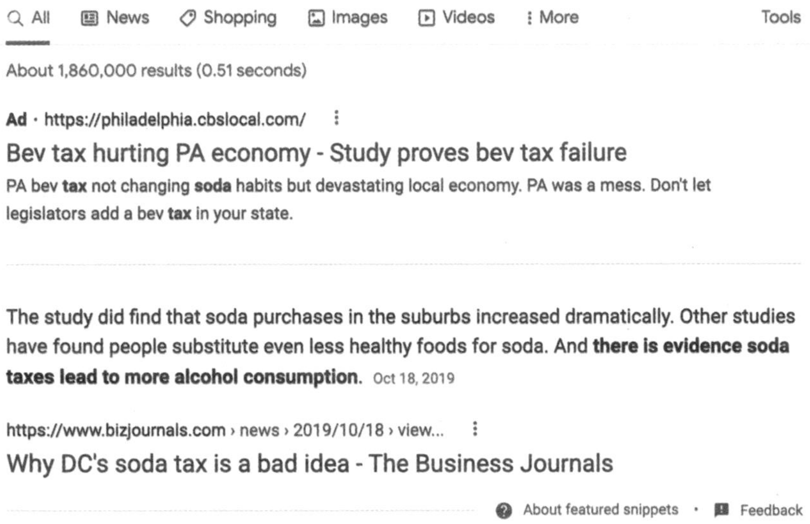

Q All   📰 News   🔗 Shopping   🖼 Images   ▶ Videos   ⋮ More   Tools

About 1,860,000 results (0.51 seconds)

Ad · https://philadelphia.cbslocal.com/   ⋮

Bev tax hurting PA economy - Study proves bev tax failure

PA bev **tax** not changing **soda** habits but devastating local economy. PA was a mess. Don't let legislators add a bev **tax** in your state.

The study did find that soda purchases in the suburbs increased dramatically. Other studies have found people substitute even less healthy foods for soda. And **there is evidence soda taxes lead to more alcohol consumption.**   Oct 18, 2019

https://www.bizjournals.com › news › 2019/10/18 › view...   ⋮

Why DC's soda tax is a bad idea - The Business Journals

                                   ❓ About featured snippets   ·   ▣ Feedback

FIGURE 3.20 Ad and featured snippet for "Are soda taxes a bad idea" search. (Google and the Google logo are trademarks of Google LLC.)

An ad at the top says that in Philadelphia the tax was a "mess" and didn't change drinking habits. A featured snippet raises the ante even more, claiming that soda taxes lead to an increase in alcohol consumption. And so on. (But note that one of the results from the "good" query, a result from the University of California, Berkeley School of Public Health, slips in too.)

Part of what's going on has to do with keywords. Results in favor of soda taxes are just more likely to include "good" (and other positive terms: "beneficial," "effective," "helpful," and so on). Likewise, results against a tax tend to include "bad" and its various synonyms. But another part of what was going on has to do with *inferred intent*. Google sees "good" or "bad" and delivers what it thinks you want. A positive or negative search term loads the dice, crafting the kind of response we want and expect. Phrasing queries in a more neutral way—for

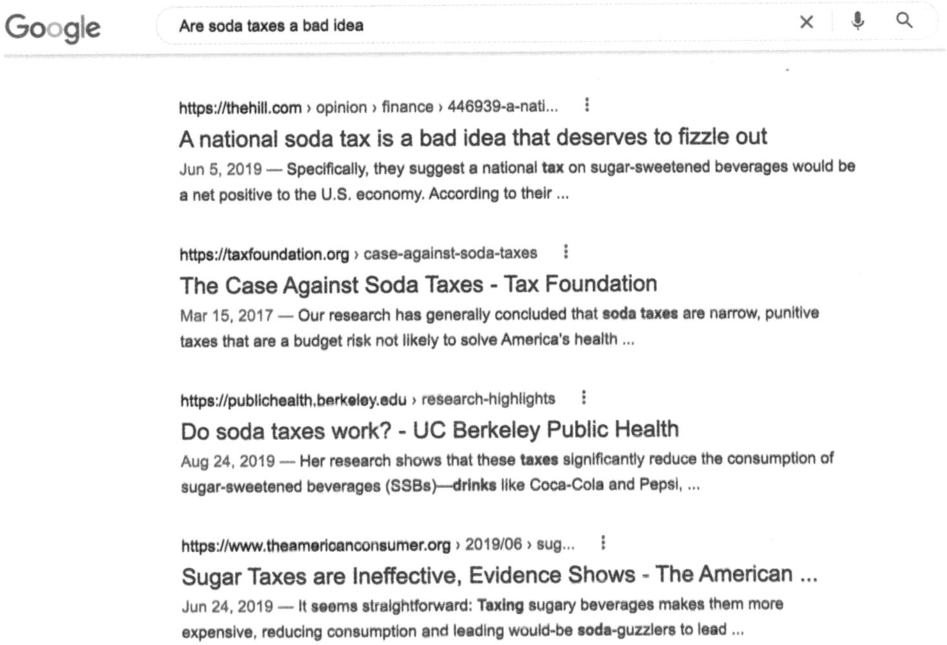

Google | Are soda taxes a bad idea

---

https://thehill.com › opinion › finance › 446939-a-nati... ⋮
A national soda tax is a bad idea that deserves to fizzle out
Jun 5, 2019 — Specifically, they suggest a national **tax** on sugar-sweetened beverages would be a net positive to the U.S. economy. According to their ...

https://taxfoundation.org › case-against-soda-taxes ⋮
The Case Against Soda Taxes - Tax Foundation
Mar 15, 2017 — Our research has generally concluded that **soda taxes** are narrow, punitive taxes that are a budget risk not likely to solve America's health ...

https://publichealth.berkeley.edu › research-highlights ⋮
Do soda taxes work? - UC Berkeley Public Health
Aug 24, 2019 — Her research shows that these **taxes** significantly reduce the consumption of sugar-sweetened beverages (SSBs)—**drinks** like Coca-Cola and Pepsi, ...

https://www.theamericanconsumer.org › 2019/06 › sug... ⋮
Sugar Taxes are Ineffective, Evidence Shows - The American ...
Jun 24, 2019 — It seems straightforward: **Taxing** sugary beverages makes them more expensive, reducing consumption and leading would-be **soda-guzzlers** to lead ...

FIGURE 3.21 "Are soda taxes a bad idea" search results. (Google and the Google logo are trademarks of Google LLC.)

example, "Do soda taxes work?"—will often produce better and more balanced results.

Google Is a Mirror Reflecting Back What You Give It

Are you an auditory learner? A kinesthetic one? Do you learn best by watching a video or reading a text? What's your "learning style"?

The field of learning styles is mired in controversy.[12] Even though the idea of learning styles has been around for years, its scientific basis is skimpy. Attempts to match people to their preferred learning style produce no better results than when they're matched to their "unpreferred" style. But scientific findings wither in the face of people's deep-seated intuitions. "I'm a visual learner! Don't try to convince me otherwise!"

In an ideal search, we'd want Google to alert us to a controversy where laypeople say one thing but the scientific consensus says another. In fact, when we asked Google if learning styles are real, that's just what we get:

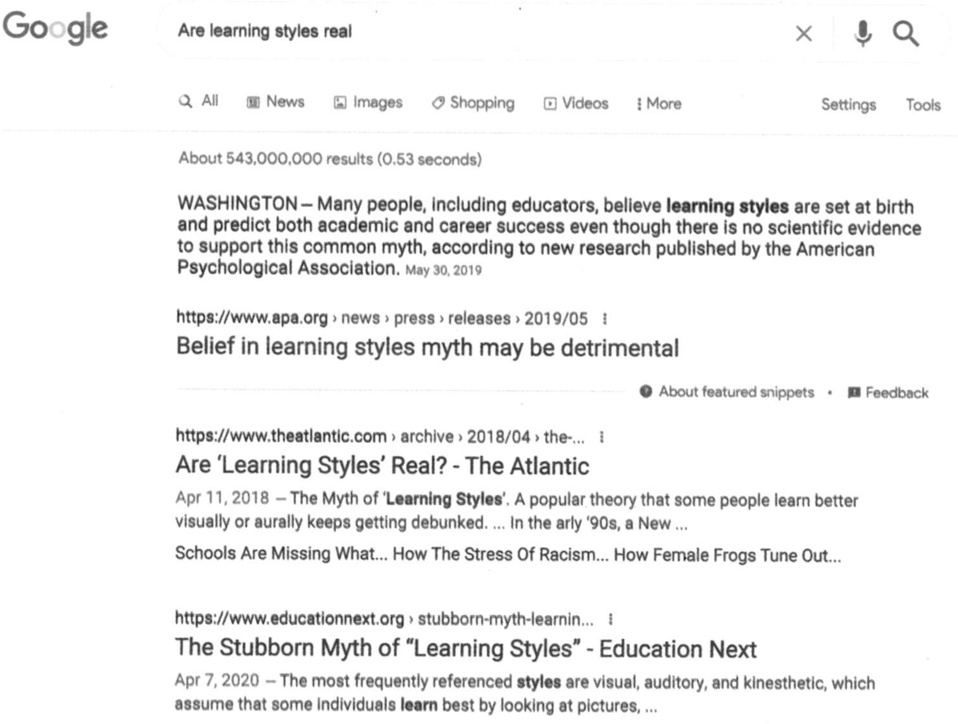

Google   Are learning styles real   ✕   🎤   🔍

Q All   🔲 News   🖼 Images   ⊘ Shopping   ▶ Videos   ⋮ More   Settings   Tools

About 543,000,000 results (0.53 seconds)

WASHINGTON — Many people, including educators, believe **learning styles** are set at birth and predict both academic and career success even though there is no scientific evidence to support this common myth, according to new research published by the American Psychological Association. May 30, 2019

https://www.apa.org › news › press › releases › 2019/05   ⋮
Belief in learning styles myth may be detrimental

                                        ❶ About featured snippets   •   🔳 Feedback

https://www.theatlantic.com › archive › 2018/04 › the-...   ⋮
Are 'Learning Styles' Real? - The Atlantic
Apr 11, 2018 — The Myth of '**Learning Styles**'. A popular theory that some people learn better visually or aurally keeps getting debunked. ... In the arly '90s, a New ...
Schools Are Missing What... How The Stress Of Racism... How Female Frogs Tune Out...

https://www.educationnext.org › stubborn-myth-learnin...   ⋮
The Stubborn Myth of "Learning Styles" - Education Next
Apr 7, 2020 — The most frequently referenced **styles** are visual, auditory, and kinesthetic, which assume that some individuals **learn** best by looking at pictures, ...

FIGURE 3.22 Search results for "Are learning styles real," December 2020. (Google and the Google logo are trademarks of Google LLC.)

At the top is a featured snippet from the American Psychological Association, the largest research group of psychologists in the world.

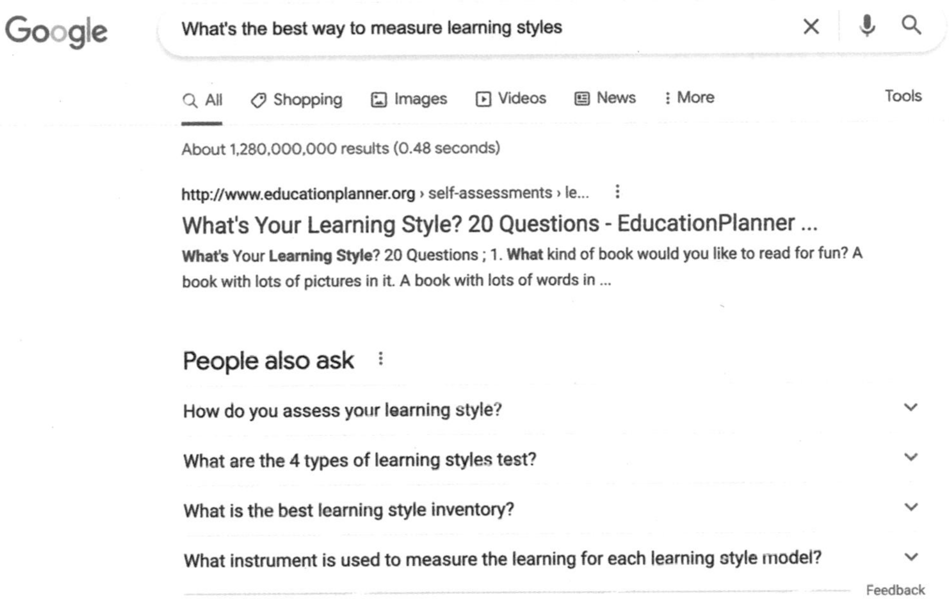

Google | What's the best way to measure learning styles | ✕ 🎤 🔍

🔍 All   🛍 Shopping   🖼 Images   ▶ Videos   📰 News   ⋮ More   Tools

About 1,280,000,000 results (0.48 seconds)

http://www.educationplanner.org › self-assessments › le... ⋮

What's Your Learning Style? 20 Questions - EducationPlanner ...

What's Your **Learning Style**? 20 Questions ; 1. **What** kind of book would you like to read for fun? A book with lots of pictures in it. A book with lots of words in ...

People also ask ⋮

How do you assess your learning style?   ⌄

What are the 4 types of learning styles test?   ⌄

What is the best learning style inventory?   ⌄

What instrument is used to measure the learning for each learning style model?   ⌄

Feedback

FIGURE 3.23 Results page for "What's the best way to measure learning styles." (Google and the Google logo are trademarks of Google LLC.)

No equivocating here: "there is no scientific evidence to support this common myth."

What happens when we assume that learning styles *are* real, but what we want to know is how to measure them? When we ask, "What's the best way to measure learning styles?" Google also obliges.

The top result takes you to a site where, in twenty questions (e.g., "Do you prefer books with words or pictures?"), you can "determine" your learning style. For fun, we answered the questions completely at random. We received an official-looking report telling us we're "visual learners" who should "sit near the front of the classroom."

There are two problems here: keywords and inferred intent. As far as keywords go, experts in education may talk about learning styles

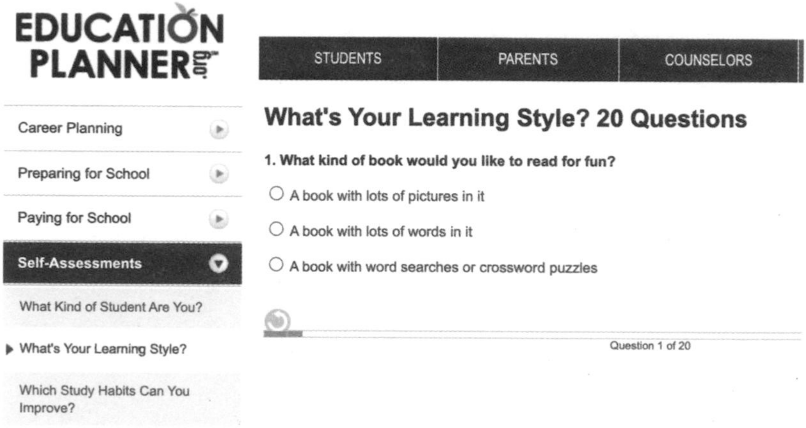

FIGURE 3.24 "What's Your Learning Style?" questionnaire from educationplanner.org (http://www.educationplanner.org/students/self-assessments/learning-styles.shtml)

in the context of whether they make a difference. But given the shaky state of research, they're unlikely to talk about "the best way" to measure learning styles because, well, it's debatable whether they even exist. So you're not going to find these keywords in documents written by experts.

But what about inferred intent—the attempt by Google's algorithms to deduce what we're looking for by the way we phrase a search? It's reasonable to assume we're already believers when we ask, "What's the best way to measure learning styles?" Google, being Google, guides us down that path.

A Search Engine, Not a "Truth Engine"

Google is not a dispassionate partner in information seeking who diligently corrects you when you've taken a wrong turn. Google is out to please, trying to determine what you want—even if doing so means giving you a dubious answer but one you want to hear. Danny

Sullivan, Google's public liaison for search, admitted as much when he stated that Google is a *search* engine, not a "truth engine." "One of the big issues we're pondering is how to explain that our role is to get you authoritative, good information, but that ultimately people have to process that information themselves," he said. "We can give you information, but we can't tell you the truth of a thing."[13]

This is exactly the case when an issue erupts that turns the internet into a raging, turbulent sea. When that happens, Google becomes especially attentive to our cues. Back in 2017, a bunch of NFL players, following Colin Kaepernick's lead, started taking a knee during the national anthem. Then president Trump tweeted that these actions hurt NFL ratings. If you searched for "NFL ratings down," your top results would have supported the president. However, had you searched for "NFL ratings up," Google would have delivered opposite results—ones that pointed to *increased* ratings.[14]

In other words, Google is not neutral. From the moment you enter your search terms, you're teaching Google what you want. Google's algorithms are masterful in picking up your personal tells: Are you on one side of an issue or the other? Favorable or hostile? Supporter or opponent? If there's any indication which way you're leaning, Google's results will nudge you *more* to that side. After all, it's Google's business model to give you what you want. "The Internet can get you to information that would back up almost any claim of fact, no matter how unfounded," wrote University of Connecticut philosopher Michael Lynch. "It is both the world's best fact-checker and the world's best bias confirmer—often at the same time."[15]

For now, just remember: you're at the poker table, and you don't want to give away your hand. If you want to understand multiple positions on a complex issue, avoid searches that broadcast your preferences, like "is X good" or "is X bad"? Choose neutral search terms. And don't forget: Google is following *your* lead.

Takeaways

▷ Anticipate the kinds of results you're looking for *before* searching. A mismatch between your expectations and the search results may signal that you need to rethink your strategy.

▷ Before you click on a result, engage in *result mining*. There's a lot you can learn just by reading the snippets that accompany each result.

▷ Specific and unique keywords will get you to your desired result a lot faster than general terms.

▷ With straight factual issues, nothing beats Google. It's when things get murky that the burden is on you. Google is a search engine, not a truth engine.

▷ Google detects your slightest tell and gives you what it thinks you want to hear. Phrasing a search in a neutral way will give you a fuller and more balanced picture on issues with multiple sides.

Lateral Reading

USING THE WEB TO READ THE WEB

You and your friends have complained for years about the bullying at your hometown school. Nothing has been done—until now. The school board is finally ready, and you've been nominated by school staff to present the issue.

You'll have one shot. You want to make sure that the school board doesn't just do something about it; you want to make sure it does something about it that *works*. You dust off those newly learned research skills and google "bullying at school."

Before you can even click, Google offers ten autosuggestions.

"Bullying at school never acceptable," the first item in the list, sounds about right. It lands you on the site of the American College of Pediatricians.

"No child should be harassed for his or her unique characteristics." Check. "Schools should encourage an environment of respectful self-expression for all students." Yes.

Weighty references accompany the article: "A Multilevel Examination of Peer Victimization and Bullying Preventions in Schools" in the

bullying at school **never acceptable**
bullying at school **statistics**
bullying at school **laws**
bullying at school **videos**
bullying at school **articles**
bullying at school **examples**
bullying at school **movie**
bullying at school **essay**
bullying at school **short film**
bullying at school **negative effects**

FIGURE 4.1 Google's autosuggestions for "Bullying at school" search, November 2020. (Google and the Google logo are trademarks of Google LLC.)

| About Us | Resources | Topics | News | Contact Us | Donate | Become a Member |

Bullying at School: Never Acceptable

American College of Pediatricians - October 2013

ABSTRACT: No child should be harassed for his or her unique characteristics. Schools should encourage an environment of respectful self-expression for all students, and no group should be singled out for special treatment. Parental involvement should be a school's primary method of resolution with programs emphasizing general respectfulness serving to set the tone in the classrooms.

FIGURE 4.2 Abstract for "Bullying at School: Never Acceptable" article from American College of Pediatricians (https://acpeds.org/position-statements/bullying-at-school -never-acceptable)

Journal of Criminology. "Association between Bullying and Psychosomatic Problems: A Meta-Analysis" in *Pediatrics.*

You skim the rest. It's science-y. You glance at the headings: "Abstract," "Forms of Bullying," "Prevention," "Conclusion"; it's signed by an MD and accompanied by this statement: "The American College of Pediatricians (ACPeds) is a national association of licensed

FIGURE 4.3 Home page of the American College of Pediatricians (acpeds.org)

physicians. . . . The mission of ACPeds is to enable all children to reach their optimal physical and emotional health and well-being."

You go to the home page.

How can you *not* trust a kid this cute?

Before you put your faith in this site, consider the fact that the American College of Pediatricians

- is labeled as a "fringe anti-LGBTQ hate group that masquerades as the premier U.S. association of pediatricians" by the Southern Poverty Law Center;[1]
- promotes "conversion" therapy for gay kids, a procedure outlawed in twenty states, the District of Columbia, and all of Canada;[2]
- publishes vile and defamatory content, like a post where it advocated adding "P" for pedophilia to "LGBT" because, it falsely claimed,

pedophilia is "intrinsically woven into [the] agenda" of LGBTQ activists;[3] and

- is condemned by Francis S. Collins, MD, the former director of the National Institutes of Health, for an "ideology that can cause unnecessary anguish and encourage prejudice."[4]

You probably couldn't find a *worse* resource for helping kids who are getting bullied at school. Especially LGBTQ kids. Compared to their heterosexual peers, LGBTQ kids are two to four times more at risk for thinking about and attempting suicide during adolescence—precisely because of the ridicule and abuse they endure at school.[5]

You may have assumed that the American College of Pediatricians was a large professional organization, dispensing authoritative information to doctors and the general public. Actually, it's a tiny splinter group of conservative doctors (estimates range from two hundred to five hundred) who, in 2002, broke from the national group, the sixty-seven-thousand-member American Academy of Pediatrics, over the issue of adoption by same-sex couples.[6]

Now that you know a bit about the American College of Pediatricians, can you spot the subtle persuasion in the abstract from the "Bullying at School: Never Acceptable" article—the phrase "no group should be singled out for special treatment"? You'd never learn from this site that LGBTQ kids are the main targets of bullying in school.[7] The American College of Pediatricians doesn't want gay kids "singled out for special treatment" because doing so, it fears, might push "temporarily-confused adolescents into adopting an atypical lifestyle," as they say later in the "Bullying at School" article.

It's easy to get duped by the site's professional look, its official-sounding name, its formal logo, and its detached scientific tone. If you got fooled, you're in good company. When Sam's research team showed this site along with that of the American Academy of Pediatrics to a

SPLC
Southern Poverty
Law Center

RESOURCES ⌄ WHAT WE DO ⌄ OUR ISSUES ⌄ HATEWATCH HATE MAP PODCAST Q

AMERICAN COLLEGE OF PEDIATRICIANS

The American College of Pediatricians (ACPeds) is a fringe anti-LGBTQ hate group that masquerades as the premier U.S. association of pediatricians to push anti-LGBTQ junk science, primarily via far-right conservative media and filing amicus briefs in cases related to gay adoption and marriage equality.

ACPeds opposes adoption by LGBTQ couples, links homosexuality to pedophilia, endorses so-called reparative or sexual orientation conversion therapy for homosexual youth, believes transgender people have a mental illness and has called transgender health care for youth child abuse.

In its own words

EXTREMIST GROUP INFO:

SPLC DESIGNATED HATE GROUP

Date Founded: 2002

Location: Gainesville, Florida

Ideology: Anti-LGBTQ

"Your public library may have a drag queen story hour where books like I am Jazz are read to children by trans activists eager to groom the next generation of victims."— *Andre Van Mol, co-chair of ACPeds' Committee on Adolescent Sexuality,* "Reinforcing Children's Sexual Identity: A Review of Ellie Klipp's 'I Don't Have to Choose,' Aug. 27, 2019*

FIGURE 4.4 Southern Poverty Law Center's description of the American College of Pediatricians (https://www.splcenter.org/fighting-hate/extremist-files/group/american-college-pediatricians)

group of Stanford students, the majority chose the splinter group as more reliable. Even professors at five different colleges wavered when asked to choose which of the two sites was more trustworthy. One of these professors confidently stated that the splinter group's site was "just a useful resource for people to learn about bullying."[8] He had no inkling that something was amiss. And amiss is an understatement.

Get off the Page!

How do we explain this? After all, the college students and university professors were good readers and critical thinkers. Why, then, did both groups go off the rails?

Part of their problem had to do with *being* smart—so smart they thought they could outsmart the web. They reckoned they could tell if a site was reliable just by looking at it.

An even bigger problem was that these smart people approached online texts the same way they approached a printed book or magazine. They read *vertically*. They started at the top of the screen and moved toward the bottom—the way we all learned to read in school. Sometimes they skimmed; sometimes they pressed on an internal link. But their eyes pretty much stayed glued to the original site, even though they were told they could do anything they normally would, like leave the site and search elsewhere. To determine a site's credibility, they placed their faith in their intelligence and reading ability. When nothing outrageous jumped out, they concluded: "pretty reasonable."

Here's the thing: what got these smart people into hot water was a category error. They took highly honed skills from the world of print and applied them to a medium, the internet, that plays by different rules. It's like a star baseball player with a sweet swing applying the same motion on the golf course. What works so well in baseball flops in golf.

Lateral Reading: Checking Information like a Fact-Checker

Now consider an approach tailored to a digital environment. It's the key to SIFT's *investigate the source*, and it is what professional fact-checkers do to cut through bluster to arrive at reliable conclusions.

Fact-checkers don't spend minutes dwelling on an unfamiliar site. They generally ignore the "About" page. They might glance at the URL, but they pay little attention to whether a site is a dot-com or a dot-org. To learn about an unfamiliar site, they do something that, at first glance, seems like a contradiction. They *leave* it.

Instead of spending minutes on a site they've never seen, fact-checkers put the name of the individual or group in their browsers and open new tabs across the top of their screen. Fact-checkers draw on the entire internet to evaluate an individual site, a strategy we call *lateral reading*. By reading laterally and scanning across a series of open tabs, every one of our fact-checkers detected the agenda of the American College of Pediatricians in seconds, leaving the college students and the university professors at the starting gate.[9]

Why Lateral Reading Works

Lateral reading works for one basic reason. The *web is a web*, a galaxy of electronically connected sources. And the way that you understand a node in a webbed network is to probe its connections to other nodes.

Think of it like this: If you wanted to understand how spiders catch their prey, you wouldn't just look at a single strand. You'd want to see how that strand connects to other strands that, together, form an elaborate geometric pattern. A similar strategy is the key to success on the internet. You evaluate a single website by seeing what the rest of the web has to say. You use the web to *read* the web.

Here's how that would work with the American College of Pediatricians. You land on the site, but before giving it your full attention (and risk falling down a rabbit hole by reading articles that con you with scientific language and fancy references), you decide to search the name of the group. When you google the group and open a few tabs, you immediately see something's askew.

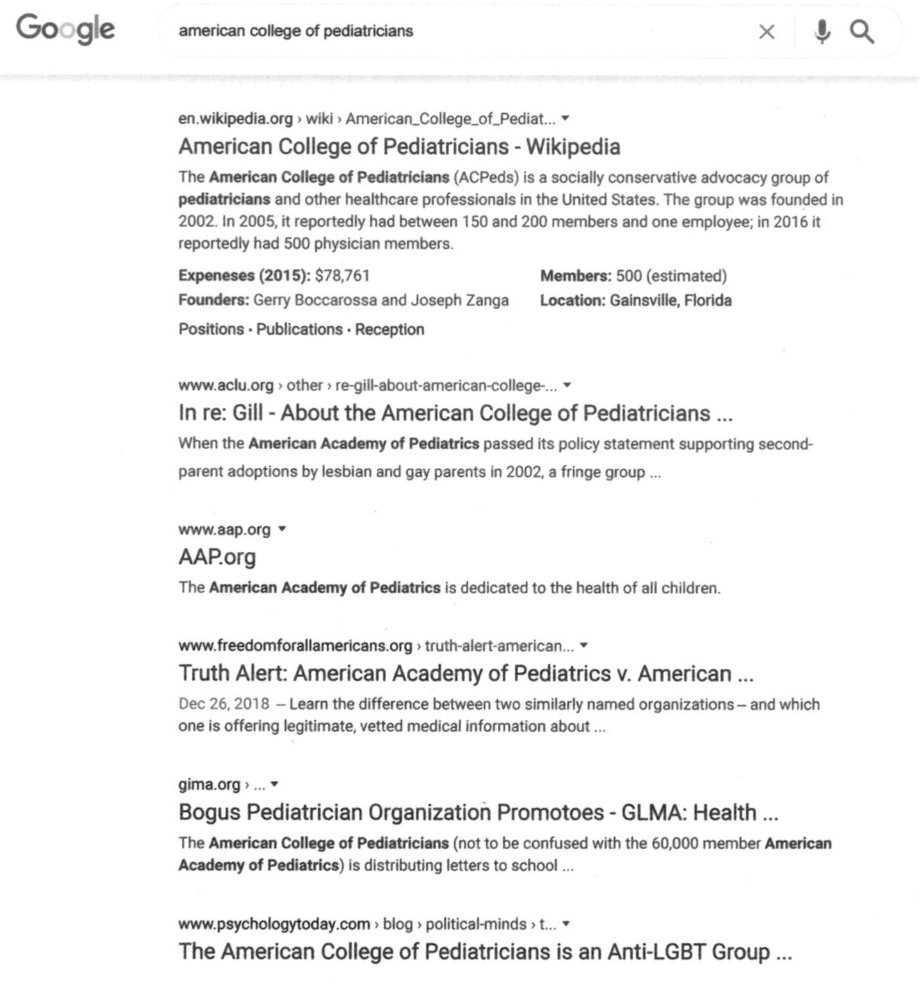

Google american college of pediatricians ✕ 🎤 🔍

en.wikipedia.org › wiki › American_College_of_Pediat... ▾
American College of Pediatricians - Wikipedia
The **American College of Pediatricians** (ACPeds) is a socially conservative advocacy group of **pediatricians** and other healthcare professionals in the United States. The group was founded in 2002. In 2005, it reportedly had between 150 and 200 members and one employee; in 2016 it reportedly had 500 physician members.

Expeneses (2015): $78,761	**Members:** 500 (estimated)
Founders: Gerry Boccarossa and Joseph Zanga	**Location:** Gainsville, Florida

Positions · Publications · Reception

www.aclu.org › other › re-gill-about-american-college-... ▾
In re: Gill - About the American College of Pediatricians ...
When the **American Academy of Pediatrics** passed its policy statement supporting second-parent adoptions by lesbian and gay parents in 2002, a fringe group ...

www.aap.org ▾
AAP.org
The **American Academy of Pediatrics** is dedicated to the health of all children.

www.freedomforallamericans.org › truth-alert-american... ▾
Truth Alert: American Academy of Pediatrics v. American ...
Dec 26, 2018 — Learn the difference between two similarly named organizations — and which one is offering legitimate, vetted medical information about ...

gima.org › ... ▾
Bogus Pediatrician Organization Promotoes - GLMA: Health ...
The **American College of Pediatricians** (not to be confused with the 60,000 member **American Academy of Pediatrics**) is distributing letters to school ...

www.psychologytoday.com › blog › political-minds › t... ▾
The American College of Pediatricians is an Anti-LGBT Group ...

FIGURE 4.5 Google's results page for the American College of Pediatricians, November 2020. (Google and the Google logo are trademarks of Google LLC.)

Wikipedia calls the organization a "socially conservative advocacy group" with one employee. The American Civil Liberties Union labels it a "fringe group." Even without knowing that glma.org is the site of GLMA: Health Professionals Advancing LGBTQ Equality (formerly known as the "Gay & Lesbian Medical Association"), we can gain clues from its description of the American College of Pediatricians as "not to be confused with the 60,000 member American Academy of Pediatrics." *Psychology Today* tells us that the American College of Pediatricians "is an anti-LGBT group." From there things go downhill. Fast.

Little Shift, Big Payoff

The shift from vertical to lateral reading makes a huge difference. Consider a second example: research into minimum wage policy. Does raising the minimum wage increase the standard of living? Or does it cause prices to rise, hurting the very people it's supposed to help? One of the first sites to come up in a search is epionline.org, from a group called the Employment Policies Institute. (This group sponsors the site minimumwage.com, which we profiled in the last chapter.)

The site piles on the cheap signals of credibility. A professional

FIGURE 4.6 Home page of the Employment Policies Institute (epionline.org)

EPI RESEARCH

A Survey of US Economists on a $15 Federal Minimum Wage

April 2022

Across the nation, lawmakers continue to grapple with the viability and impact of increasing the minimum wage to $15 an hour. The debate continues to be heated and some cities have already enacted increases they believe will benefit workers. While the impact of these increases is becoming more clear, recent surveys of businesses, franchises and other groups confirm that such minimum wage raises actually harms...

The Case for the Tip Credit: From Workers, Employers, and Research

February 2021

The tipping system provides substantial earning opportunities for workers across many industries, especially restaurant servers and bartenders – well beyond the current minimum wage, and even beyond the proposed $15 minimum wage. Saving the tip credit is a worker-organized, bipartisan issue. Thousands of tipped workers across the country have pushed to save the tip credit, against the infringement of outside interests and activists. Yet, interest...

Tipped Workers, Minimum Wage Workers, and Poverty: Analyzing the Redistributive Impact of Eliminating Tip Credits

February 2021

Key takeaway: According to a new study by economists from the University of California, Irvine, tipped workers are significantly less likely to be poor than are standard minimum wage earners. Tipped workers, many of whom are in the food and beverage service industry, have lower statutory minimum wages than other workers (under federal and most state laws). However, the lower minimum wages for tipped workers...

FIGURE 4.7 Research reports on the site of the Employment Policies Institute, April 2022 (https://epionline.org/studies/)

layout bathed in tasteful maroon and gray hues. A nonprofit designation from the IRS. A physical address and contact number. A dot-org URL. A "Research" tab listing reports by professors at established universities: the University of New Hampshire; University of Connecticut; University of California, Irvine; Carnegie Mellon; and others.

Rather than clicking on any of these research reports or dwelling on the "About" page, here's how one of the fact-checkers we observed approached the site. He left it in a split second and googled "Employment Policies Institute." In a half minute, he had seven open tabs across the top of his screen. One, from the online magazine *Salon*, wasted no time calling out the Employment Policies Institute: "Corporate America's New Scam: Industry P.R. Firm Poses as Think Tank."[10]

The Employment Policies Institute dresses up in the costume of "nonpartisanship." In actuality, it's the handiwork of a public-relations firm, Rick Berman and Company, which specializes in cooking up websites for corporate and political clients. As for those research reports, which all conveniently stack up *against* raising the minimum wage? One of the professors received a $180,000 grant from the Employment Policies Institute to fund his study.[11] That doesn't mean he fudged his data. Let's just say the optics don't look great.[12]

FIGURE 4.8 Fact-checker's open tabs when reading laterally. (Google and the Google logo are trademarks of Google LLC.)

Lateral Reading Puts You in Control

When you dwell on a site before you know who's behind it, you play into the hands of the Rick Bermans of the world. But when you marshal the web's web-like qualities, it's you who's in the driver's seat. As the journalist Steve Daly explained, "Think of lateral reading as sending up multiple signal flares in a barrage instead of one at a time. The bombardment lights up a wide swath of terrain. It lets you see quickly which part of this landscape might provide the fastest gauge of reliability."[13]

The big message of lateral reading is this: get off the page. Once you're off—once you've entered your keywords, hit return, and sit staring at the results—how, then, do you decide which result to click? Many of us never look beyond Google's first few results—some studies have found that over 50 percent of searchers never go beyond the third result.[14] A joke among disgruntled web advertisers goes like this: "Where's the best place to hide a dead body?" Answer: "Page 2 of the search results."

Google tells us that by using the criteria of expertise, authoritativeness, and trustworthiness, or E-A-T, it tries to array the most relevant results at the top of the search.[15] And that sort of works. Sometimes. For certain subjects. Given the right keywords.

But Google's search algorithms, like all things human, betray the flaws of human design—racism, sexism, ableism, antisemitism, and every other *ism* that afflicts humankind. (More on this later. For now, let's give the company credit where credit is due: Google generally tries to fix these problems when they are pointed out). Each year the company adjusts its search algorithms with hundreds, if not thousands, of tweaks. The process is never-ending. However, given the monetary value of being at the top of page 1, Google is engaged in a cat and mouse game with legions of site owners who try to outgame the algorithms by manipulating keywords, planting links on other sites, spamming, reconfiguring their content, and doing everything imaginable to get a leg up on the competition. Pushing results to the top of Google's list, a process known as *search engine optimization*, is an eighty-billion-dollar-a-year business focused on a singular goal: figuring out how to land a site on Google's prime real estate while kicking the competition to the bottom of the page—or even better, to the mortuary of page 2.

Avoid Promiscuous Clicking: Practice *Click Restraint*

Rather than immediately clicking on the first three results, we suggest that you follow step one of SIFT: *stop*. Take a deep breath. Look around. Figure out where you've landed. If it helps, take those sticky fingers off the mouse so you don't click the first thing that pops up. Then do what professional fact-checkers do: practice *click restraint*.

How? By resisting the impulse to click. Click restraint is about surveying the *information neighborhood* into which you've landed. Who occupies the palatial mansion at the top of the page? Who's dwelling in the row houses in the middle? What about the cellar dwellers at the bottom of the screen who, despite their lowly placement, might just be the best sources for your question?

Obviously, the importance of click restraint varies depending on what you want to know. Ask Google "Where was Beyoncé born?" and you'll get an answer faster than it takes to type the question. Things start to get wonky when you put a question to Google that has multiple answers, or controversy.

For example, a post in your social media floats by that China has bought Walmart, and the chain will now be redubbed "the Great

Wallmart," with signs in English and Mandarin. You're tempted to share the post—the new moniker is kinda clever—but since you've taken to heart what we've written, you do a thirty-second fact-check by googling "Did China buy Walmart?" Here are four results that come up:

did china buy walmart 🔍

All   News   Shopping   Videos   Images   More   Settings   Tools

About 32,800,000 results (0.31 seconds)

China Buys Walmart, Will Rebrand As GreatWallmart - The Final Edition
thefinaledition.com/article/china-buys-walmart-will-rebrand-as-greatwallmart.html ▼
In a move that took both Wall Street and Main Street USA by surprise, the world's largest nation has announced the acquisition of the world's largest retailer.

Does China own Walmart? - Quora
https://www.quora.com/Does-China-own-Walmart
Jan 10, 2017 - No, **Walmart** is a Transnational Corporation (TNC) which sets up in different ... lower **prices** at other stores while you shop on Amazon and tells you where to **buy**.

Does **Walmart** own Dollar Tree?   Dec 28, 2016
Why **Walmart** and Best **Buy** both failed in **China**?   May 12, 2016
Is **Walmart** owned by **Chinese** interests? How?   Jan 30, 2016
Who owns **Walmart**?   Mar 19, 2015
More results from www.quora.com

Walmart Sells To Chinese Investment Group For Over $500B | Empire ...
empirenews.net/walmart-sold-to-chinese-investment-group-for-over500b/ ▼
Jan 28, 2015 - BENTONVILLE, Arkansas –. Sam Walton founded **Walmart** on July 2, 1952 after working for retail giant J.C. Penny for several years. Walton ...

Rob Walton sells Walmart shares - Business Insider
https://www.businessinsider.com/rob-walton-sells-walmart-shares-2017-8 ▼
Aug 28, 2017 - Analysts are split on **Walmart**, according to CNBC: 14 have buy, 15 hold and , ... A **Walmart** spokesperson has did not immediately respond to ...

FIGURE 4.9 Search results for "Did China buy Walmart," December 2017. (Google and the Google logo are trademarks of Google LLC.)

There's your answer—right at the top. "China Buys Walmart, Will Rebrand as GreatWallmart." You're tempted to click, but you've turned over a new leaf: *look but don't click.*

That first result? It comes from a site called thefinaledition.com, which claims that "the world's largest nation has announced the acquisition of the world's largest retailer." Have you heard of thefinaledition .com?[16] We haven't either. We'll move on.

Result two is from quora.com, a helpful question-answering site that offers a lot of useful material. There's even a question relevant to our search: "Does China own Walmart?" We make a mental note and move on to empirenews.net. We haven't heard of that site either. But the title's pretty clear, and it even says the sale was valued over five hundred billion dollars. Maybe we *will* be shopping at the Great-Wallmart.

We get to the last result, businessinsider.com, an established trade magazine (the site, with an expanded purview, is now called "Insider," insider.com), and we read the snippet. Nothing about China. We make a wise first click and arrive at an article about how Rob Walton, the son of Walmart founder Sam Walton, sold less than 1 percent of his shares for a cool sixty-two million dollars. Nothing in the article about China. So, aside from that first link, which turns out to be from a satirical site, and empirenews.net, which, no surprise, is also a parody site, there seems to be no evidence that China bought Walmart. You can breathe a sigh of relief. (If you still need convincing, check out Quora and confirm there's nothing to the rumor.)

The "Vibe" of the Search Engine Results Page

Remember those optical illusions where, depending on how you look at them, you see two different things: in one case, a vase or two faces; in another, an old or a young woman?

Seeing both images simultaneously requires stepping back and gaining perspective. The goal is to take in the image as a whole, what

FIGURE 4.10 Vase or two faces? (Image by OpenClipart, licensed under Creative Commons 1.0 Universal.)

in German is called *gestalt*: an organized figure that is greater than the sum of its parts. If you'll excuse the use of a newer term, think of it as the "vibe" of the whole. Gestalt is the vibe.

A list of search results is also a gestalt. Yes, each result is a separate entity. But when you step back from the list, you can discern a pattern—a forest rather than a bunch of individual trees. Seeing the whole forest is key to understanding where on the internet you've landed. And who's controlling the territory.

In the GreatWallmart example, we made a smart first click. But the truth is, we realized something was wrong even before clicking. If China had bought Walmart, that would be a big news story, right? So why did the results page have no recognizable news stories at the top? It's not just about the individual results; it's the *whole* page. Did

FIGURE 4.11 Old woman or young woman? (Illustration by William Ely Hill, "My Wife and My Mother-in-Law," *Puck*, November 6, 1915.)

it look like the results page for a huge breaking news story? Obviously not.

Here's another example: a search about Margaret Sanger (1879–1966), the founder of what would become Planned Parenthood. Because the topic of abortion is so polarizing—fierce battles rage between pro-choice and pro-life advocates—Sanger has become a lightning rod that attracts intense feelings depending on where you stand. In one of Sam's research studies, participants were asked to investigate whether Sanger supported euthanasia (also known as mercy killing or assisted suicide), the practice in which someone with an incurable disease is painlessly helped to die.

Here's what people found when they typed "Margaret Sanger euthanasia" into their browser:

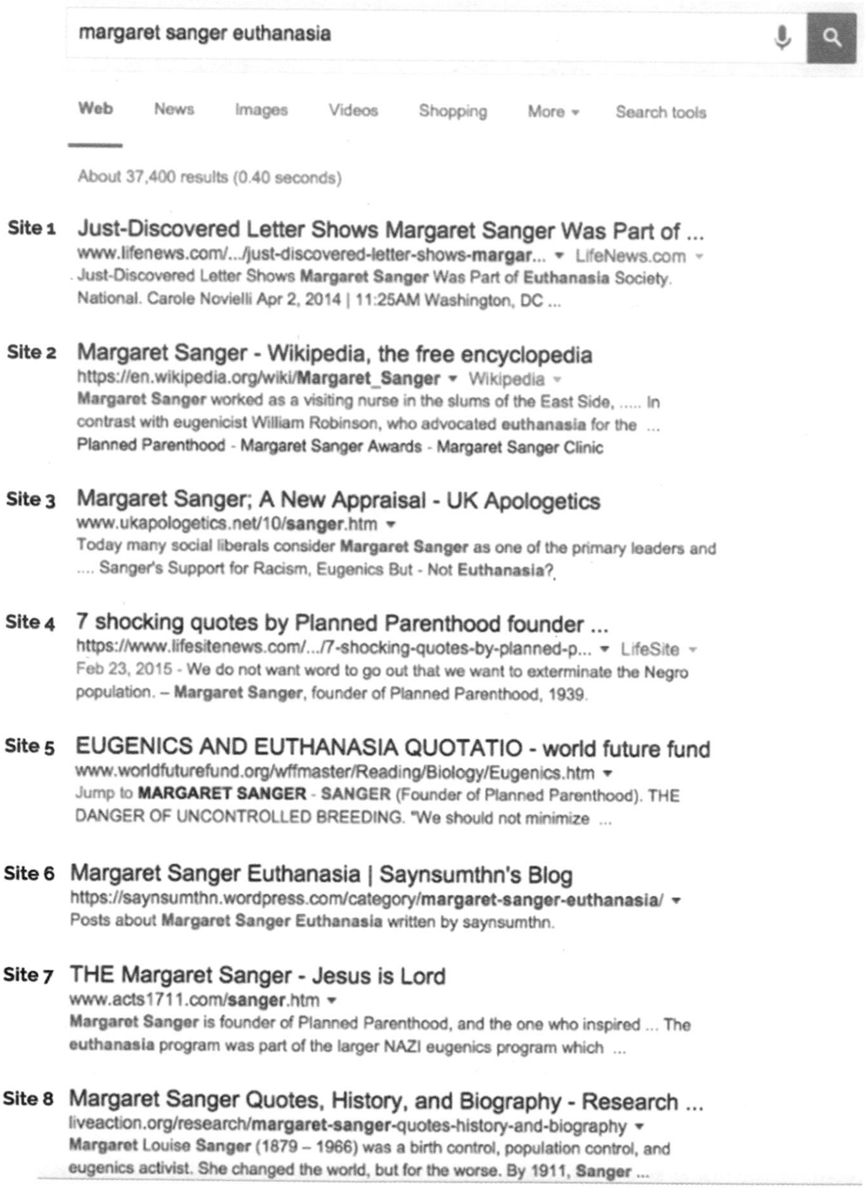

margaret sanger euthanasia

Web   News   Images   Videos   Shopping   More ▾   Search tools

About 37,400 results (0.40 seconds)

Site 1 Just-Discovered Letter Shows Margaret Sanger Was Part of ...
www.lifenews.com/.../just-discovered-letter-shows-margar... ▾ LifeNews.com ▾
. Just-Discovered Letter Shows **Margaret Sanger** Was Part of Euthanasia Society.
National. Carole Novielli Apr 2, 2014 | 11:25AM Washington, DC ...

Site 2 Margaret Sanger - Wikipedia, the free encyclopedia
https://en.wikipedia.org/wiki/**Margaret_Sanger** ▾ Wikipedia ▾
Margaret Sanger worked as a visiting nurse in the slums of the East Side, ... In
contrast with eugenicist William Robinson, who advocated **euthanasia** for the ...
Planned Parenthood - Margaret Sanger Awards - Margaret Sanger Clinic

Site 3 Margaret Sanger; A New Appraisal - UK Apologetics
www.ukapologetics.net/10/**sanger**.htm ▾
Today many social liberals consider **Margaret Sanger** as one of the primary leaders and
.... Sanger's Support for Racism, Eugenics But - Not **Euthanasia**?

Site 4 7 shocking quotes by Planned Parenthood founder ...
https://www.lifesitenews.com/.../7-shocking-quotes-by-planned-p... ▾ LifeSite ▾
Feb 23, 2015 - We do not want word to go out that we want to exterminate the Negro
population. – **Margaret Sanger**, founder of Planned Parenthood, 1939.

Site 5 EUGENICS AND EUTHANASIA QUOTATIO - world future fund
www.worldfuturefund.org/wffmaster/Reading/Biology/Eugenics.htm ▾
Jump to **MARGARET SANGER** - SANGER (Founder of Planned Parenthood). THE
DANGER OF UNCONTROLLED BREEDING. "We should not minimize ...

Site 6 Margaret Sanger Euthanasia | Saynsumthn's Blog
https://saynsumthn.wordpress.com/category/**margaret-sanger-euthanasia**/ ▾
Posts about **Margaret Sanger Euthanasia** written by saynsumthn.

Site 7 THE Margaret Sanger - Jesus is Lord
www.acts1711.com/**sanger**.htm ▾
Margaret Sanger is founder of Planned Parenthood, and the one who inspired ... The
euthanasia program was part of the larger NAZI eugenics program which ...

Site 8 Margaret Sanger Quotes, History, and Biography - Research ...
liveaction.org/research/**margaret-sanger**-quotes-history-and-biography ▾
Margaret Louise Sanger (1879 – 1966) was a birth control, population control, and
eugenics activist. She changed the world, but for the worse. By 1911, **Sanger** ...

FIGURE 4.12 Results page for "Margaret Sanger euthanasia" search, April 2016. (Google
and the Google logo are trademarks of Google LLC.)

Step back from this list of results. Can you discern a gestalt for the whole page? Has this search welcomed us to the Margaret Sanger fan club or catapulted us in an information neighborhood seething with rage at the mention of Sanger's name?

Apart from Wikipedia, none of the sites is familiar (at least not familiar to us). Another thing you notice is that site 1 (lifenews.com), site 4 (lifesitenews.com), and site 8 (liveaction.org) all have "life" or "live" in their URLs. The hostility is evident: site 3 accuses Sanger of racism; site 7 yokes her to Nazis; site 8 says she "changed the world, but for the worse." Apart from Wikipedia, the gestalt leaves no room for doubt. Sanger is public enemy number one.

One of the fact-checkers we observed scrolled through these results, spending twenty seconds practicing click restraint, just trying to get a sense of where she landed: "A lot of the sites that are coming up . . . seem to be very anti–Planned Parenthood sites. So, lifenews .com, lifesitenews.com, 'Sanger's support for racism,' so clearly these are people who are not very fond of her." That's putting it mildly.

She concluded that the anti-Sanger forces controlled the top real estate and that she could find better information by scanning books about Sanger. On the toolbar under "More" are a list of options. The second option is "Books."

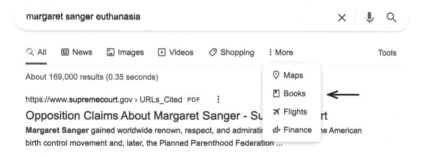

FIGURE 4.13 Restricting a Google search to "Books." (Google and the Google logo are trademarks of Google LLC.)

After scanning a few scholarly books, the fact-checker realized that the question of Sanger's stance on euthanasia was far more complicated than any quick soundbite or thirty-second foray would provide.[17]

We've focused on doing quick searches because we don't want you to waste your time. If you know what you're doing, it's astounding how much context can be gleaned in thirty seconds. But, as this example shows, quick searches can also show you the *limits* of quick searches. Trying to figure out where Margaret Sanger stood on the issue of euthanasia would require an investigation across multiple books and articles. Even then, the answer is not so clear-cut.

There's no formula that guarantees your first click will be the best one. Click restraint is far from an exact science. But taking in the full set of results *before* you click increases the chances you'll find something reliable rather than clicking away at the first thing that catches your eye.

Takeaways

▷ Rather than spending precious minutes on an unfamiliar website, get off the page. Practice the *I* in SIFT, investigate the source, by *reading laterally*.

▷ Put the name of the group or individual into your search and see what the rest of the web has to say. Use the web to read the web.

▷ If something looks fishy, lean into the *F* of SIFT and *find a better source*.

▷ Once you have that list of results in front of you, resist the temptation to click the first thing that catches your eye. Practice *click restraint* by scanning the full list of results to get a sense of the information neighborhood. Then, make a wise first click.

Reading the Room

BENEFITING FROM EXPERTISE WHEN
YOU HAVE ONLY A BIT YOURSELF

In his fact-checking workshops, Mike tells a parable of sorts about someone called Jill. Apologies if your name is Jill. But, as you'll see in a minute, Jill is really *all* of us.

Here's how the parable goes. One day, Jill is walking by a lake, and in the lake, she sees a bottle. Just bobbing up and down. A wave comes and tosses it onto the shore. She walks up to the bottle and sees a note inside.

It's interesting, right? She pulls out this note, and it's a full article. At the top is a headline: "N95 Masks Don't Work."

This is very shocking information. But Jill's no dummy. She does what she's learned in school. She looks at the tone of the text below the headline, at the article itself. And it's very scholarly. She looks for footnotes, and she finds lots of them, to all sorts of impressive-sounding journals. The author has an NMD. Jill doesn't know what that is, but it sounds like medical credentials.

There's more. The article has a *ton* of data, and Jill is very impressed. It not only makes claims—it backs them up with *numbers*, which is what she was taught to look for. There are statistics. There are charts. And at the core of the article is a very compelling, seemingly bullet-proof argument. The article states that the size of an N95 mask weave is .3 microns. The size of the coronavirus? Only .1 micron. And so, the article states, the coronavirus is going to sail through that mask like a "marble through a chain-link fence."

Jill sits there and sorts through the evidence. Coming to her own conclusion, she runs and tells her friend Antonio that she has discovered something quite disturbing: N95 masks don't work!

What would you say if you were Antonio? We hope it would be something like the following: "Jill, it's great that you've thought so much about this—but, in the end, you still got the information from a bottle floating in the lake."

Why You Can't "Just Do the Math"

It's good to think about things. It's good to try to understand the various arguments around issues of public or personal concern. But to come to better understandings of issues we care about, we rely heavily on the expertise and fair-mindedness of those we read, watch, or listen to.

Take Jill. Jill had a "just do the math" moment with the N95 argument she examined. The coronavirus is almost two-thirds smaller than the weave that is supposed to stop it, so it made sense to her that the mask would be ineffective. But the note in the bottle failed to mention a couple of other important things.

First, the coronavirus doesn't float around as the coronavirus, all alone. It needs a *medium*. Usually, that medium is a water droplet, and the size of the droplet, not the virus itself, is what is relevant.

Second, N95 masks benefit from an *electrostatic charge*, which pulls particles toward the fibers of the mask when the particles come near. So, the weave of the mask may be .3 microns, but in effect the weave can catch particles smaller than that.

Third—and perhaps most important—particles that are less than three microns engage in an erratic movement pattern called "Brownian motion." When a particle is over three microns, you can model it with standard physics. When it gets under three microns, something weird happens. The particle zigzags around because it is so small that the air molecules themselves affect its path. This zigzag pattern is hard to predict, but it makes particles *easier* to catch, since they can't pass straight through the weave. This means that, in practice, it is easier for a mask to capture a particle just under .3 microns than one that is exactly .3 microns.

We could go on. Most people test masks experimentally, of course, by just seeing how many particles get through them (no surprise, the masks work here too). But if we wanted to take Jill's "just do the math" approach, it turns out it takes a lot of math: the Brownian motion formula, the size of the medium, the relative humidity, the static charge of the mask, and, at least according to a prominent paper on the subject, a few dozen other variables and several pages of calculus.

In a way, Jill was doomed from the start. She was given the dots to connect, and then she dutifully connected them. But she wasn't given *all* the dots, and some of the dots she was given were downright wrong. No amount of Jill tallying numbers or thinking through the problem logically was going to fix that. She doesn't have enough knowledge to know what she isn't being told.

What's the solution? Ultimately, for most things in life, it's not getting better at math, more knowledgeable about biology, or spending more time looking at the details of a document that happens to wash up onshore in front of you. Ultimately, the solution is the *F* of SIFT:

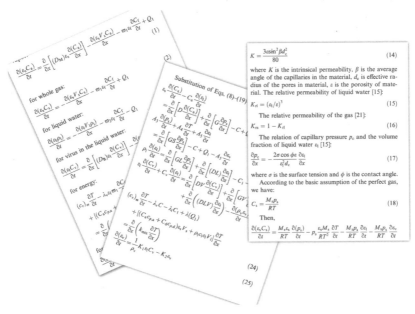

FIGURE 5.1 A taste of what's required to determine the effectiveness of an N95 mask through mathematical modeling. (Adapted from Yi, Fengzhi, and Qingyong, "Numerical Simulation of Virus Diffusion in Facemask during Breathing Cycles," *Int J Heat Mass Transf.* 48, no. 19 [2005]: 4229–42, https://doi.org/ 10.1016/j.ijheatmasstransfer.2005.03.030.)

find a better source, and learn what people with more knowledge than you think. For that you're going to have to learn to "read expertise."

Reading the Room: Quick Assessment
of a Range of Expert Views

For a lot of things in life, you can trust a single person. A good doctor or trusted mechanic will give you a lot of advice that just might be worth taking.

For issues where you do not have a trusted expert at hand, your best bet on getting a good treatment is usually not to put your faith in a single expert or professional. And even where you do have an expert handy, if the decision is particularly important (for example, around surgery), you might want a second opinion. For things that matter, you're going to want to understand what a range of experts think.

Let's start with some definitions of types of agreement and disagreement you find in expert communities.

COMPETING THEORIES: There are multiple explanations, and most experts buy into one or another of them, but no one idea is dominant.

MAJORITY/MINORITY: There is one widely accepted theory, but a nontrivial number of respected experts support one or more alternative theories that the majority concedes are worth consideration.

CONSENSUS: A rare condition where the majority of experts consider the evidence so compelling that the question is effectively closed. At the margins, a few folks may continue to pursue alternative theories, but most of the discipline has moved on to other questions.

UNCERTAINTY: This situation might initially look like majority/minority or competing theories, but when you look deeper, you find that most experts are so uncertain they have not invested deeply in any one hypothesis. (This is the sort of situation where the expert in a news article says pointedly, "We just don't know.")

FRINGE: For certain issues, in addition to a majority or minority expert viewpoint, you will find fringe viewpoints. Fringe viewpoints are not minority viewpoints—experts may disagree with minority viewpoints, but they consider them, nonetheless. Those espousing minority viewpoints argue their case with those espousing majority viewpoints, and vice versa. Fringe viewpoints, on the other hand, are viewpoints that have no support among the vast majority of respected scholars in the field. As such, these views are not even in dialogue with scholars in related disciplines or most individuals in a profession.

So how do you go about "reading the expert room" on various issues? This doesn't mean you have to agree with the smartest expert or the most people. In fact, it's quite the opposite. You may look at a majority/minority divide on the benefits of taking a given medication and go with the minority. You might have to wade in and make your best guess in choosing between competing theories. Or, sensing the level of uncertainty on an issue, even among experts, you might wisely decide to take no position at all—at least for now.

But we do want you to avoid what we call *trust compression.*[1]

GOING DEEPER
Why We Call This "Reading the Room"

"Read the room!" is the common rebuke to someone who jumps into a conversation without understanding its history or participants. It's also good advice when wandering into scholarly debates.

Why? If you look at our different categories of expert agreement and disagreement, you'll notice something. They aren't static. Scholarly conversations have a history. New issues arise, and experts propose a variety of explanations. In their field, they are expected to argue for those ideas in ways that allow others to review and challenge their work. Over time, experts come to various conclusions. A question might initially provoke uncertainty among experts, then competing theories. Certain approaches win out. What starts out as a competing theory might become consensus, or a majority theory. Likewise, from the fringe, people may make claims but not engage in the conversation in ways that abide by scholarly norms. Trying to figure this out can be a challenge. When you first wander into a new issue, you may think you are responding to a paper or a claim. In fact, you are wandering into an ongoing *conversation.*

So why do we call this chapter "reading the expert room?" Our metaphor here is that you arrive late to a party or dinner to find everyone deep in vigorous conversation. Asking a friend what's going on, you find out that the discussion has been in progress for hours.

Do you just jump in with your opinion? Or do you take a few minutes to understand what that conversation has covered until now, who the participants are, and the positions these people hold? You're trying to figure out what issues are resolved (the things that will elicit a communal groan if you drag the conversation back to them) and the things that are of current interest. If you follow the same practices when entering a scholarly conversation, you'll benefit richly from the room's expertise.

Trust Compression, or How to Avoid Info-Cynicism

Imagine you are trying to figure out the best person to drive you to the airport. You ask your friend whether Pedro, Leann, or Koko would be the best person to drive you. "Oh, I've asked them all at one point or another," she says. "I think they all have problems if you ask me."

Taking this to mean they're equivalent, you decide on Leann. She turns up forty-five minutes late, manages to get in a fender bender on the way there, and then insists that you reimburse her for mileage "plus 20 percent" before you get out of the car. You head back to your friend and relay the story. "Yeah," she says, "she did the exact same thing to me."

Stunned, you ask why she didn't warn you. "Well," she says, "Leann *is* always late and *did* crash her last four cars. But Pedro plays the radio too loud, and Koko never stops talking about her cat. Like I said, they all have problems."

We think you would agree that your friend here failed you in offering a recommendation, even if it is technically true that "they all have problems." What you really needed to know was how reputable each one was relative to the others. And one of the choices was very far apart from the others in that respect. The way your friend described them didn't convey the vast differences in reliability. Instead, the differences among them were minimized.

This minimizing of difference in quality or reliability is what we call "trust compression," because it takes the vast distances between different sources in reliability and shrinks them to the point where they all look roughly the same. And while it's unlikely one would make the sort of mistake in real life described in our going-to-the-airport example, people make it on the web *all the time*.

For instance, there's a huge distance between a site like the Mayo Clinic, a research hospital in Rochester, Minnesota, and Dakota Bob's All-Natural Holistic Health Supplements.[2] But if you start to think of both sites as being compromised—the Mayo Clinic is dependent on people getting sick and coming to it for treatment, and All-Natural Health Supplements is trying to convince you you're sick and need to buy sugar pills—then what we have is trust compression. What starts out as a chasm between a reputable site known all the world over and a fly-by-night holistic remedies site shrinks to the point of being negligible. Both are compromised. Neither can be trusted.

What's at stake is not just a bad ride to the airport. When trust compression reaches this level, where it seems like everybody's got an agenda and no one can be trusted, well, you've reached a state where unscrupulous people have you in their clutches. There's a reason why trust compression is often the goal of disinformation campaigns, whether the campaign is run by a foreign country, a global corporation, or a domestic lobbying group. When we believe no source is more trustworthy than any other, how do we decide who's right?

History tells us this works out various ways, none particularly good. In authoritarian regimes, creating a broad cynicism about all sources of expertise—the press, academics, professionals—serves to make sure political power, not truth-seeking, is the ultimate arbiter of what's true. If the best reporter is no better than the worst tabloid hack, why not just get the news directly from your leader or your political faction? Or why not choose academics based on their political allegiance rather than their credentials and expertise? They're all the same, right? Pick the one best for your cause. Or dispense with them altogether.[3]

When it comes to corporate disinformation, creating trust compression is a way to hide that a former competing theory has moved to a majority/minority or even consensus status. The classic example of this is cigarettes. Early on, there was much debate about whether smoking caused cancer, but by the 1950s there was a consolidation of the research. It became clear that what had initially just been one theoretical position among many (that smoking caused cancer) was quickly approaching consensus status. The tobacco industry came up with a plan: "flood the zone" with so much low-quality conflicting information that instead of interested citizens seeing the overwhelming consensus on the issue, they would be confused about who to believe and conclude that the matter was still one under debate.[4] (It wasn't, and even now, 480,000 people die from tobacco-related illnesses each year, partly as a result of the industry's success in creating confusion. This is about one out of every five deaths in the United States.)[5]

To sum up: we tend to think of a gullible person as someone who believes everything they hear. But on the web, it's more often the *opposite*. Gullibility presents itself as the *inability* to believe anything, no matter how authoritative, proven, and trustworthy that source may be. And the social consequences of this inability can be devastating.

Reading the Room on the Mask Issue

Back to Jill and her mask issue. It's clear (we hope) that trusting a note in a bottle without understanding the expertise and motivations of the individual who put it there is not a bright idea. But let's consider another scenario. Let's suppose that article was better—that it didn't make such outrageous mistakes, but that it still expressed doubt that N95 masks were effective. Can we dive in *now*?

You're probably sick of hearing us saying this, but no. You need to slow down. If you're already well grounded in what the current research says on an issue and adept at computing the Brownian motion formula, fine, go ahead, dive in. However, if you're not, the first thing you should do is *take bearings*, a concept drawn from navigation. A lot of what happens when we search is like parachuting into unfamiliar territory. When you don't know the terrain, it's easy to get spun around in circles. Only foolhardy paratroopers go traipsing off toward the first mountain peak they see. Instead, they use their compass to "take bearings"—measuring the angle between true north and their desired destination, so that even with poor visibility, they can look at their compass and proceed at, say, forty-five degrees north and not get lost when fog sets in. Obviously, taking bearings on the web is not an exact science, and certainly not as exact as measuring an angle. But the premise is analogous—when landing in unfamiliar terrain, head off only after you've gotten the lay of the land.

On a topic where you lack vital background information, how should you start? Let's return to the issue of masks to find out.

To get a bird's-eye view of the terrain, we might forgo papers that focus on a single topic and see what a group like the Occupational Safety and Health Administration (OSHA) has to say. Take this page, which gives a clear summary of the factors in play:

FIGURE 5.2 COVID-19 FAQs on the Occupational Safety and Health Administration site (https://www.osha.gov/coronavirus/faqs)

Will an N95 respirator protect the wearer from the virus that causes COVID-19?

Yes, an N95 respirator is effective in protecting workers from the virus that causes COVID-19. . . . The National Institute for Occupational Safety and Health (NIOSH) tests respirators using particles that simulate a 0.3 micron diameter because this size particle is most likely to pass through the filter. If worn correctly, the N95 respirator will filter out at least 95% of particles this size. *An N95 respirator is more effective at filtering particles that are smaller or larger than 0.3 microns in size.*[6]

Who is OSHA, you wonder, and what the heck does it know? Well, if you practice the *I* in SIFT, you'll find OSHA is the government entity responsible for setting workplace safety standards—for things like masks. (It started doing this long before COVID-19, often in workplaces that have contact with hazardous substances.) And to do that, it relies on the advice of not just one expert but the larger expert community. So you're getting the benefit of OSHA summarizing the expert landscape for you.

But maybe you don't trust OSHA. Fine. Who do you trust, then, to accurately summarize not just a single researcher's opinion but the state of knowledge in the field? You should be careful where you invest your trust, but you have to invest it somewhere. If you throw up your hands and say, "Maybe the truth is in the middle, or maybe it's all lies," then you're exactly where the media manipulators want you to be.

Maybe in this case you go and see what the American Medical Association (AMA) says. This is an association that represents the vast majority of doctors in the United States. Like most professional organizations, it is hesitant to put out guidelines if its members disagree; the AMA is there to communicate the knowledge of the field not referee squabbles between rival factions. But we find in this case that it, too, says that N95 masks work (while adding that they should be used primarily by health-care workers).

You don't trust the largest medical organization on the planet? OK. Maybe pick a publication with a dedicated health beat (e.g., one that has a reporter with extensive experience reporting on health issues). Again, you're looking for an article where a reporter relies on a variety of respected experts in the field and tries to summarize the current state of knowledge regarding the issue of certainty (how certain experts are that masks work) and the issue of consensus (how much agreement there is on this issue).

Maybe you think the US institutional infrastructure is hopelessly compromised by Democratic rule (it's not) or Republican rule (it's not). But if you *do* think that, you're free to look at the advice issued by other countries. Does that advice differ substantially from the United

States? To check, you may want to look at the *Lancet*, the top medical journal in the United Kingdom.

We hope you get the point. You can choose any one of these, depending on what strikes you as the most trustworthy. But any one of these, as a summary of the current state of knowledge in an entire field, is going to be a better starting point than a single paper. That single paper may be useful once you're ready to do a deep dive. But when you first start, you need a bigger, more inclusive map of the terrain, and you're more likely to get that from a broad research summary. Start digging deep into the weeds of comparing individual papers in an area outside your expertise, and you'll quickly find yourself at the bottom of the trust compression sinkhole.

Note that even here we can see the importance of consensus. OSHA is saying the same thing as the AMA, which is saying the same thing as most experts. If OSHA had said something very different from the AMA, or the AMA had disagreed with experts quoted in health reporting, we might recommend slowing down a bit. Instead, we found strong consensus across multiple sources of expertise. Throw that bottle, along with the note it contains, back into the lake.

The Perils of the Single Academic Contrarian

It's good to have contrarians in a discipline. It really is! As a matter of fact, our own work in media literacy started out being a bit contrarian. The methods and approach we propose in this book initially went against a lot of the advice dispensed in college classrooms.[7]

But they didn't stay contrarian. Though it can be a slow process, researchers are interested in new ideas, and good ideas are valued when they prove to be effective. And professionals (in our case, the teachers and professors who have been teaching media literacy) want to do well at their jobs and are in the market for ways to improve. It can be slow going at first. Fortunately, over time, good ideas generally attract at least a subset of researchers and gain momentum in society at large.[8] And that's the sort of story a lot of people romanticize when they think about contrarians—starting at the edges and slowly building a following for an idea in a community of professionals and academics.

Crank contrarians are a different matter. Fringe ideas are not simply ideas with a smaller than usual following. They are ideas that *are not in dialogue* with the profession at all. They are not reading the room. More often than not, they aren't even *in* the room.

Judy Mikovits is one such crank. She is the "star" of the video *Plandemic: The Hidden Agenda behind COVID-19*, which had more than seven million views on YouTube before it was taken down.[9] It is sometimes difficult to disentangle her claims from that of the filmmaker, Mikki Willis. But between statements from the two of them, the video asserts that

- Mikovits was known as one of the "most accomplished scientists of her generation";
- her 1991 doctoral thesis revolutionized the treatment of HIV/AIDS;
- the new coronavirus was being wrongly blamed for many deaths;
- face masks "activate" the coronavirus and cause more sickness; and
- the National Institutes of Health head Anthony Fauci was responsible for millions of deaths during the HIV/AIDS epidemic by suppressing the work of Mikovits's team.[10]

None of this was true. And it is almost certain that the video caused the death and long-term disability of many people. Whatever their intentions, Mikovits and Willis are to blame for some portion of those deaths.

But what about the people who forwarded the video to family and friends? Certainly, everyone who spread it contributed, in whatever small fraction of a fraction, to the damage the video caused. But were those who spread it responsible for that damage? Could they have known, without substantial background knowledge of virology, that Mikovits was not simply someone expressing the opinion of a respected minority in the field but actually a fringe crank?

The answer, unfortunately, is yes. We will SIFT through it to show you why.

First, let's examine Mikovits's credentials. A big part of the schtick is that Mikovits is not only a person who has been in the field of virology but a *leader* in the field, including playing a key role in research related to the treatment of HIV/AIDS.[11] And to establish that, the video claims that her doctoral dissertation revolutionized the treatment of that disease. This in itself wouldn't be enough to argue her ideas were right, but if she was, in fact, one of the leading lights of virology, then you might be excused for thinking she was expressing a minority rather than a fringe view.

So, let's do a bit of lateral reading and see what we come up with.

FIGURE 5.3 Searching for information on a claim to expertise—results for "Mikovits research HIV treatment" search, June 2022. (Google and the Google logo are trademarks of Google LLC.)

Notice we get two results at the top (there are more results, but let's just focus on these two). The first is an article from science.org. Looking at the snippet, we can see it seems to be analyzing the claims made in the video and presenting an assessment of them for a general audience. The second result is a paper that looks like it is on HIV, authored (maybe?) by Mikovits. Which one should you choose?

The paper looks legit—186 citations is not exactly a sign that you revolutionized a discipline, but it's decent for the medical field. But your first click shouldn't be the paper. Instead, click the article from science.org, which looks like it speaks directly to these claims.

Why? The first reason is what we've been calling the *context of you*. Papers like Mikovits's aren't set up to tell you what you need to know. If you had a level of knowledge of virology where you could look at a research paper from someone and say, "My God! This is revolutionary virology work," we're going to guess you wouldn't be getting your COVID-19 information from *Plandemic* in the first place.

But the broader issue is much like Jill's issue with the note in the bottle. This video has washed up on your information shore. (Yes, we know, we're stretching that metaphor a bit). But at this point, the risk is wading deeper and deeper into complexity. Instead, you need to start with a few basic questions. Who are the people who made this video? What do people "in the know" say about them and their claims? It looks like the first result is going to get you those basics.

Of course, you still need to check that the top result is actually from people "in the know" and not, say, from some blogger with a keyboard and a grudge. This top result comes from "science.org." What's that?

Using Google's "three dots," which we demonstrated in chapter 3, we click and bring up the "About this result" pop-up, and then we click again for more information. The most important part of the page is up

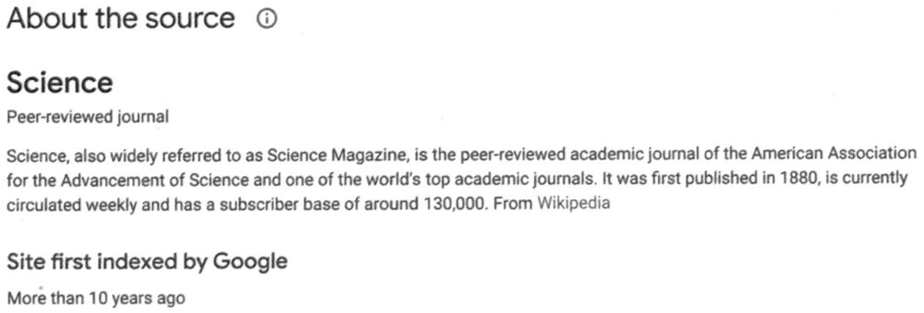

About the source ⓘ

Science

Peer-reviewed journal

Science, also widely referred to as Science Magazine, is the peer-reviewed academic journal of the American Association for the Advancement of Science and one of the world's top academic journals. It was first published in 1880, is currently circulated weekly and has a subscriber base of around 130,000. From Wikipedia

Site first indexed by Google

More than 10 years ago

FIGURE 5.4 Using Google's "About the source" feature. (Google and the Google logo are trademarks of Google LLC.)

toward the top—this is not only the site of a peer-reviewed journal but one of the world's *top* journals. Probably worth a click!

Remember, if you want more information, you can always click the Wikipedia link or explore links to news articles that appear lower down.

Science is one of the world's top academic journals. That doesn't mean that things published in it are always correct. It's a research publication, and all research publications publish some things that later turn out to be wrong. And this particular article is from its news department; this isn't peer-reviewed research. But on something like a fact-check, it should be pretty solid.

Is Mikovits a well-known figure in the world of virology? Yes, but not in the way most would think. Far from being vital to early HIV/AIDS work in the 1980s and '90s, she was relatively unknown until 2009, when she published a paper on xenotropic murine leukemia virus–related virus, or XMRV, as a potential cause of chronic fatigue syndrome (CFS) in (ironic twist time) *Science*!

That's actually pretty impressive. What happened next was less so.

Two months later, the entire *Science* paper was retracted. Mikovits refused to sign the retraction notice, but she took part in another major replication effort. That $2.3 million study, led by Ian Lipkin of Columbia University and funded by the National Institutes of Health, was "the definitive answer," Mikovits said at a September 2012 press conference where the results were announced. The new study looked for XMRV in blinded blood samples from nearly three hundred people, half of whom had CFS; it turned out none of the subjects had XMRV. In other words, the original study had been wrong. "There is no evidence that XMRV is a human pathogen," Mikovits conceded.[12]

People get things wrong, of course. But the claim that Mikovits was a leading researcher here is simply not true. She is not well known for work on HIV/AIDS, and her only previous claim to fame seems to have been a retracted paper in *Science*. You can read the article about her in *Science* and see how things went downhill from there. The fact that this supposed expert claimed false authority (and has had to walk back her "extraordinary" claims before) should by itself be enough of a red flag to move on.

From there, the *Science* article goes on to eviscerate many of *Plandemic*'s main claims. And it does so not by pitting one crank's opinion against another but by trying to accurately summarize what is known about the claims.

Of course, for any given claim you can "read the room," just like we did with the mask issue, looking at a variety of sources and trying to get a sense of whether experts agree, disagree, or just don't know. In this case, you won't find much debate. It's clear that Mikovits doesn't represent a "minority" view. Rather, she's out there on the fringe, making false claims about her supposed authority. And establishing that, if you know how to read the room, is easier than you might think.

GOING DEEPER
What Makes a Good Summary Source?
When reading the room, it helps to start by reading high-quality *summary* sources. What do those look like?

First, look for a source in a *position to know*. People in such a position are likely to know more than the average person due to their expertise (e.g., academic) or their job (e.g., reporter). Keep in mind that specificity matters—a physicist summarizing health info is not necessarily helpful; neither is a paranormal practitioner making claims about history (more on that later).

Second, check that these sources have incentives to be *careful with the truth*, or a good track record of doing so. We trust the meteorologist to try to get the weather right because she pays a price when wrong about the weather. We trust her less on health policy, in part, because the professional consequences for messing up are lower.

Third, and this is a point that is particularly applicable to summaries, consider whether sources *are fully engaged in providing a summary of research*. Beware of quick summaries that are just being used to set up another, less trustworthy claim.

Takeaways

▷ You don't always realize what you don't know, so "zooming out" to get a summary of expert opinions is a good first step. Before diving headfirst into a new topic, start off by "reading the room."

▷ Cynicism doesn't make you any smarter than gullibility. To avoid "trust compression," distinguish between little problems and giant failings in the sources you evaluate.

▷ Avoid relying on a single self-proclaimed expert. Instead, try to assess and understand the range of credible expert opinion on a subject.

Show Me the Evidence

WHY SCHOLARLY SOURCES ARE BETTER
THAN PROMOTIONAL MATERIALS,
NEWSLETTERS, AND RANDOM TWEETS

Can playing chess make you smarter? Why not? The game demands concentration, forethought, and cool-headed logic—the same virtues that define critical thinking.

Before you reach for that dusty chessboard, let's look at the evidence.

When you ask Google about the connection between chess and intelligence, one of the first results to come up is a 104-page document called *The Benefits of Chess in Education*, compiled by Patrick S. McDonald, the youth coordinator for the Chess Federation of Canada. McDonald's report claims that the movement of knights and rooks not only "makes kids smart" and "improves academic performance" but also "enhance[s] creativity, problem solving, memory, concentration, intellectual maturity, self-esteem, and many other abilities."[1] A veritable jackpot of benefits.

OK, clearly this author has a lot of skin in this game and may not be the most objective source. But the report backs up its claims with a staggering list of references—titles like "Scientific Proof: Chess Improves Reading Scores," "Utilizing Chess to Promote Self-Esteem in

Perceptually Impaired Students," and "The Effect of Chess on Reading Scores: District Nine Chess Program Second Year Report."

When you look a bit closer, however, an unmistakable pattern emerges. Most of the references cite magazine articles (including one that itself needs dusting off—from a 1931 *National Geographic*), along with newsletters from organizations like the "Commission of Chess in Schools," scattered doctoral dissertations from the 1990s, and a mishmash of presentations delivered at random conferences. What ties them all together is not something they possess but something they lack. Almost all these references do an end run around the process known as *peer review*.

What's Peer Review?

If you've ever attended an intro session at your school's library, you've listened to the librarians lower their voices and speak in reverential tones about peer review: the touchstone that separates rigorous research from mere opinion, hearsay, and the untutored opinions of your know-it-all roommate. At its most basic level, peer review is a form of quality control, a process that scholars came up with in the 1700s to protect the public from shady information. It gets its name from the fact that before a study is published, it's evaluated by experts in the field—"peers"—who decide whether the work passes muster.

Here's how the process is supposed to work, at least in theory. A researcher designs a study, gathers data, writes up results, and sends it off to a journal. The editor scans the study to make sure it fits the publication's scope and then forwards it to reviewers. The reviewers assess the article's merits: Have the authors interpreted their data correctly? Do the claims fit the evidence? Were the procedures used the correct ones? Are the conclusions justified? If the reviewers deem

CHILD DEVELOPMENT

A Publication of the Society for Research in Child Development

Willard W. Hartup, Editor
University of Minnesota

Linda P. Acredolo, Associate Editor
University of California, Davis

Susan Crockenberg, Associate Editor
University of California, Davis

Robert Kail, Associate Editor
Purdue University

June 23, 1987

Mr. Samuel S. Wineburg
Room 407, Center for Education Research
Stanford University
Stanford, Ca 94305

Dear Mr. Wineburg:

    Re: Manuscript #16APR87-143
          "Growing Older and Giving Less: A Field Study of
          Children and Charity"

This manuscript is not publishable, in my opinion, nor in the opinion of the three reviewers who read it. It is our view that you cannot treat your data in the way you have, especially to conduct the analyses of variance that you report. The standard deviations in Table 1 appear to be indices of session-to-session variations in class means, not individual-to-individual variations. You interpret the results, though, as if they were the latter.

FIGURE 6.1 Rejection letter Sam received early in his career from *Child Development*

that the paper is flawed beyond repair, it receives a flat-out rejection. When Sam was starting out, he had the dubious honor of being rejected by some of psychology's most prestigious journals.

If, on the other hand, a paper shines so brilliantly that there's not a single thing to fix, it merits a straight acceptance (Sam's still waiting). What tends to happen a lot of the time is that an article is placed in a nebulous category, known as "revise and resubmit," that wavers between "reject" and "accept." In this all-encompassing catch basin, the editor summarizes the reviewers' criticisms and offers the authors a chance to fix their paper and give it another go. However, the opportunity to resubmit carries no guarantee that the resubmission will be published. If the revised manuscript is sent to new

Journal of Educational Psychology

© 2022 American Psychological Association
ISSN: 0022-0663

https://doi.org/10.1037/edu0000740

Lateral Reading on the Open Internet: A District-Wide Field Study in High School Government Classes

Sam Wineburg[1], Joel Breakstone[1], Sarah McGrew[2], Mark D. Smith[1], and Teresa Ortega[1]

[1] Graduate School of Education, Stanford University
[2] College of Education, University of Maryland, College Park

In a study conducted across an urban school district, we tested a classroom-based intervention in which students were taught online evaluation strategies drawn from research with professional fact checkers. Students practiced the heuristic of *lateral reading:* leaving an unfamiliar website to search the open Web before investing attention in the site at hand. Professional development was provided to high school teachers who then implemented six 50-minute lessons in a district-mandated government course. Using a matched control design, students in treatment classrooms ($n = 271$) were compared to peers ($n = 228$) in regular classrooms. A multilevel linear mixed model showed that students in experimental classrooms grew significantly in their ability to judge the credibility of digital content. These findings inform efforts to prepare young people to make wise decisions about the information that darts across their screens.

> *Educational Impact and Implications Statement*
> This study tested the effectiveness of an intervention that taught high school students to make sound decisions on the Internet. Less than 6 hr of classroom instruction significantly improved students' judgment about the credibility of online sources.

Keywords: media literacy, digital literacy, civic education

FIGURE 6.2 Abstract from intervention study in the *Journal of Educational Psychology* (Wineburg et al., "Lateral Reading on the Open Internet")

reviewers—something that can and does happen—the manuscript can languish in revise-and-resubmit-land for ages.

Even if a study is competent and avoids fatal errors, it can still be rejected if the reviewers conclude that it says nothing new or rehashes points already in the scholarly literature. Conversely, reviewers will sometimes accept a paper that's not ready for prime time if they think it might spur researchers to take up new questions and open new lines of inquiry. If you think the process of peer review sounds complicated, laborious, time-consuming, and pulling-your-hair-out frustrating for anxious authors, you're right. Case in point: a 2022 study that Sam's team did on teaching students the techniques in this book took a year and a half and three different revisions before it finally appeared in print![2]

Peer Review: "The Worst Way to Judge Research, Except for All the Others"

We wish we could say that every article that makes its way through the gauntlet of peer review is printworthy. No system is perfect, and peer review is no exception. Peer review runs on the backs of unpaid volunteers who have agreed to serve as the guardians of quality control in their respective disciplines. Some reviewers take their job seriously and write detailed and helpful reviews. Others dash off perfunctory comments barbed with stinging insults. There's even a whole website where disgruntled authors post the nasty things reviewers have written.[3] And let's not forget about the biases and prejudices that creep in whenever humans express judgment. Many journals try to compensate for these foibles by following a "double-blind" procedure: reviewers don't know who the authors are and vice versa. But experts often have a sense of who is doing what in their field, and the pretense of anonymity turns out to be a hollow shell game.

For some journals, like the prestigious *New England Journal of Medicine*, peer review is only the first stage in a rigorous publication process. If reviewers agree that a manuscript is of sufficient merit, it's forwarded to a group of in-house editors who go through it with a fine-tooth comb. But the *New England Journal of Medicine* is the exception. Only a dozen or so of the ten thousand biomedical journals can afford a staff of paid editors.[4] The vast majority rely on the kindness of volunteers. When the system works, it does a decent job of separating good scholarship from bad. When it doesn't, slipshod work finds its way into print. Yet, despite its many problems, the tendency of peer review to produce better results *on average* than other methods has spurred many of the advances we see today. An article by an editor at the *Journal of the American Medical Association* put it like this: "Peer Review: The Worst Way to Judge Research, Except for All of the Others."[5]

The Problem of the Single Study

You've probably seen the chilling commercials of emphysema patients wheezing through a breathing tube telling us they wished they never started smoking. There's little argument today that smoking causes cancer. But you'll always find some know-it-all who harrumphs that their grandfather smoked three packs of Camels a day and lived till he was 97.

An analogous phenomenon goes on with journal articles—even one that's peer reviewed. With two million articles churned out each year, you can almost always find one that provides backing for the wackiest claim someone wants to offer—even if this one-shot, stand-alone study flies in the face of a thousand others.[6]

Which brings us back to chess. A Google search produces a study conducted by researchers at Iran's Islamic Azad University. Groups of fifth-, eighth- and ninth-grade boys practiced chess for six months and afterward posted modest gains in their metacognitive ability as well as their math skill.[7] Does this study put to rest, once and for all, the question of chess's benefits? Or is it the peer-reviewed equivalent of that chain-smoking granddad?

Literature Reviews: A Bird's-Eye View of Multiple Studies

As we said in the last chapter, when you're wading into a new topic, our advice is to avoid single studies until you've read the room and gotten a lay of the land. You do this by starting with a *literature review*, a bird's-eye view of multiple studies that conveys the "state of the art" on a question of scholarly concern.

To answer whether chess makes you smarter, two psychologists at the University of Liverpool conducted a type of literature review known as meta-analysis, where the results of individual studies are aggregated across studies to estimate how successful (or negligible) a given intervention might be.

The researchers located sixty-four different studies but found that the vast majority, over 60 percent, contained so little information about the experimental procedures that they had to be eliminated from analysis. Combining the twenty-four remaining studies, the researchers found "small to moderate effects" of chess's benefits on working memory, cognitive ability, and academic skill. However, the researchers' conclusion came with this crucial caveat: the more rigorous the study, the smaller the effects. They researchers concluded that the chief benefit of playing chess is that it . . . makes you better at playing chess. There's "little evidence," they wrote, that the game "makes people smarter."[8]

GOING DEEPER
Journals That Prey on Unsuspecting Victims
A consequence of the academic imperative to "publish or perish" is the growth of online "predatory journals" that prey on academics pressured to bulk up their résumé. These journals charge authors a fee to publish their work (euphemistically called "article processing charges") and typically have weak (or no) editorial standards, lax (or nonexistent) review processes, and no editorial board (or one filled with dead scholars). They often falsely claim that they are included in prestigious scholarly databases (like PubMed in medicine or ERIC in education). Predatory journals spam academics with invitations to publish their work in journals with scopes so expansive that it strains the imagination (for example, a predatory education journal solicits papers in English, computers, engineering, psychology, law, social work, business, economics, and the arts—nothing short of the entire corpus of human knowledge). How can you tell if an article comes from a bona fide journal instead of one created by schemers out to make a buck? You can start with Wikipedia, which has a decent database of the leading journals across a range of fields. Also, many college libraries subscribe to JSTOR (jstor.com), a digital repository that allows you to search more than two thousand online journals.

(continued)

Finally, there's a website called Think Check Submit (thinkchecksubmit.org). The site is intended for researchers who want to check if a journal they're considering is legit. Even though the site is geared to researchers, anyone can access it and benefit from its tips for sniffing out rogue journals.

Real History, Fake History: How to Tell the Difference

In an unregulated internet, scholarly sources compete with blogs, tweets, TikTok videos, memes, and just about everything else, each claiming to possess the truth. Consider the following two items appearing in your social media feed. The first claims that the Union army, not the Confederates, committed the most horrific act of genocide during the Civil War, herding twenty thousand free Black people into a "concentration camp" and starving them to death in an area of Natchez, Mississippi, known as the "Devil's Punchbowl." The second claims that on the morning of January 28, 1918, in Porvenir, Texas, a small town about one hundred miles southeast of El Paso, a group of Texas Rangers "went door-to-door, ordering the inhabitants of the community out of their homes," and massacred a group of fifteen unarmed men.

Neither event was covered in your history book, a fact that doesn't actually mean that much. Many injustices committed against BIPOC (Black, Indigenous, People of Color) communities have been covered up or simply ignored in official textbook accounts of history. The most gruesome race massacre in US history occurred in 1921 in the Greenwood area of Tulsa, Oklahoma, when the neighborhood was firebombed from the air, turning thousands of Black families into race refugees. Until just a few years ago, US history textbooks were mute on this horrific crime. So, just because you haven't heard of the Devil's Punchbowl or the massacre in Porvenir doesn't mean they didn't happen. How, though, would you check?

· Feb 9, 2020   ...

The devil's punchbowl in Natchez, ms. was a concentration camp manned by union soldiers.

Within one yr, over 20,000 freed Black slaves were rounded up, barricaded in, and starved 2 death.

We celebrate these murdered ancestors on 2day.

#BlackHolocaust #BlackHistory #FBA

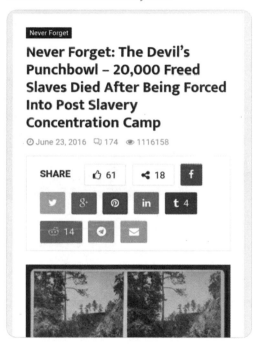

FIGURE 6.3 Tweet about a "concentration camp" in Natchez, Mississippi. (Poster's name and handle are redacted.)

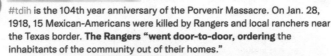

· Jan 28   ···

#tdih is the 104th year anniversary of the Porvenir Massacre. On Jan. 28, 1918, 15 Mexican-Americans were killed by Rangers and local ranchers near the Texas border. **The Rangers "went door-to-door, ordering** the inhabitants of the community out of their homes."

♡ 1   ↻ 8   ♡ 7   ⬆

FIGURE 6.4 Tweet about Texas's Porvenir Massacre. (Poster's name and handle are redacted.)

Using Google Scholar to Find Scholarly Sources

We'll start with the claim that there was a concentration camp in Natchez, Mississippi, during the Civil War. You could search "Natchez + concentration camp" but doing so brings up a slew of unfamiliar sites and random YouTube videos. If an event of such magnitude happened—twenty thousand deaths at the hands of a liberating army that was supposed to protect these freed men, women, and children—there's bound to be some kind of *scholarly* footprint, even if it didn't make it into your history book. To evaluate this and other claims, a great place to start is Google Scholar (scholar.google.com), which, according to Google, "provides a simple way to broadly search for scholarly literature."[9]

Google Scholar operates on the same principles as a regular Google search. You put in keywords and see what comes up. A search for "Devil's Punchbowl + Natchez + concentration camp" turns up little—almost nothing. The only result is a thesis by a master's student at Louisiana State University, who heard about the Devil's Punchbowl but found little concrete evidence.[10] When he consulted historians, "most had not heard about the story, and some were doubtful of the story."[11]

That an event of this immensity lacks a scholarly footprint should, by itself, raise a red flag. At the same time, the tweet about it has a link to an article on a website called *Black Main Street*.

FIGURE 6.5 Article on the Devil's Punchbowl in Natchez, Mississippi (https://blackmain street.net/never-forget-devils-punchbowl-20000-freed-slaves-died-forced-post -slavery-concentration-camp/)

The article repeats the claim that "20,000 freed slaves died" after being herded into a "post slavery concentration camp." But the article contains no footnotes to the source of this information. Instead, there's a reference to a researcher named Paula Westbrook. Putting her name into Google Scholar comes up empty—red flag number two. A regular Google search yields slightly more. Paula Westbrook, it turns out, is no historian. She's not an academic or an archivist. She's not a teacher. What, then, *are* her qualifications?

Westbrook is part of something called the Southern Paranormal & Anomaly Research Society, a "Mississippi based paranormal investigation team." Her bio explains that while growing up in Louisiana's backwoods, she became skilled in the practices of voodoo, sparking "her interest in the paranormal." Probably not the kind of "expert" you'll want to cite in your history paper.[12]

The Vibe of Google Scholar's Results Page

When we use Google Scholar to investigate the tweet about the Porvenir Massacre, a different picture immediately emerges.

Thirty seconds of mining the results shows that, unlike the Devil's Punchbowl, the Porvenir Massacre is a real and shameful episode in American history. In the early morning of January 28, 1918, a band of Texas Rangers, accompanied by the US Army cavalry and Anglo cattle ranchers, marched fifteen men, the youngest being sixteen years old, to a bluff overlooking the banks of the Rio Grande and shot them in cold blood. The first reference is to the official website of the Texas Rangers, which describes this loathsome act without pulling punches. The second is to the Oxford University Press, which publishes the *American Historical Review*, the official journal of the American Historical Association, the largest organization of historians in the world. The link goes to a review of University of Texas historian Monica

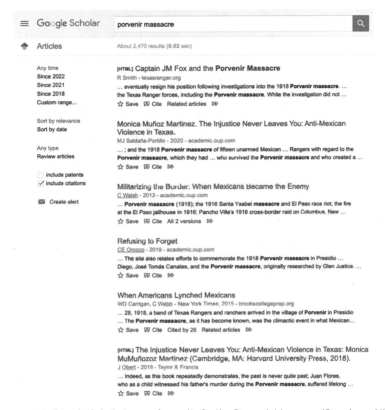

FIGURE 6.6 Google Scholar's search results for the Porvenir Massacre. (Google and the Google logo are trademarks of Google LLC.)

Muñoz Martinez's book *The Injustice Never Leaves You: Anti-Mexican Violence in Texas*, published by Harvard University Press. (Books published by university presses also go through peer review.) The next to last link brings up a *New York Times* column about the massacre by two more history professors, William Carrigan and Clive Webb. Long covered up, the Porvenir Massacre is now recognized by the Texas Historical Commission, which in 2019 placed a historical marker on the site of the bloodshed.

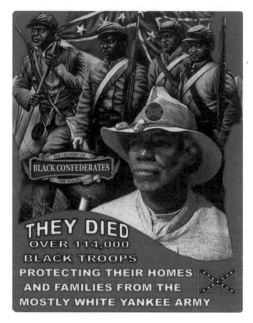

FIGURE 6.7 Meme claiming thousands of Black troops fought for the Confederacy (https://deadconfederates.com/2016/02/10/do-the-guinness-people-know-about -this/)

Using Google Scholar as a Quick Reputation Check

The internet swarms with memes that make claims about the past. Here's one about the Civil War and "Black Confederates": "Over 114,000 Black troops protecting their families" (who, we should note, were still in bondage) from the "mostly white Yankee Army." Can that be right?

You google "Black Confederates" and find two articles: one by a professor named Bruce Levine, who debunks the idea, and another by Vernon Padgett, a professor who defends it. Each article is stuffed with footnotes to original sources. How would you figure out which is a better source without spending the whole day on it?

Google Scholar allows you to see how many times an article or book has been cited by other researchers. Obviously, just because an article has been cited doesn't mean it's true, and one with few citations doesn't necessarily mean that it's false. But if a publication has been around for years, with plenty of time to marinate in scholarly circles and hardly anyone cites it, it's an indication that it has had little impact.[13]

When we put Bruce Levine's name into Google Scholar with the keywords "Civil War," we see that he has written multiple books and been cited by other scholars hundreds of times.

When you do the same for Vernon Padgett (who turns out to be a

FIGURE 6.8 Google Scholar results for "Bruce Levine Civil War." (Google and the Google logo are trademarks of Google LLC.)

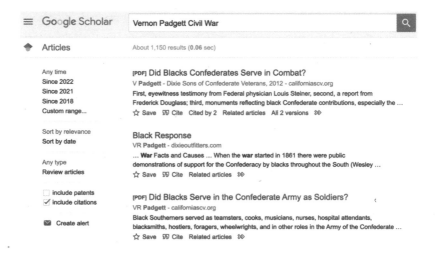

FIGURE 6.9 Google Scholar results for "Vernon Padgett Civil War." (Google and the Google logo are trademarks of Google LLC.)

professor of psychology, not history), the only result cited is an article appearing on the website of the Sons of Confederate Veterans, the "oldest hereditary organization for male descendants of Confederate soldiers." The article has been cited only twice—both times as an example of how *not* to do historical research. The claim that "over 114,000 Black troops" took up arms to defend their own bondage? Hogwash.

Takeaways

▷ Peer review is not a perfect system—not by a long shot. But it's an important first step in the line of defense against junk scholarship.

▷ When wading into broad scholarly questions, get your feet wet by starting with a review of the literature rather than fixating on a single study.

▷ Google Scholar is a quick way to judge scholars' reputations as well as to check if other scholars cite their work.

Wikipedia

NOT WHAT YOUR MIDDLE SCHOOL
TEACHER TOLD YOU

Your middle school teacher threatened to give you an F if you cited it. A menacing reminder hung in the computer lab: a thick black line slashing the word in two. Even now, you can find blanket dismissals bellowing from college websites: Wikipedia "isn't a credible resource because anyone is allowed to be a contributor."[1]

In its early days, Wikipedia had no shortage of problems. Errors propagated like fruit flies. People used the site to spoof their friends and exact revenge on their enemies. The site's flaws were legendary, sometimes scandalous. A 2006 article accused John Seigenthaler, an assistant to Robert Kennedy in the 1960s, of having a hand in Kennedy's assassination. The false charge stayed on the site for 132 days before it was finally removed. But not before Seigenthaler denounced Wikipedia in the pages of *USA Today* as a site run by "volunteer vandals."[2] The head of the American Library Association compared professors who let students use Wikipedia to nutritionists who prescribe a diet of Big Macs.[3]

Scandals like John Seigenthaler's gave Wikipedia a black eye. They also prompted the site to clean up its act. Today's Wikipedia bears little resemblance to its earlier self. The world's biggest and deepest-pocketed tech companies shamelessly grab content from the site. Google poaches on Wikipedia to populate its knowledge panels. Ask Amazon's Alexa or Apple's Siri a question, and you're likely to get an answer that begins, "According to Wikipedia." Chances are, your doctor consults the site too. A 2015 study found that Wikipedia was the single leading source of medical information for 50 to 70 percent of physicians. And among medical students, the percentage was even higher: 94 percent consulted the site.[4] Each month, an estimated one billion people across the globe spend the equivalent of sixty thousand *years* on the site (that's no typo).[5] Today, Wikipedia is the fifth-most visited website on the entire internet and the only nonprofit among the top ten.[6] Still, many people—not just middle school teachers—have misgivings about the site. Let's consider the most widespread.

What about the Mistakes?

Aren't there still mistakes on a site with fifty million articles written in three hundred different languages? Well, uh, yes. Wikipedia is written by human beings, and last we heard, human beings make mistakes. But unlike in its early years, today's Wikipedia is armed with sophisticated mechanisms for weeding out errors, both technological (automated bots that gobble up changes from unidentified contributors) and human (hawk-eyed administrators who monitor lists of controversial pages). These procedures go a long way in catching problems before they turn scandalous. Instead of festering on the site for 132 days, as in John Seigenthaler's case, it now takes about thirty minutes before vandalized content is scooped up and erased.[7] The more popular an article, the more eyeballs that track it and the faster malicious content is vaporized.

GOING DEEPER
Wikipedia to Britannica: "He That Is without Sin . . ."
Paid professionals make mistakes too. Back in 2005, the prestigious journal *Nature* compared forty-two different science articles in Wikipedia to the "gold standard" of encyclopedias, *Britannica*. The study found that the typical Wikipedia entry, written by volunteers, contained on average four mistakes per article. The same study found that *Britannica*, for all its hype and supposed expertise, contained about three errors per article. When *Nature* released its findings, *Britannica* published full page ads demanding a retraction. *Nature*'s editors held firm. "Entries were blinded—reviewers did not know which entry came from Wikipedia and which from *Britannica*," retorted *Nature*, not budging an inch. "Our comparison was unbiased, and we reject *Britannica*'s allegation that we have acted in a dishonest manner. We stand by the story."[8]

Anyone Can Change Wikipedia, Can't They?

It's true that anyone with a laptop and an internet connection can edit most Wikipedia pages. But that doesn't mean the edits survive. If someone hasn't registered with Wikipedia, chances are that person's edits will be apprehended by tireless bots on the hunt for unfamiliar IP addresses. Plus, there's a whole category of "protected pages." They are often Wikipedia's most trafficked and most controversial pages, the ones that enflame passions and bring out the worst human tendencies (entries like "Barack Obama," "Donald Trump," "Gamergate," and "Causes of transsexuality," to name some of the most recognizable entries, but also the "Coat of arms of Lithuania"—go figure). If you consult these articles, you'll see some features you might not have noticed before. See that teeny lock to the right of "Donald Trump"? That tells you the page is protected. Also, did you notice that the "Edit" tab

FIGURE 7.1 Wikipedia article on Donald Trump showing lock icon (https://en.wikipedia.org/wiki/Donald_Trump)

(which usually appears after the "Read" tab) has gone AWOL? Unless you already have Wikipedia editing privileges, you won't be able to lay your hands on these pages.

The system of locks is another way that Wikipedia has erected guardrails that prevent newbies, trolls, and just plain goofballs from making drive-by edits.[9] As Wikipedia maven Jake Orlowitz notes, it's no big deal to say "I changed Wikipedia." The real mark of achievement is "being able to say I made an edit to Wikipedia—*and it stuck.*"[10]

Isn't Wikipedia Biased?

Yes, Wikipedia is biased—if by "biased" we mean that Wikipedia reflects the proclivities of its contributors, who overwhelmingly skew male, white, college educated, and middle class. Wikipedia is acutely aware of its bias (there's an entire Wikipedia page devoted to it) and has made strides to enlist more women and people of color to its editing ranks. Over the past few years, the phenomenon of "edit-a-thons" has taken hold, where groups come together to create Wikipedia content to rectify imbalances in coverage. The first edit-a-thons focused on increasing the coverage of women scientists. But there have also been editing events on Black history, the history of Indigenous peoples, and the status of lower caste peoples in India, as well as events on many other underrepresented groups.[11]

Wikipedia still isn't where it wants to be—not by a long shot. But it's trying. Between 2015 and 2018, the site increased the number of entries about women from 15 to 17 percent. This might not seem like a lot until you realize that the change resulted in 83,600 new entries.[12] While the rest of the internet peddles clickbait, tracks our every move, and auctions our data to the highest bidder, Wikipedia—free, ad-less, and staffed by volunteers—is headed in the right direction. The site, notes internet theorist Yochai Benkler, captures our imagination not because Wikipedia is "so perfect" but because in so many cases it is "reasonably good . . . a proposition that would have been thought preposterous a mere half-decade ago."[13]

Wikipedia as a Tool for Research

Since we brought up your middle school teachers, we need to give credit where credit is due. When they warned you not to cite Wikipedia, they echoed Wikipedia's own cautions: Wikipedia articles "are designed to introduce researchers to topics, not to be the final point of research."[14]

Encyclopedias are considered "tertiary" (a fancy word for "third") sources. That means that they draw on information already contained in primary sources (original documents or research reports) and secondary sources (books, magazines, newspapers, TV broadcasts, and other published sources that are matters of public record). One of Wikipedia's ironclad rules goes by the acronym of NOR, or "no original research." This means that claims in a Wikipedia article must be anchored to already existing sources. As we'll see, this is a godsend for all kinds of research, from the simplest fact-checks to finding your sea legs when embarking on a new research project.

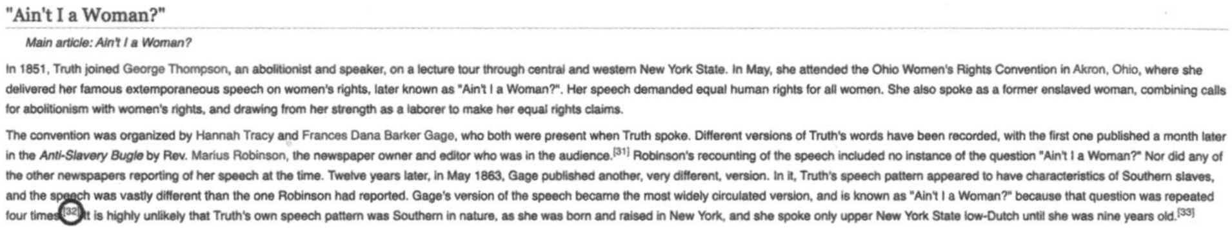

"Ain't I a Woman?"

Main article: Ain't I a Woman?

In 1851, Truth joined George Thompson, an abolitionist and speaker, on a lecture tour through central and western New York State. In May, she attended the Ohio Women's Rights Convention in Akron, Ohio, where she delivered her famous extemporaneous speech on women's rights, later known as "Ain't I a Woman?". Her speech demanded equal human rights for all women. She also spoke as a former enslaved woman, combining calls for abolitionism with women's rights, and drawing from her strength as a laborer to make her equal rights claims.

The convention was organized by Hannah Tracy and Frances Dana Barker Gage, who both were present when Truth spoke. Different versions of Truth's words have been recorded, with the first one published a month later in the *Anti-Slavery Bugle* by Rev. Marius Robinson, the newspaper owner and editor who was in the audience.[31] Robinson's recounting of the speech included no instance of the question "Ain't I a Woman?" Nor did any of the other newspapers reporting of her speech at the time. Twelve years later, in May 1863, Gage published another, very different, version. In it, Truth's speech pattern appeared to have characteristics of Southern slaves, and the speech was vastly different than the one Robinson had reported. Gage's version of the speech became the most widely circulated version, and is known as "Ain't I a Woman?" because that question was repeated four times. It is highly unlikely that Truth's own speech pattern was Southern in nature, as she was born and raised in New York, and she spoke only upper New York State low-Dutch until she was nine years old.[33]

FIGURE 7.2 "Ain't I a Woman?" section of Wikipedia article on Sojourner Truth (https://en
.wikipedia.org/wiki/Sojourner_Truth)

Using Wikipedia to Validate Sources

If you're not supposed to cite Wikipedia, what *should* you cite? The simple answer is that you cite the sources that Wikipedia cites. Let's walk through an example.

Your Speech and Rhetoric professor makes an offhanded remark about one of the most famous speeches in American history, Sojourner Truth's "Ain't I a Woman?" "You know," she says, with a sly, myth-busting smile, "She actually never said those words."

No way! You studied the speech in high school. You even remember seeing a video of actor Alfre Woodard performing a stirring rendition.[15]

You go to Wikipedia and scroll through the article on Sojourner Truth until you see a separate subsection for "Ain't I a Woman."

The first recorded version of the speech was published in an abolitionist newspaper in 1851 and included no instance of the question "Ain't I a Woman?" It was a white abolitionist who rewrote Truth's speech in the middle of the Civil War to conform to the speech patterns of southern Black women. Truth (née Isabella "Bell" Baumfree) was born into slavery in 1791 in upstate New York. She spoke Dutch until age nine.

How do we know this? That's where Wikipedia's policy of "no original research" comes in. That little number "32" directs us to the references, where we find this note:

32. ^ Craig, Maxine Leeds. *Ain't I a Beauty Queen: Black Women, Beauty, and the Politics of Race*, Oxford University Press USA, 2002, p. 7. ISBN 0-19-515262-X

Now, if you're just trying to fact-check your professor, you can stop here. Really. Odds are that between her PhD and a book published by Oxford University Press (a very good press, by the way), there's something to the claim. However, should you decide to go deeper—perhaps even write a paper about Sojourner Truth—you should take the next step. You'll need to look up Maxine Leeds Craig's book to verify that it says what Wikipedia says it does. (For quick ways to do this, see "Going Deeper: Quickly Validating a Reference from a Book.")

GOING DEEPER
Quickly Validating a Reference from a Book
In the preinternet days, checking references involved going to the library, looking up the call number (and not on a computer either—in a massive chest of drawers called a "card catalog"), and then wandering around in dimly lit stacks to locate a physical book. Ah, the marvels of the internet! Now, you could begin your search by going online to your library's website to see if it has an e-book of *Ain't I a Beauty Queen: Black Women, Beauty and the Politics of Race*. You could do that. We recommend, however, a quicker step. First, check to see if Amazon has digitized the book. If Amazon hasn't, check to see if Google Books has (books.google.com). Both have a feature where you can search for terms inside of a digitized book (but both purposely exclude key sections, so it's hit or miss). When we search for "Sojourner Truth" in Amazon's e-version of *Ain't I a Beauty Queen*, the first entry that comes up is the same page 7 that Wikipedia quotes: "Ain't I a woman," as Craig explains, "was an embellishment added by white feminist abolitionist Frances Dana Gage." Now, instead of citing Wikipedia in your bibliography, your citation can read: "Craig, Maxine Leeds. *Ain't I a Beauty Queen: Black Women, Beauty and the Politics of Race*. New York: Oxford University Press, 2002."

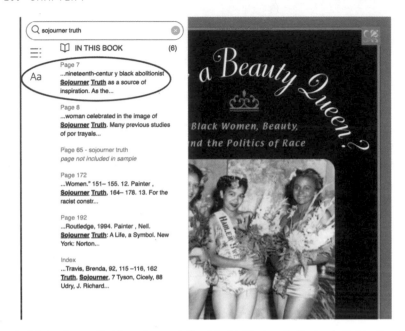

FIGURE 7.3 Screenshot from Amazon's "Look Inside" feature for the book *Ain't I a Beauty Queen?* by Maxine Leeds Craig

Using Wikipedia for Quick Checks of Unfamiliar Websites

INSTITUTE FOR HISTORICAL REVIEW

You find yourself reading something about World War II, and a few clicks later you land on ihr.org, something called the Institute for Historical Review.

It's a dot-org, which by this point in the book you realize means diddly-squat. The tag line at the top seems reasonable enough: "For a more just, sane and peaceful world." Then you start to notice the articles clustering around Nazi Germany, US foreign policy, and Israel. Especially Israel. Lots of articles about Israel and Jews. You could continue reading more deeply—or you could take a thirty-second

FOLLOW US: 🔵 🟦 🐦 📷 ✴️ [ENHANCED BY Google] [🔍]

ⓘHR INSTITUTE FOR HISTORICAL REVIEW
For a More Just, Sane and Peaceful World

| HOME | ABOUT | STORE | VIDEO | ARCHIVE ▾ | AUDIO | CONTACT | SUPPORT | EVENTS | LINKS |

FIGURE 7.4 Masthead of the Institute for Historical Review (ihr.org)

Wikipedia detour. It's a smart use of thirty seconds because Wikipedia's opening sentence confirms your gut: the Institute for Historical Review is "an organization best known for promoting Holocaust denial," a statement backed by five references. You're outta here.

NATIONAL CONSTITUTION CENTER

You were reading something about the Second Amendment and ended up at constitutioncenter.org. Is it right-wing, left-wing, a gathering point for conspiracy theorists? Should you dig in only to learn an hour later that you stumbled on a site that says the Constitution guarantees the right to child sacrifice?

FIGURE 7.5 Wikipedia entry for the National Constitution Center (https://en.wikipedia .org/wiki/National_Constitution_Center)

Nothing in Wikipedia sticks out. The Center was funded as part of the Constitution Heritage Act of 1988, supported by President Ronald Reagan, a Republican. Both George H. W. Bush, another Republican, and Bill Clinton, a Democrat, served as chairmen of the board. The Center seems to be the rare bipartisan institution that tries to preserve the heritage of the Constitution for adherents in both parties. You conclude: "Looks OK."

Quick Investigation of a Claim

You hate flossing. You see this tweet, which implies you don't have to—even the "Health Dept" says so. Before you toss the floss, there are a couple of steps to take. Hover over WINK News. Despite its cheesy name, you learn that it's a legitimate TV station in southern Florida. On to Wikipedia's article on dental floss.

You skip the introductory material and beeline to "Efficacy." The first line reads: "The American Dental Association has stated that flossing in combination with tooth brushing can help prevent gum disease and halitosis."[16] Preventing disease and smelly breath seem like good reasons to keep flossing, no? As for the "Health Department"? There's a whole subsection about it. True, the 2015 US Dietary Guidelines for Americans eliminated reference to flossing. But when the American Dental Association investigated why, it learned that the new guidelines focused only on diet and that "the omission was not

WINK News @winknews · Aug 2, 2016   ···
Dentists say all the time to floss your teeth. Except there's little proof that flossing works. Health Dept quietly removed recommendation.

FIGURE 7.6 Tweet from @winknews proclaiming "little proof" that flossing works (https://twitter.com/winknews/status/760432456935825408)

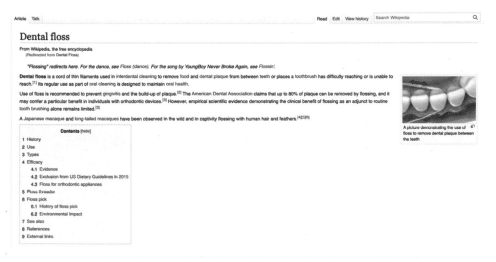

FIGURE 7.7 Wikipedia page for "Dental floss" (https://en.wikipedia.org/wiki/Dental_floss, September 2021)

because the Department questions the efficacy of flossing." For now, continue to strangle your fingers to save your teeth.

Quick Checks of an Unfamiliar Academic Source

You've stayed away from cigarettes. You've learned about the dangers of vaping. But a friend invites you to a hookah bar with the assurance that it's safe: "The chilled water and the charcoal filter remove the toxins. There's research on it." Your friend texts you a link to a study in something called *Medical Hypotheses*.

You *could* read the article and do battle with sentences like "Even the level of NNAL, metabolite of the potent carcinogen NNK, was not different from that of controls." Or, you could see if Wikipedia says anything about this source so you can better answer the question, "Is this what I think it is—a respected medical journal?"

Medical Hypotheses

Volume 74, Issue 5, May 2010, Pages 843-846

A critique of recent hypotheses on oral (and lung) cancer induced by water pipe (hookah, shisha, narghile) tobacco smoking

Kamal Chaouachi [a] ☕ ✉, Khan Mohammad Sajid [b] ☕ ✉

Show more ∨

+ Add to Mendeley ⌁ Share ❞ Cite

https://doi.org/10.1016/j.mehy.2009.11.036

Get rights and content

Summary

The medical hypothesis that the mainstream smoke (the one inhaled by the user) from "water pipes" (mainly: shisha, hookah, narghile) causes oral cancer is certainly acceptable. However, most of the recent reviews on this issue, including an attempt to develop an hypothesis for hookah carcinogenesis, have not cited key references of the world available literature which, so far, generally do not support such an hypothesis. Besides, the proposal is biased since it is apparently an adaptation of the cigarette model whereas cigarette and hookah smokes are, chemically to start with, completely different. Furthermore, all water pipes, despite their striking varieties and the consequences on the chemical processes, are, according to the same cancer-hypothesis, considered as one. The reason is the use, in the cited mainstream literature, of a nominalism ("waterpipe", often in one word) which does not allow any distinction between devices. This critical article suggests to take into account all the peculiar characteristics into consideration in order to come up with another (or several other) carcinogenesis model(s). "Firmly believ[ing] that water pipe smoking can provoke lung cancer as well as oral cancer", based on what may be seen as a rather reductionist view of the issue, is not enough.

FIGURE 7.8 Abstract from article from *Medical Hypotheses* (https://doi.org/10.1016/j .mehy.2009.11.036)

Medical Hypotheses

From Wikipedia, the free encyclopedia

Medical Hypotheses is a not-conventionally-peer reviewed[1] medical journal published by Elsevier. It was originally intended as a forum for unconventional ideas without the traditional filter of scientific peer review, "as long as (the ideas) are coherent and clearly expressed" in order to "foster the diversity and debate upon which the scientific process thrives."[2] The publication of papers on AIDS denialism[3][4][5] led to calls to remove it from PubMed, the United States National Library of Medicine online journal database.[4] Following the AIDS papers controversy, Elsevier forced a change in the journal's leadership. In June 2010, Elsevier announced that "submitted manuscripts will be reviewed by the Editor and external reviewers to ensure their scientific merit".[6]

FIGURE 7.9 Wikipedia article on the journal *Medical Hypotheses* (https://en.wikipedia .org/wiki/Medical_Hypotheses, September 202)

Medical Hypotheses, you learn, is a lightning rod for controversy. During the HIV/AIDS crisis, it published articles denying the existence of the disease and got booted from PubMed, the medical database maintained by the US National Institutes of Health. The hookah bar? You take a pass.

Using Wikipedia to "Read the Scholarly Room"

Wikipedia is an indispensable resource for reading the room when you're still finding your way into a topic and don't know who the players are, the differences that separate them, and the big issues still under debate. For example, you've heard that near the end of World War II there was a lot of controversy around the decision to drop the atomic bomb. When you google "Atomic bomb + debate," this article comes up.

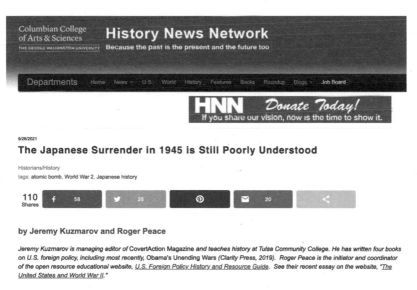

FIGURE 7.10 Article from the website of the History News Network (https://historynews network.org/article/181372)

It appears on historynewsnetwork.org, a site for history buffs out of the College of Arts and Sciences at George Washington University. The authors argue that when the bombs were dropped, the Japanese were already on the "verge of defeat." Surrender, claim authors Jeremy Kuzmarov and Roger Peace, "could likely have been achieved without the atomic bomb."[17]

A bold claim that, if true, could have prevented untold human suffering. It's not quite what you remember from your history books. Then again, textbooks lag years—sometimes decades—behind the latest scholarship. Is this what the latest research says? Would a room full of historians nod in unison?

Wikipedia's entry on the "Atomic Bombings of Hiroshima and Nagasaki" is long—excruciatingly long. It runs thirty-seven pages, with a five-page bibliography and over 350 references. It's easy to get lost. Since our goal is to read the room, not immerse ourselves in every detail, we do a quick scan of the table of contents. Near the end, we spy a subsection called "Debate over the Bombings." It's blissfully short. Two paragraphs.

The first sentence hints that things are, well, let's just say a bit more complicated than authors Kuzmarov and Peace let on. The role of the bombings, according to Wikipedia, are "the subject of scholarly and popular debate."[18]

The short section lays out three positions:

1   The atomic bomb was responsible for bringing the war to a swift end. Had the Allies attempted a land invasion, there would have been an even greater loss of life among the Allies as well as the Japanese defending their homeland.

2   It wasn't the bomb that brought Japan to its knees but the Soviets' declaration of war in August 1945.

3   Japan was indeed ready to surrender. The Americans dropped the

bombs anyway to intimidate the USSR in what would become the first round of the Cold War.

So how do the claims of Kuzmarov and Peace fare? Their position is not beyond the pale—it's not "fringe." On the other hand, it's by no means universally accepted. It's one position among several in an ongoing historical debate.

Using Wikipedia to Jump-Start Your Research

Reading the room is bit like arriving at a party where you don't know anybody. You're standing off to the side watching the action, trying to get a feel for what's going on. But when you're exploring a topic for a research paper, you need to do more than spectate: the observer in you must become a participant. The goal, as Gerald Graff and Cathy Birkenstein explain in *They Say, I Say*, is to "join the conversation."[19] You need to learn enough about a topic to be able to stake your own claims—to make a case for which positions *you* think are strong and which don't hold water.

In research, the biggest challenge is knowing where to start. Getting off on the wrong foot—diving headfirst into a densely written book that promotes a single position while ignoring all others—gives you a distorted view of the terrain and eats up precious time. You want to begin with a source that plays fair, that gives you a bird's-eye view of the different positions, laying out their strengths and weaknesses, while putting undecided issues in the foreground.

Here's where Wikipedia is super helpful. Its policy of "no original research" provides you with a ready-made bibliography. But taking advantage of this bibliography requires a bit of code breaking, along with some familiarity with Wikipedia's quirky conventions.

Let's return to the same two-paragraph "Debate over Bombings" section we looked at earlier. It's accompanied by seven references, a soup of last names spiced with the title of a TV broadcast.[20]

319.   ^ Walker 2005, p. 334.
320.   ^ Jowett & Andrew 2002, pp. 23–24.
321.   ^ Selden & Selden 1990, pp. xxx–xxxi.
322.   ^ Walker 1990, pp. 97–114.
323.   ^ Stohl 1979, p. 279.
324.   ^ "Historians: Soviet offensive, key to Japan's WWII surrender, was eclipsed by A-bombs." Fox News Channel, Associated Press. 14 August 2010. Retrieved 18 September 2013.
325.   ^ Orr 2008, pp. 521–29.

Wikipedia employs this shorthand when its references come with a full-length bibliography. To find out, for example, what note 319, "Walker 2005, p. 334," refers to, you have to cross-reference with the bibliography (we've made it easier by cross referencing for you).

Remember, our goal is to get off on the right foot. We're looking for a source that not only allows us to read the room with greater resolution but puts us in the middle of the conversation and gives us tips for next steps.

1. Walker 2005, p. 334.
    Walker, J. Samuel (April 2005). "Recent Literature on Truman's Atomic Bomb Decision: A Search for Middle Ground." Diplomatic History. 29 (2): 311–34. doi:10.1111/j.1467-7709.2005.00476.x. ISSN 1467-7709. S2CID 154708989.
2. Jowett & Andrew 2002, pp. 23–24.
    Jowett, Philip S.; Andrew, Stephen (2002). The Japanese Army 1931–45: 2 1942–45. Oxford: Osprey Publishing. ISBN 978-1-84176-354-5. OCLC 59395824.

3. Selden & Selden 1990, pp. xxx-xxxi.

   Selden, Kyoko Iriye; Selden, Mark (1990). The Atomic Bomb: Voices from Hiroshima and Nagasaki. Armonk, New York: M.E. Sharpe. ISBN 978-0-87332-773-2. OCLC 20057103.

4. Walker 1990, pp 97–114.

   *Walker, J. Samuel (January 1990). "The Decision to Use the Bomb: A Historiographical Update." Diplomatic History. **14** (1): 97–114. doi:10.1111/j.1467-7709.1990.tb00078.x. ISSN 1467-7709.*

5. Stohl 1979, p. 279.

   Stohl, Michael (1979). The Politics of Terrorism. New York: M. Dekker. ISBN 978-0-8247-6764-8. OCLC 4495087.

6. "Historians: Soviet Offensive, Key to Japan's WWII Surrender, Was Eclipsed by A-bombs." Fox News Channel, Associated Press. 14 August 2010. Retrieved 18 September 2013.

7. Orr 2008, pp. 521–29.

   *Orr, James J. (2008). "Review of Hiroshima in History: The Myths of Revisionism and The End of the Pacific War." Journal of Japanese Studies. **34** (2): 521–28. doi:10.1353/jjs.0.0036.*

Right from the start, the process of elimination allows us to get rid of number 6, "Historians: Soviet Offensive, Key to Japan's WWII Surrender, Was Eclipsed by A-bombs." Too narrow. Number 7 is a book review. Reviews can be incredibly helpful when you've already determined that a particular book is key to your research. However, since we're still getting our feet wet, we'll skip that for now. Numbers 2 (Jowett and Andrew), 3 (Selden and Selden), and 5 (Stohl) are references to full-length books. Judging from their titles, they seem too specific. That leaves just two references, numbers 1 and 4, both by J. Samuel Walker. The subtitle of the 2005 reference, "A Search for Middle Ground," seems to hit the bullseye—a discussion of different positions rather than a partisan harangue.

We could download it and jump in. We could—and that would be fine. But since we're already on Wikipedia, there are two more stops, both quick, that boost our confidence we're on the right track. Remember the check we did for *Medical Hypotheses*? When we do the same for the journal *Diplomatic History*, we see it has been around for nearly fifty years with no red flags. We can also look up the author, J. Samuel Walker. He has his own Wikipedia page, a good sign because Wikipedia doesn't consider every writer to be "notable." He, too, checks out.

We can now dig in. The article's introduction lays out the big question of the debate: "Whether the use of the bomb was necessary to achieve victory in the Pacific." We learn about the key historians associated with each of the positions we encountered earlier. We also learn about the open questions historians are still debating. The article's twenty-three pages won't turn you into an expert, but you're no longer going to be a wallflower either. You're armed with a list of questions about the evidence for each position and, using Walker's footnotes, a roadmap for cutting your own path into this conversation.[21]

GOING DEEPER

Deciphering the Hieroglyphics of a Bibliographical Reference

It's easy to get lost in Wikipedia's references. But if you know what all these parentheses and slashes and weird acronyms stand for, you'll end up saving yourself a ton of time. Let's dissect one of them:

Walker, J. Samuel (April 2005). "Recent Literature on Truman's Atomic Bomb Decision: A Search for Middle Ground." *Diplomatic History*. 29 (2): 311–34. doi:10.1111/j.1467-7709.2005.00476.x. ISSN 1467-7709. S2CID 154708989.

After the title of the journal, you see this string of numbers: 29 (2): 311–34. The "29" refers to the volume of the journal (most often, the number of years the journal has been around). The "(2)" refers to the issue number. If there are twelve issues in a year, the "(2)" would refer to the February issue. The numbers after the colon ("311–34") are the actual page numbers of the article.

What about all these other letters and numbers, like this curious creature: "doi:10.1111/j.1467-7709.2005.00476.x"? "DOI" is library-speak for "Digital Object Identifier." It's a string of numbers assigned to an article (sometimes a book, but mostly articles) that allow you to find it on the web without having to type in the title. An active DOI link is a time-saver because all you have to do is click and you go right to the article (provided, of course, your library subscribes to the journal). With journals, you'll see a different string of numbers, preceded by the letters ISSN. This stands for "International Standard Serial Number." It's an older system than DOI but still useful. When you put the ISSN in your browser, results about the article come up (provided your library subscribes to the journal) without you having to put in the title or author's name. If you are looking at a book, you can use its International Standard Book Number, or ISBN. Typically, an ISBN search also brings up reviews of the book, which are great starting points for deciding whether a book is relevant to your research. Finally, there's the odd concoction that begins with "S2CID." This stands for "Semantic Scholar Corpus ID." Semantic Scholar (semanticscholar.org) is another means to quickly locate an article, but one that carries the unique advantage of finding material that is not imprisoned behind a paywall.

The Messiness of Making Knowledge

Making knowledge is messy. Interpretations conflict. Scholars argue about which facts to include and which to downplay—even whether a statement *is* a fact. Textbooks often hide these debates and serve up just the conclusions, delivered in neat little bundles. But Wikipedia's transparency gives us a peek into how the sausage of knowledge is made. You might not have noticed the tab hiding in plain sight next to Wikipedia's "Article" tab, the "Talk" tab. When you click on "Talk," you enter a raucous world of knowledge negotiation in which

Article Talk

WIKIPEDIA
The Free Encyclopedia

Atomic bombings of Hiroshima and Nagasaki

From Wikipedia, the free encyclopedia

FIGURE 7.11 Article on atomic bombing of Hiroshima and Nagasaki with Wikipedia's "Talk" tab highlighted (https://en.wikipedia.org/wiki/Atomic_bombings_of_Hiroshima _and_Nagasaki)

Wikipedians hash out challenges to an article, discuss new evidence, and deliberate if a change is warranted. All these discussions (some of which get out of hand and have to be curtailed by top-level Wikipedians) are conducted in public view. All you have to do is click, and you're into the middle of a knowledge party. It's Wikipedia's commitment to transparency and a great way to peek behind the curtains of how knowledge is haggled over and agreed upon.

Takeaways

▷ Wikipedia has made great strides in the last decade and become an invaluable resource for anyone using the internet.

▷ Use Wikipedia for all kinds of quick fact-checks.

▷ Use Wikipedia to "read the room" and quickly figure out who's whom and what the big issues are on topics of public and scholarly debate.

▷ Use Wikipedia's references to "enter the conversation" and jump-start your research.

Video Games

THE DIRTY TRICKS OF DECEPTIVE VIDEO

People often think persuasion is about facts. This is not wholly wrong. The good news, especially over the past few years, is that research shows facts can change beliefs. We're not logical engines when it comes to the beliefs we hold. But we're far from being the hostages to our emotions that many would have us believe. Particularly when presented with a new phenomenon—let's say the safety of new induction-style stovetops—we're open to explanations.

It's when we turn to issues about which we already have strongly held beliefs that the story gets more complicated. It's often said that "facts don't care about your feelings," but the real problem is your feelings don't particularly care about the facts. Take nuclear power. Stop a minute and consider how you feel. When you think of nuclear power, what images come to mind? What connections?

Now let us introduce a fact. A recent-ish study looked at the impact of nuclear power on death rates. They calculated the various harms that nuclear power has caused historically, from meltdowns to worker radiation exposure. Then they compared the harm that coal-fired plants have caused. Every aspect was studied, from mining for materials to operation to pollution to radiation-caused disease. The result? The use of nuclear power in lieu of coal may have saved 1.8 million lives.[1]

Does that change how you feel about nuclear power? If you're like most people, you may now know something you didn't before. But does this knowledge change your *feelings* toward it? They probably haven't changed that much, especially if they were strongly held before.

One relatively popular conclusion from this is that better information doesn't matter when it comes to belief, as shown in the *New Yorker* article "Why Facts Don't Change Our Minds."[2] While the move away from a naive view of the influence of facts on behavior is useful, it misses a crucial insight that has been part of propaganda and public relations since before we had names for these things. Abstract knowledge may not shift our positions much. When our feelings and our positions do shift, it's because something stirs our emotions, gets us roiled up, or causes us to care about something we didn't know we cared about.

Propagandists have known this for a long time. Edward Bernays, one of the founders of modern public relations, wrote in 1923 that to create emotion in their audience, the "public relations counsel must create news around his ideas," isolating those ideas and "develop[ing] them as events."[3] For Bernays, this did not mean trickery. An early example he provides is of a hotel fighting a rumor that it is going out of business. It's a dangerous rumor for the hotel because people don't book rooms at hotels they believe may close. And it's a difficult public-relations situation for the hotel: to deny the rumor would only look defensive. His solution is to make a public event of a five-year renewal of a contract of a world-famous manager there. People hearing such a story, he reasoned, will have an impression that the hotel is on good financial footing to make such an expensive, long-term contract.[4] By creating events, one shapes experience, and experience shapes opinion.

In that case, the event may have been a bit stage-managed, but it was real, and meaningful in its way. However, most propaganda is not bounded by such constraints. The term "fake news" has fallen out of favor with academics for a variety of (mostly valid) reasons, but at the heart of the term is an insight. To the unethical propagandist, the quickest way to shift public sentiment is not to change what they *know*, but what they *think is happening*. Luckily, the tricks propagandists use to manipulate reality are relatively predictable, and we'll cover some of them here.

False Context

On the night of November 3, 2020, election workers in Fulton County, Georgia, were tired. Up early to help with Election Day, by ten o'clock at night, many were exhausted and decided to go home and get some rest. A number stayed at the vote-counting center, packing the ballots in the standard black security bins used to protect them from being tampered with overnight. Shortly after they had finished, they received a call. Under pressure to announce a result as soon as possible, the state wanted them to continue counting through the night. After letting out what we imagine was the huge sigh all workers know when bosses reverse direction, registration officer Wandrea "Shaye" Moss went and retrieved the security box from under the table where it was stored. Under the eyes of an independent state investigator and 24/7 surveillance cameras, she and others restarted the counting process.[5]

Those cameras were there to build confidence in the process, but the video they produced was put to a more devious use. If you were to have encountered a video snippet of that event in one of hundreds of viral YouTube, Instagram, Twitter, or TikTok videos circulated about a month later, here's how it would have been described:

"Video shows suitcases filled with ballots pulled AFTER supervisors told poll workers to leave"[6]

"Suitcases Filled With Ballots; Hidden Under Table; Counted Without Oversight"[7]

"Fulton County supervisors in Georgia tell poll workers, press and observers to leave the room . . . And then pull out SUITCASES of ballots."[8]

Attached to most of these lurid headlines? A short video showing the worker pulling the security bins out and coordinating the resumed count according to standard procedure. But to the viewer, convinced by the framing text and shortened clip that these were secret suitcases filled with fake ballots, to the person who was told the count was not supervised or made to believe that other workers had been sneakily sent home—to all these people—the video, so innocuous to one who knows what it actually shows, was an outrage. It seemed to show an election being stolen in plain sight.

What happened next was sadly predictable. Threats against the worker and her mother (who was featured in another miscontextualized video) began to propagate on social media. Further photos and claims were presented, with similar skewing. As Moss and her mother went into hiding, fearing for their lives, many citizens watched video after video of this sort, on Facebook, on Twitter, on less-than-honest television programs.

That sensational coverage of events would circumvent our critical faculties is hardly novel. Going back to the example of nuclear power:

in the United States, perceptions of nuclear power changed rapidly in the late 1970s; this change was partly the result of sensational coverage of the Three Mile Island disaster in 1979. People watching TV at that time watched an event that bypassed formal debate and formed lasting impressions of the danger of nuclear power, and, in the words of one writer, sent the American romance with nuclear power into a "deep freeze."[9] The effects were substantial and durable, and it is possible that the impressions formed may have had unfortunate social consequences. In that case, at least, the event being experienced was real—there really had been an accident at Three Mile Island.

But here was another thing entirely. A substantial portion of the country was experiencing nightly events that were largely fabricated. To these viewers, the election was being stolen in front of them. They could see it, right there in the video.

Exploiting "Seeing Is Believing"

Doubt is a healthy thing in a democracy. If someone sends you a video of supposed election misdeeds, it's more than reasonable to find that compelling and potentially important. But how do you make sure that in looking at videos and other evidence you are asking valid questions about an event of social importance—and not taking the off-ramp into a fictional world full of false experiences meant to manipulate and enrage you?

As always, the first thing to ask yourself when you encounter such content is *not* whether it is true or false. That comes later. The first question is always, Do I understand what I'm looking at here? And to answer that, you need to think about our three contexts. For the video shared, the most obvious factor is the *context of you*. What riles you up? Do you know what normal election procedures look like? Can you tell the difference between a valid ballot container and a suspicious one? Have you become a sudden "elections expert" two minutes after watching something on YouTube?

You might note, as well, that you have very little information on the other contexts. On the *context of the source*, it might seem initially obvious: the video is from a surveillance camera. But the video is also two minutes long, not twelve hours: Who decided where it would start and stop? Who supplied the description of these as "suitcases of ballots," and who is saying these were counted without oversight? An objective source? An expert? Or someone with an ax to grind? And while we're at it, what's the context of the claim? What happened before? What happened after? What would an actual expert in elections say is happening in this video?

When we say to stop and take note of these issues, we're not talking about doing a research project. If you take as long to do it as it took to read the preceding paragraph, you're doing it wrong. This isn't a checklist or a worksheet. Your inability to answer even *one* of these questions is enough to realize that you *don't actually know* what you're looking at. And that's enough to push you to a decision—either wait until a better-sourced and contextualized video comes out, or, if you still find this compelling, do the moves.

With video, we almost always go straight to the *F* in SIFT, *find other coverage*, particularly if the video is an excerpt from something longer. Most deceptive video is "real" in the sense that it usually depicts something that happened somewhere: it's the context—the who, what, when, where, and why—that gets hacked by bad actors. So, getting the bigger story by finding out what others have said about the video is a good first stop.

While we can't precisely simulate what it would have been like to search for this video when it first emerged in the context of a Georgia legislative session, the search we are about to describe is a half-decent guess. When new evidence emerges, it's often the case that context isn't immediately available. Even in the best of circumstances, it takes a few hours for reporters, researchers, and other experts to reconstruct the full context of a decontextualized video. And so, looking to find out more, you might get something like this, where a search for context on a short video provides a bunch of irrelevant results, and one result that just sends you right back to the video itself:[10]

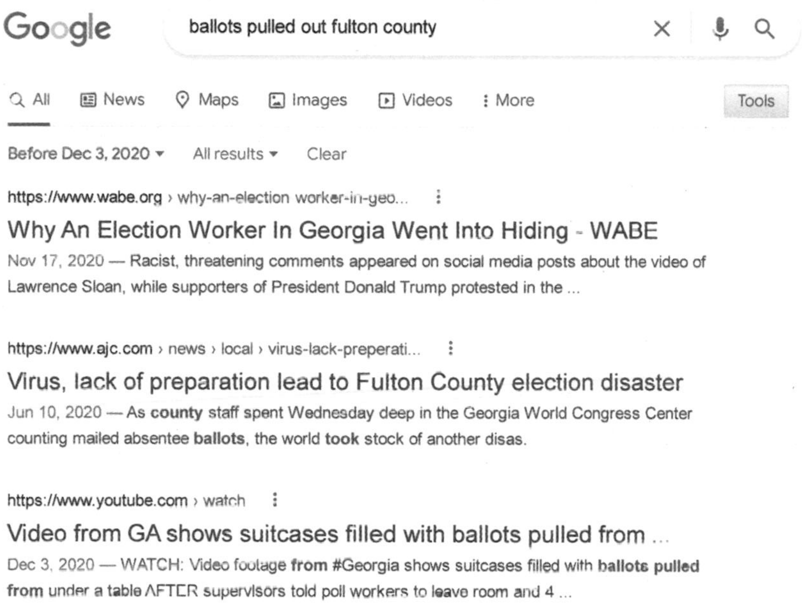

Google   ballots pulled out fulton county   ✕   🎤   🔍

Q All   🗐 News   ◯ Maps   🖾 Images   ▶ Videos   ⋮ More   Tools

Before Dec 3, 2020 ▾   All results ▾   Clear

https://www.wabe.org › why-an-election worker-in-geo...   ⋮
Why An Election Worker In Georgia Went Into Hiding - WABE
Nov 17, 2020 — Racist, threatening comments appeared on social media posts about the video of Lawrence Sloan, while supporters of President Donald Trump protested in the ...

https://www.ajc.com › news › local › virus-lack-preperati...   ⋮
Virus, lack of preparation lead to Fulton County election disaster
Jun 10, 2020 — As **county** staff spent Wednesday deep in the Georgia World Congress Center counting mailed absentee **ballots**, the world **took** stock of another disas.

https://www.youtube.com › watch   ⋮
Video from GA shows suitcases filled with ballots pulled from ...
Dec 3, 2020 — WATCH: Video footage **from** #Georgia shows suitcases filled with **ballots pulled from** under a table AFTER supervisors told poll workers to leave room and 4 ...

FIGURE 8.1 Search for "ballots pulled out Fulton County" scoped to the day of the video's release. (Google and the Google logo are trademarks of Google LLC.)

This lack of results is in itself a signal—a signal communicating one of the hardest messages for human beings to comprehend: maybe you should wait. Before you get incensed, before you rage-share it, before you decide to *experience it as fact*, maybe wait and get the context. Trust us: if there are legs to a video, people are frantically looking into it. You won't have to wait long.

Keep in mind that after a video like this goes viral, the first "reporting" on the scene is not likely to be reporting at all but various rage merchants wrapping a blog post around a YouTube video with various levels of exclamation points and caps-lock use. Reliable reporters need time to work. Rage merchants do not. When it comes to breaking events, the greatest information literacy superpower is often just learning to wait before allowing yourself to form deep beliefs about the event. Remember that both the con artist and the propagandist feed on the impatient, because time to investigate and reflect does not favor liars.

Of course, you don't have to wait long. Relatively quickly, the search results will shift. And they will reveal the backstory you need to understand the video. They weren't suitcases. They weren't hidden ballots.

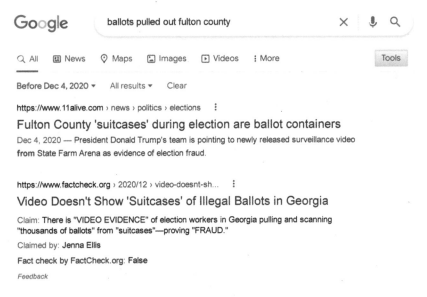

FIGURE 8.2 Search for "ballots pulled out Fulton County" scoped to the day after the video's release. (Google and the Google logo are trademarks of Google LLC.)

They weren't unsupervised. Workers were not forced to go home. If you think back to all the things that made this video compelling or enraging—none of those things are true.

GOING DEEPER

Online News Is Often More Credible Than You Think

In this chapter, we talk a lot about fakery, so it may surprise you to know that in most cases, the news people see on social media is pretty credible. People across all ages and demographics consistently overestimate the prevalence of false news in their timelines. Additionally, most people *share* very little false news: the spread of toxic information online is driven by a small number of people who share a lot, have followers who share a lot, and aren't particularly careful with the truth.[11] The majority of people recognize the fundamental asymmetry of reputation building. You can undo the reputation of sharing true things daily by sharing one false item.[12] People want to preserve their reputation and act accordingly.

We assume that if you're reading this book, you're probably on the cautious side of the equation already. So, what should you, the cautious reader of this work, take away? There are numerous lessons, but we hope you will consider a surprising one: we want you to share more news, not less.[13] What we find with most students is a growing reluctance to share *any* news, based on the fear that it may turn out to be false, and an unwillingness to challenge false stories they see, based on the fear they may be wrong about them. This in turn produces what Mike has called elsewhere a "Yeats effect," based on a line from an old poem about the end of the world: "The best lack all conviction, while the worst are full of passionate intensity."[14]

So, read about the tricks the devious use. When you see something compelling, run your quick checks. But if it looks good after walking through SIFT and is something people should know, share it! If you see falsehood, correct it! We want these skills to empower you, and we want to get voices like yours back to the social media table.

Falsely Implied Date

What other types of false context can be used to manipulate people? One common trick is to portray old footage as if it's happening in the present, thus shifting the meaning. Often the deception is subtle; unless dates are explicitly mentioned, people usually assume the story they are looking at is new and current.

We worked on this book after the extent of Russia's brutal invasion of Ukraine had become known and documented. Early on, however, many people were making the case that the war was overblown, a show put on for the cameras. According to this theory, there were no attacks, no bombings, no fighting. Russia, according to this theory, was being *framed*. The invasion of February 23, 2022, had never really happened.

A couple days after the invasion, a video appeared claiming to show such fakery. The video, shown as being from cable news station CNN, started by showing Ukrainian troops on maneuvers in snowy terrain. They work as a group, impressively advancing up a road while providing cover for each other. Then the camera pulls back and reveals something shocking: this isn't a war scene at all. Behind this military maneuver is a horde of press filming it. As one poster asserts, this is a "FAKE WAR," staged like a film for the sheeple masses.[15]

Again, the principle of "Do I know what I'm looking at?" applies here. In this case, you probably don't know. This one is difficult to find, but after searching through a few CNN videos and trying different search terms, we were able to trace it to the source and see the original context. And the context changes everything.

First of all, we note that the press involved is not some sort of deep-state secret. It's in the original CNN video. But it's the date that makes all the difference. As you can tell from the original title, this is a video of troops preparing *before* the invasion. It's not a video

Jonathan Doe
@jonathandoe_693

Ukraine War is FAKE... this thread and this video shows just how fake it is! This is a production not a WAR! Who's getting paid again and making money?

423 Retweets   **207** Quote Tweets   **1.2K** Likes

FIGURE 8.3 Tweet and selected frames from video allegedly showing war footage from Ukraine was faked. (Poster's name and handle are redacted.)

In Chernobyl, Ukrainians prepare for war

Chernobyl has been abandoned since the world's worst nuclear disaster here three decades ago. But with Russian troops amassing on Ukraine's border, the ghost town is now playing host to security forces training for war. Source: CNN

Meat. Cheese. Treat.
Sponsored by Hillshire Farm®

See More

World News (15 Videos)

In Chernobyl, Ukrainians prepare for war

See Chinese police show of force in response to assaults on women

Yair Lapid takes over as Israel's caretaker prime minister

Hear what this Parmesan producer has to say about worst drought in 70 years

NATO Secret General: Mac summit a 'vic the alliance

FIGURE 8.4 Original CNN video showing press covering training exercises weeks before Russia invaded Ukraine, cnn.com, February 2022 (https://www.cnn.com/2022/02/07 /europe/ukraine-chernobyl-belarus-intl-cmd/index.html)

of the war, and it was never presented as such. The invasion occurred on February 24, 2022. This video of troops training was posted by CNN on February 8, 2022.[16]

When there's no fact-check available, tracing something like this to the source can be tricky. But again, the trickiness can be a signal. If you see several people sharing a video like this, but no one provides a link to the original or provides a date or location of where the video was supposedly filmed, it might be best to hold off deciding whether a brutal and tragic war that killed thousands is all a media-cooked-up illusion.

Connect My Dots, or Creating a False Sense of "Research"

Sometimes the problem is not the absence of a link but that the link you're provided comes shorn of the context you need to understand it. This can be particularly pernicious: on the one hand, you *feel* like you're verifying something (after all, isn't following a link to a source the last part of SIFT?). On the other hand, the false framing you've been fed prevents you from understanding the real meaning of the materials you've pulled up.

Consider the odd TikTok conspiracy that circulated in spring of 2021. A user on that site made a video that pointed at the party-supply pages of a seller on Amazon, saying that they were suspiciously overpriced. A party hat for fifteen thousand dollars? Was it possible that this store was actually a front for child sex-trafficking? That the party hat was really a secret way to "order up" an abducted child?

If you're reading this book, we hope that you're not gullible enough to fall for such nonsense. But such conspiracies, when presented this way, do have a compelling element. After all, you can go and look at the Amazon listing yourself, right? It feels like verification; you're "doing your own research," after all. And when you get to the link

jane doeish_ Jane Doe

what you all think? 🫤 #amazon #fyp #viral #trending

♫ original sound - jane_doeish1

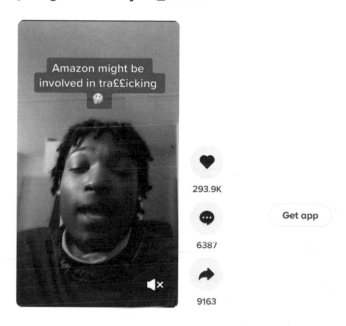

FIGURE 8.5 Screenshot of TikTok conspiracy theory video, February 2021. (Poster's name and handle are redacted.)

and find there *are* party-themed fedoras for fifteen thousand dollars, maybe you don't necessarily buy the conspiracy. But you have to admit, something seems fishy.

Except you've been had. That research you're doing is a set up. The facts are presented without context. Then you are invited to verify these contextless facts. But what you're *not* given is the information that would allow you to make sense of them. We call this technique "Connect My Dots": you feel like you are drawing a picture yourself, directly from evidence, but in reality, you have been given the dots to connect and the order in which to connect them. The dots that don't fit the chosen narrative are not supplied.

In this case, the crucial piece of context? Sometimes people buy party supplies in bulk for large events. And if, for example, you buy a bulk order of three thousand hats, the price will be, more or less, fifteen thousand dollars.[17] In cases like this, it's not always clear if the conspiracy theorists know the context and don't supply it, or if they're confused themselves. But the consequences are pretty horrific. Spreading like wildfire on TikTok, this video received over six million views! Viewers confused by it went on Amazon and left outraged comments. Employees received threats, the police were called, and users down-ranked the store on Amazon, dealing the small business of seventeen years a financial blow. In the mind of the conspiracy theorists, of course, they were sure that *they* were the critical thinkers. After all, hadn't they used reasoning to figure out whether this was "plausible"? They hadn't taken the TikTok poster's word for it; they had verified these prices on Amazon directly.

We see this technique in even more weighty cases. As we noted in chapter 2, one technique of antivaccine activists is to link people to the VAERS website, an unverified database of things that people claim to have experienced within a certain period after getting a vaccine. It's meant to alert researchers to issues they may want to research; it is not a running record of vaccine issues. A lot of things happen to people every day, including the days after they get a vaccination, and the vast majority of those things are not related in any real way to vaccines. If you look carefully at the page itself, it will tell you that, just as Amazon's interface was pretty clear you were ordering three thousand hats. But the wrong person presenting the database as something else—and providing a link—can make people blind to cues that should be obvious.

The techniques you should use here are not that different from what we have shown before. For the TikTok conspiracy, it's notable that there was another video debunking it and explaining it before the theory went viral. So, by the time most people shared it, a search for "TikTok conspiracy Ionized" (Ionized is the name of the company) would have turned up the debunking video and provided the context. For a deep-linked source like VAERS, our standard "Investigate" advice applies: don't assume that how a source has been described by the person sending it to you is necessarily accurate.

Deceptively Cropped Video

A time-honored tradition in political campaign advertisements is to take a quote from one's opponent out of context and present it as the full story. "Some people say if we enact this law, there will be starving in the streets," says an incumbent for office, "but the opposite is true." Several months later, a campaign ad runs from the opposition. Now the video is cut so that the incumbent says, simply, "If we enact this law, there will be starving in the streets."

With the internet and cheap video editing, what used to be the province of professionals is now available to the masses. Any person can crop a video, frame it as an outrage, and get it trending before the full context catches up. We saw that in the "suitcases of ballots" example. In that case, the video would have needed to be pretty long to show the full context. But in many cases, just getting a bit of video on each side of the crop changes everything.

For example, a video was circulated where the US director of the Centers for Disease Control and Prevention (CDC) said, regarding COVID-19, "The overwhelming number of deaths, over 75% occurred in those with over four comorbidities. So really these were people unwell to begin with." In this case, the video was from *Good Morning*

America—not exactly a hotbed of antivaccine activism—and featured the director of the CDC saying this directly.

Social media went berserk. Had the CDC director just admitted—after pushing everyone to get vaccinated—that COVID-19 wasn't dangerous to people of moderate health? Hadn't this been what the antivaccine activists were saying all along: that COVID was less dangerous than the flu? "We were told (COVID-19) killed like that of the Spanish flu or the Black Plague," said one poster, "but finally the truth is beginning to resound and I pray it sets you free."[18] And while you might think that this is a statistical argument, its significance to those viewing the tightly edited clip was not the statistics but the fact that they finally had proof it had all been a deception.

So, was this a sign that vaccines weren't necessary? Had it all been a sham? You can probably guess the rest. When you take that partial quote and throw it into Google, a different picture emerges.

Here's the full context of what the CDC director said: "A study of

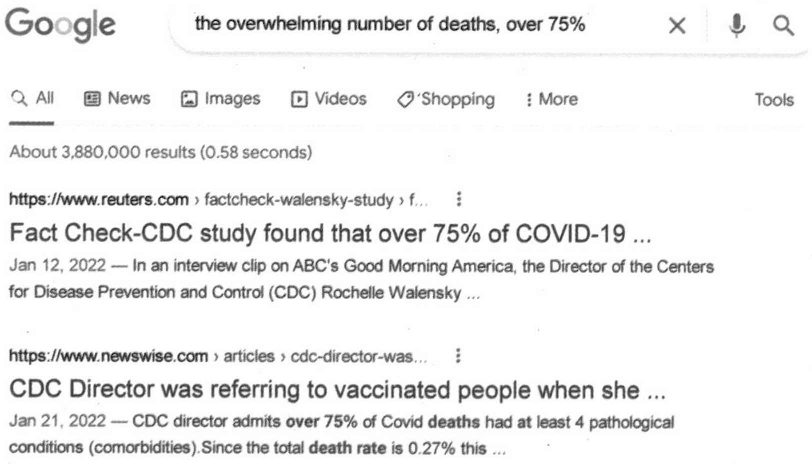

Google   the overwhelming number of deaths, over 75%   ✕ 🎤 🔍

🔍 All   📰 News   🖼 Images   ▶ Videos   ◇ Shopping   ⋮ More   Tools

About 3,880,000 results (0.58 seconds)

https://www.reuters.com › factcheck-walensky-study › f...   ⋮
Fact Check-CDC study found that over 75% of COVID-19 ...
Jan 12, 2022 — In an interview clip on ABC's Good Morning America, the Director of the Centers
for Disease Prevention and Control (CDC) Rochelle Walensky ...

https://www.newswise.com › articles › cdc-director-was...   ⋮
CDC Director was referring to vaccinated people when she ...
Jan 21, 2022 — CDC director admits **over 75%** of Covid **deaths** had at least 4 pathological
conditions (comorbidities). Since the total **death rate** is 0.27% this ...

FIGURE 8.6 Search for "the overwhelming number of deaths, over 75%," February 2022. (Google and the Google logo are trademarks of Google LLC.)

1.2 million people who were vaccinated between December and October and demonstrated that severe disease occurred in about 0.015% of the people who received their primary series and death in 0.003% of those people. The overwhelming number of deaths, over 75 percent, occurred in people who had at least four comorbidities."[19] That's right—the CDC director was referring to *vaccinated* people, and the full context says that the vaccines were startlingly *effective*.

Could we have known this just by looking at the cropped video? Should we have suspected it? Our general advice is to do quick checks on anything we find compelling—suspicious or not. But in this case—just as in the case with the ballot bins and the case with the Ukrainian soldiers—there was a particular tell. The shorter a video is, the easier it is to create a false context. This is part of what we call Molloy's Law, named after Parker Molloy, a researcher who has documented dozens (perhaps hundreds) of falsely contextualized videos over the years: "The tighter a video is clipped, the less inclined you should be to share it."[20] If the content is compelling and the video is short, seek out the longer version (please!).

What can we do? Because it is important to keep up with events, we can't mistrust every video that comes across our feeds. But we can take a few seconds to seek context before engaging with it and setting our emotions on fire. We should particularly do that when the video or quote is short. And we can seek our *own* context instead of relying on the links that others feed us to verify their claims. Once we have the context and re-engage with the video, quote, or news article, we sometimes come to see the event in a very different light.

We want you to be careful, but we don't want to turn you into cynics. So many things that shape our world for the better start out with an unexpected video, inspiring picture, or disturbing news item. We should be open to it all and share it if it is useful to others. But before handing over the keys to our emotional reactions, we need to exercise a bit of restraint. The old adage of the master carpenter—"measure twice, cut once"—can be adapted here: think twice, share once.

Takeaways

▷ Social media can bamboozle you with false facts, but it is equally dangerous how it creates a stream of false experiences and events to which we react.

▷ False context can be used to warp your interpretation of real events, creating scandals out of relatively ordinary occurrences.

▷ Taken out of context, the links posters give you to verify something often warp the context even more.

▷ The tighter a video is clipped, the less inclined you should be to share it.

Stealth Advertising

WHEN ADS MASQUERADE AS NEWS

Five women peer out from a picture on *Teen Vogue*'s website: "How Facebook Is Helping Ensure the Integrity of the 2020 Election." The article praises Facebook's efforts to combat misinformation by profiling the women leading the charge. Posting on social media in January 2020, Sheryl Sandberg, Facebook's chief operating officer, gushed: "Great *Teen Vogue* piece about five incredible women."[1]

The article let on nothing of Facebook's problems: nothing about the site letting Russian propaganda run amok, nothing about allowing landlords to discriminate by placing restrictive ads, nothing about how the site experimented on users without their knowledge.[2] Pure puffery: sweet, light, vapid.

A perplexed reader named Lauren Murphy detected something fishy. She asked on Twitter, "What is this @TeenVogue . . . ?" The official *Teen Vogue* account replied in a tweet deleted soon thereafter: "Literally idk." Lots of people, however, *did* know—including Sheryl Sandberg. Sandberg was smitten by the piece because her company had paid for it.[3]

Teen Vogue, it turns out, had struck two deals. First, with Facebook.

FIGURE 9.1 *Teen Vogue* article touting Facebook (Abrams and Kang, "The Mystery of *Teen Vogue*'s Disappearing Facebook Article")

← **Thread**

Lauren Murphy   •••
@laurenmurphypho

What is this @TeenVogue teenvogue.com/story/how-face... ⑦

9:08 AM · Jan 8, 2020 · Twitter for iPhone

10 Retweets   **4** Quote Tweets   **76** Likes

FIGURE 9.2   Tweet by @laurenmurphypho asking @TeenVogue about the *Teen Vogue* Facebook article (https://twitter.com/laurenmurphypho/status/1214956959700529152)

Teen Vogue ✔
@TeenVogue

Replying to @laurenmurphypho

literally idk

12:32 PM · Jan 8, 2020 · Twitter Web App

FIGURE 9.3 @TeenVogue's response to @laurenmurphypho's question about the *Teen Vogue* Facebook article. (Tweet has been deleted.)

Second, with the devil—by agreeing to deceive readers with ads that look like legitimate news stories. "Stealth ads," unlike their detested but more recognizable cousins—flashing banner ads, multicolored display ads, obnoxious pop-ups—are designed to fade unobtrusively into the surrounding news content. The article looks like a news story, written by an independent and trustworthy journalist, when in reality it's tainted by the agenda of the company that paid for it. You think you're being informed only to find out—if you *do* find out—you're being swindled.

The Federal Trade Commission (FTC), the government agency responsible for regulating these kinds of things, stipulates that "native ads" (so called because they appear "native" to the website, sharing the same fonts, color schemes, style, etc.) must carry a warning label—an indication that alerts readers they're reading an ad. But in *Teen Vogue*'s case, the warning label went AWOL. Then it mysteriously reappeared. Then, just as mysteriously, it disappeared again. When the Twitterverse caught wind of this fiasco and erupted in outrage, *Teen Vogue* removed the Facebook "story" and hung its head in shame.

Native ads were created for one simple reason: we ignore regular ads. We've installed extensions to zap them. Your mouse steers clear of ads like real mice steer clear of cats. The click-through rate on regular digital ads is stupendously low, a minuscule fraction of 1 percent. Yet, people *do* click on native ads. How come? Could it be, as media expert Bob Garfield put it in an article aptly titled "A Conspiracy of Deception," that people "don't realize native ads are ads"?[4]

The Problem: Stealth Advertising Works

Stealth advertising has proven effective—chillingly so. By 2018, it was estimated to be a $32.9 billion business, eclipsing all other forms of online advertising and growing astronomically.[5] That's because stealth advertising works. When undergraduates at Purdue University

FIGURE 9.4 Graphic accompanying news article from *The Atlantic* (https://www.the atlantic.com/science/archive/2015/10/why-only-a-technocratic-revolution-can-win -the-climate-change-war/410377/)

were shown a news article and an eye-catching infographic on climate change on the website of the *Atlantic*, 78 percent said the infographic was more reliable than the article. Students failed to notice—or if they did, it didn't register—the tiny "sponsor content" label lurking in the upper left-hand corner. Next to it was a miniature icon for none other than Shell.[6] A fossil fuel company casting itself as the source of objective information on climate change? Smell anything wrong here?

It's not only college students who get hoodwinked by the shifty practices of native advertising. We all do. A study by the marketing company Contently showed people native ads that appeared on the websites of six different publishers. The results were, well, let's just say, concerning. Eighty percent of respondents mistook a native ad in the *Wall Street Journal* for a news article. The percentage was only slightly lower for an ad disguised as news from the *New York Times*. The

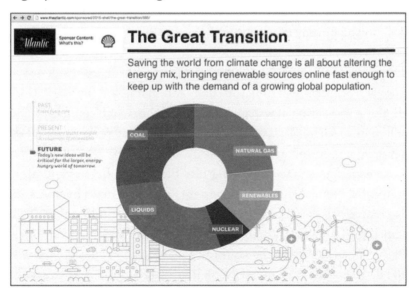

FIGURE 9.5 Infographic from oil company Shell appearing in *The Atlantic* (www.theatlantic .com/sponsored/2015-shell/the-great-transition/595/; see also Forte, "Civic Online Reading in First-Year Composition")

study's author, an advertising insider with reasons to cast the whole smarmy business as perfectly legit, had to admit the obvious: "There's little doubt that consumers are confused by native ads."[7]

And confused we are. Researchers at Boston University and the University of Georgia surveyed people across age levels and backgrounds after they had read a 515-word article, "America's Smartphone Obsession Extends to Online Banking." The piece came with a label saying that it was created for Bank of America. But this disclosure was overshadowed by the masthead of the *New York Times* and the article's headline. Only one in ten respondents were able to identify the article as an ad.[8] A blizzard of other studies confirm this troubling pattern.[9]

A Con Is Born

Back in the heyday of print, publishers raked in piles of cash from ads. Then along came the internet, raining on the parade. Ad dollars decamped from traditional news outlets and took up residence at Google, Facebook, Twitter, YouTube, and Instagram. By 2012, Google alone was eating newspapers' lunches: the search company's $46 billion in ad earnings was more than double the ad revenue for *all* US newspapers—print and digital.[10]

Newspapers started dropping like flies. Ad dollars evaporated. Journalists joined the unemployment lines. The news business today employs less than half the number of people it did in 2010. To stanch the bloodletting, publishers adopted an idea laid out by David Ogilvy, head of one of the country's leading ad agencies: "There is no need for advertisements to look like advertisements. If you make them look like editorial pages, you will attract about 50 percent more readers."[11] In other words, *make advertisements undetectable*. Just like that, a con was born.

The New York Times

America's smartphone obsession extends to mobile banking

by DAVID RABINOWITZ Nov 29, 2016, 9:20am EST

Partner Content **Bank of America**

(BPT) - There's no denying it -- smartphones have become essential to daily life. From the smallest to the most complex of tasks, we've adopted a mobile-first mindset. For an increasing number of adults, this means their smartphone is never too far out of reach.

In fact, if you're like most Americans, your smartphone is your first and last interaction of the day. Nearly 71 percent of consumers sleep with their smartphones nearby and 35 percent say it's the first thing they reach for in the morning, according to the second annual Bank of America Trends in Consumer Mobility Report. What's more, 36 percent report checking their mobile devices "constantly," and 38 percent never disconnect from their smartphones.

The survey, which explored broad mobile trends and banking behaviors among adults across the country, found the need for constant connectivity also extends to banking. Of those respondents who use a mobile banking app, 62 percent say they access it a few times a week or more, while 20 percent check once a day or more.

"We recognize how essential smartphones are to everyday life and banking is no different," says Michelle Moore, head of digital banking at Bank of America. "For many of our customers, mobile has become the bank in their pocket, allowing them to bank with us when, where and how they want."

The report revealed further insights into how consumers are using mobile to manage their money.

Mobile banking is the new normal. More consumers are using mobile banking to stay in control of their finances, with the survey revealing nearly six in 10 (57 percent) have at least tried mobile banking and 48 percent are active users. Fifty-one percent use either mobile or online as their primary method of banking, while just 23 percent complete the majority of their banking at a bank branch.

Mobile check deposit is on the rise. Consumers are increasingly benefitting from the convenience of mobile check deposit, using the feature to save themselves a trip to the bank. Sixty-three percent surveyed have used mobile check deposit, with older millennials (ages 25-34) the most likely to use it (72 percent).

Consumers trust alerts to stay in-the-know. Mobile banking alerts give consumers the flexibility to manage their finances via a range of customizable notifications. Many Americans are already taking advantage — the majority (81 percent) of mobile banking app users report receiving banking notifications via mobile, such as low balance (43 percent), unusual activity (41 percent) and bill pay (35 percent) alerts.

Mobile phones becoming mobile wallets. Consumers are increasingly receptive to new and emerging technology, particularly when it comes to mobile banking and payments. Approximately six in 10 (56 percent) surveyed would consider paying someone using person-to-person payments via mobile banking app. Additionally, 34 percent would consider or have already used their smartphone or wearable device to make a purchase at checkout.

For additional insights into consumer mobility and mobile banking, view the full Bank of America Trends in Consumer Mobility Report at http://newsroom.bankofamerica.com/press-kits/bank-america-trends-consumer- mobility-report.

FIGURE 9.6 Prompt used in a 2019 research study, November 29, 2016 (Amazeen and Wojdynski, "Reducing Native Advertising Deception")

At first, it was only the scrappy upstarts like BuzzFeed (masters of clickbaity stories like "Ten Important Life Lessons You Can Learn from Cats") that pioneered this new form of deception. But as ad income plummeted at publications like the *New York Times*, the *Wall Street Journal*, and the *BBC*, they, too, decided that the devil was a legitimate business partner. The price, at first, didn't seem too steep: sacrifice a little bit of integrity to stay afloat. But the slope downward was slippery. If the long-standing commitment of journalism was to protect journalistic standards by erecting a wall of separation between the news side and the business side, native advertising dissolved the mortar in that wall. The resulting seepage blurred the boundaries beyond recognition. Sure, journalists found ways to convince themselves they weren't doing anything wrong. But, in their hearts, they knew something different. "When I explain what I do to friends outside the publishing industry," wrote one publishing insider, "the first response is always 'so you are basically tricking users into clicking on ads.'"[12]

Newspapers Become Ad Agencies

In the days of print newspapers, ads were set off from regular content, often with a blue box marked by the word "advertisement." The people who worked on the business side and who sold these advertisements would hit the streets rounding up business. Professional ad agencies would design the copy, and the newspapers would print it.

Not anymore. Newspapers now have their own in-house ad agencies, writing, designing, and tweaking their client's message. As for those salespeople? Today they are more likely to be called "creative directors" or "content strategists" or "video producers"—often former journalists pitching ads to their *own* newsrooms a flight of stairs below.[13]

Among mainstream newspapers, the acknowledged leader in

stealth advertising is the *New York Times*, which established T Brand Studio in 2014. Ad industry insiders lauded one of T Brand Studio's first "stories," "Women Inmates: Why the Male Model Doesn't Work," paid for by Netflix to promote the show *Orange Is the New Black*. Soon, all the big media players were in on the game. The *Wall Street Journal* has Custom Studios, with a staff of thirty-two.[14] The BBC has StoryWorks, which uses "BBC's creative excellence and rigorous editorial quality to help brands connect through beautifully crafted storytelling."[15] The *Guardian* has its "Branded Content from the Guardian" squad. CNN has Courageous, which "specializes in bold, culturally-relevant creative documentary-style premium storytelling that captivates audiences."[16] The *Atlantic* has its Re:think studio. What will they *re:think* up next?

Publishers contort themselves into pretzels trying to explain why

FIGURE 9.7 Paid post appearing in the *New York Times* to promote the Netflix show *Orange Is the New Black* (https://www.nytimes.com/paidpost/netflix/women-inmates -separate-but-not-equal.html)

all of this "premium storytelling" is kosher. An executive from Turner Broadcasting, CNN's parent company, waxed poetic about upholding journalist ethics: "This isn't about confusing editorial with advertising. . . . This is about telling advertisers' stories—telling a similar story but clearly labeling and differentiating that. . . . This is CNN. We're not here to blur the lines."[17] Responding to these overblown statements of faith, Janine Jackson of the media watchdog group Fairness & Accuracy in Reporting quipped: "Advertisers aren't stupid. When they pay money for something they expect to get money in return . . . whether it's called storytelling or content or co-branding. An ad is an ad is an ad."[18]

The Problem in Three Words: *Conflict of Interest*

What's the big deal if you don't notice that the story you just forwarded was an ad from ExxonMobil? To start, these kinds of companies are not in the business of helping humanity or adopting stray cats. Their goal is to make shareholders giddy by increasing profits. Fossil fuel companies may want us to think they're on the right side of history when it comes to climate change. But actions speak louder than ads. Clean energy investments by big oil companies ("renewable resources" as the Shell ad calls them) represent a sliver, 1 percent, of their yearly capital expenditures, a pittance compared to what they spend exploring and discovering new ways to extract fossil fuels from the earth and sea.[19] Shell might not be outright lying in its infographic, but you can bet on one thing: companies are not going to pay for something that casts them in a negative light. The whole point, after all, is to spiff up their image. Instead of having us view Shell as climate change enemy number one, its ads are designed to soften us up, to plant a seed of doubt.[20] "Sure, it's an oil company, but look, maybe it's really trying."

Three words explain why we should think hard before accepting what Shell tells us about climate change: *conflict of interest*. It goes against Shell's interest to be forthcoming about the harmful effects of fossil fuels. Big oil companies like Shell, ExxonMobil, BP, and the rest "may be a reliable source of information on oil and gas extraction," writes Harvard professor Naomi Oreskes, but they are "unlikely to be a reliable source of information on climate change." Why? Simple: "The former is its business and the latter threatens it."[21]

Disappearing Warning Labels

Aren't there supposed to be warning labels? Uh . . . yes. The FTC is supposed to protect us from all this monkey business. In 2015, it issued guidelines for publishers to follow. Labels were supposed to be "clear and conspicuous," displayed in a "font and color that's easy to read."[22] The labels weren't supposed to beat around the bush either. The FTC recommended that publishers use words understandable by a ten-year-old: "ad" or "advertisement." Even better: "paid advertisement."

Did you notice the weasel word "recommended" in the FTC statement? At the same time the FTC specified guidelines, it provided publishers with an escape hatch as big as the Grand Canyon. Publishers, it wrote, should be transparent about paid ads. However, the "required nature of transparency is situation specific." *Ah, yes, situation specific.* You didn't need laser vision to see where all this was headed.

First, a whole bunch of slithery alternatives to "ad" and "advertisement" started to sprout: "sponsored content," "presented by," "crafted by," "partner content," "brand voice," "in association with," "brought to you by," "co-created with," "hosted by," or the most unobtrusive of them all, just one word: "with"—as in, "*with Shell.*" What's "with Shell" supposed to mean, anyway?

It gets worse. The deals publishers work out with clients are based on clicks. So, inside T Brand Studio at the *New York Times* or *The Atlantic*'s Re:think, you have "audience development teams" tracking clicks and making little tweaks to ads—changing the font, altering the color scheme, enlarging a headline, changing the picture—until they arrive at just the right camouflage to garner the most clicks.

You'd think that if you wanted people to see a warning label, no matter what weasel word you slap on it, you'd put it at the top of the story. Not only does this seem like common sense—it's what the FTC recommends. And here's where the slime achieves its thickest viscosity. It turns out that when researchers studied what happens when a label comes at the top of an ad, they found that most people—60 percent—overlook it. But when it's in the middle, nine out of ten people notice it. Guess where publishers put that label. Right you are: at the top, safely concealed by the blinding masthead-headline-picture trifecta. When most of us look at an online story, our eyes focus on this combination and glaze over the small print. The FTC's guidelines about warning-label placement ("immediately before the ad or at the top left corner of the content") may actually help morally challenged journalists sharpen their claws of deception.[23]

Sponsored Propaganda

It's not just the Shells, the ExxonMobils, and the AT&Ts who've gotten in on the game. With China and Russia leading the pack, foreign governments spend millions of dollars to place their "news" stories in leading digital publications like the *Washington Post*, the *Wall Street Journal*, and the *Chicago Tribune*. In the twelve months from November 2019 to October 2020, the China Daily Distribution Corporation funneled over nine million dollars to influence American audiences. A favored venue was MSN, Microsoft's web portal, which featured a positively bubbly story about how Tibet, ravaged by China in a brutal

1950 takeover, had "broken free from the fetters of invading imperialism and embarked on a bright road of unity, progress and development" (see screenshot from MSN). Nowhere does it say the story was paid. You only know that if you recognize "Xinhua" as China's state-run news agency.[24]

In another story, MSN repackaged a Xinhua story critical of Taiwan originally published in the Philippines' *Manila Times*. When the

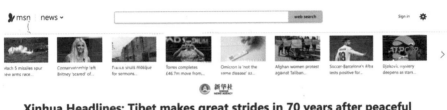

FIGURE 9.8 Chinese government story appearing on msn.com in May 2021 (link no longer available)

story resurfaced on MSN's website, even the Xinhua logo vanished, replaced by the words "Global Times." Did you recognize the innocuous sounding "Global Times" as the English-language newspaper of China's Communist Party?[25] Neither did we.

Like other "successful" native ads, these political puff pieces lull unsuspecting readers into consuming state-sponsored propaganda. Researchers from New York University and Hong Kong Baptist University showed people a web page from *The Telegraph*, a London newspaper founded in 1855. In big letters at the top of the screen was the word "News" followed by "World news" in red. Underneath were glowing stories about China, each with an accompanying photo or illustration. In cramped small print—the smallest print on the screen—came this warning: "This content is produced and published by China

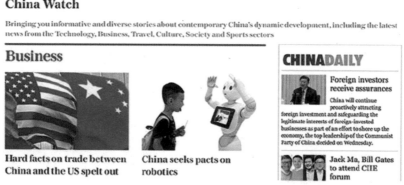

FIGURE 9.9 Chinese government content appearing on *The Telegraph*'s website (Dai and Luqiu, "Camouflaged Propaganda")

Daily, People's Republic of China, which takes sole responsibility for its contents." When asked afterward about the content they viewed, 86 percent of viewers were unable to identify its origin.[26]

Half Truths Are Not Whole Truths

Whether it's Shell, AT&T, Facebook, or the Chinese government, the goal is the same. To persuade you when your guard is down. They know, and you know, that if the message were plastered with the word "ad" in big red letters, you'd ignore it. We would be remiss, however, if we didn't acknowledge that just because something's an ad doesn't mean it is false. Big companies are wary of ads backfiring. They fear the consequences of being outed as liars. But there are many forms of persuasion besides outright lying. An ad can tell only part of the story. It can leave out the broader context. It can ignore evidence that goes against the story the company wants to tell. It can emphasize some facts and de-emphasize others. It can use examples that tug at our heartstrings, even when those examples misrepresent general trends. A partial truth is often more dangerous and less easy to detect than a pack of lies. So, before fixating on the results of a new study, make sure you understand the broader context, that you have read the room, and that you resist the glow of the shiny new object until you've scoped out the territory and gotten the lay of the land.

When Stealth Ads Move to Social Media

Just when you thought things were already bad, stealth ads moved to social media.

A native ad about 5G technology appeared on the website of the *Washington Post*. The *Post* did a decent job making the warning label prominent and visible. AT&T's blue logo stands out on the right

The dawn of the 5G world

How 5G technology will ultimately alter the DNA of the digital experience

By WP BrandStudio
DECEMBER 14, 2018

CONTENT FROM

AT&T Business

Introduction

We stand on the doorstep of the 5G world.

When the Wright brothers invented the airplane, it fundamentally altered how we experience traveling.

It wasn't just about speed. Yes, it was great getting from Chicago to Miami in less time. But flight also gave us thrill of defying gravity and soaring to new heights.

MORE FROM AT&T BUSINESS

FIGURE 9.10 Advertising from AT&T on the website of the *Washington Post* (https://www.washingtonpost.com/brand-studio/wp/2018/12/14/the-dawn-of-the-5g-world/)

Follow

5G is going to change more than we could possibly realize...The Washington Post: The dawn of the 5G world

The dawn of the 5G world
Introduction We stand on the doorstep of the 5G world. When the Wright brothers invented the airplane, it fundamentally altered how we experience traveling. It was...
washingtonpost.com

12:05 PM - 7 Jan 2019

FIGURE 9.11 Warning labels disappear when paid content goes social. (Reproduced from Amazeen and Vargo, "Sharing Native Advertising on Twitter," 927.)

side of the screen, and you don't need a magnifying glass to find the words "Content from AT&T Business" at the top. But a funny thing happens when ads migrate from the publisher's site and land on social media as cards—those little boxes we scroll though in our feed. That blue AT&T logo and the words "content from"? Poof. Gone. Kaput.[27]

WARNING LABELS DISAPPEAR WHEN PAID CONTENT GOES SOCIAL

You might think Twitter's to blame. But it's the *Washington Post*, not Twitter, that generates these cards. Some human or humans decided it was against the newspaper's interest to post a big warning label when the ad migrated to social media. When clicks drive ad revenue, it doesn't take a genius to figure out why. (See "Going Deeper: How Stealth Ads Lose Their Warning Labels.")

GOING DEEPER
How Stealth Ads Lose Their Warning Labels
Sadly, examples like the AT&T card from the *Washington Post* are not the exception but the rule. A study of over fifteen hundred native ads revealed that when a native ad journeyed from a publisher's website and resurfaced on Twitter, its original warning label disappeared more than half the time, a pattern that the study's authors characterized as a "blatant breach" of FTC guidelines.[28] And it's not just on Twitter but all over social media. Researchers tracked seventy-six native ads that migrated from news outlets and ended up on Facebook. More than half shed their warning label. Even when a label appeared, the rarest one was the humble but too-easily-recognized "ad." Instead, the labels employed the full battery of weasel words, including the most bizarre and misleading we've yet seen: "content solutions."[29] Solutions, we wonder, to what?

Protecting Yourself in an Age of Slimy Advertising

How can you avoid getting bamboozled by stealth ads when they were invented for the sole purpose of bamboozling you? We can't guarantee you'll never be fooled. But if you keep a couple of principles in mind, you'll be fooled a lot less.

First, realize that the internet is one giant marketing experiment. Smart people work overtime to figure out how to sell you stuff without you noticing. When you're scrolling through your feed and see the headline "New Study Shows the Dangers of Eating Chicken," for all you know it could be planted by the beef industry. Worse, when these paid stories make their way from the publisher's website and land on social media, these "stories" slough off any warning label they might've carried. To put this another way: deception is not an aberration or bug in the system—it's how the game is played. You're scrolling through social media and see a story on, say, the nutritional benefits of coffee. Before you forward it, pause. *Please, pause.* Ask yourself: *Is this what I think it is?* Is it a news story by a health reporter, or is it an ad from a company that wants you to go out and order a double tall macchiato? So, remember: Practice the *T* of SIFT. Click on the link in the card and *trace* the story back to the reporting source. Once you're back on the site of the *Washington Post*, *Vice*, *Slate*, *CNN*, or whomever (sadly, they're all in on it), clean your glasses. You'll need your best eyesight for the next move.

Don't expect to find the word "advertisement" flashing in neon. Instead, be on the lookout for grayish type strategically placed in the upper left-hand corner of the page, where it's overshadowed by a thirty-two-point headline, a dazzling photo, and an eye-catching infographic. And make sure you're up to date on the latest menu of weasel words: "sponsored content," "brand partner," "presented with," "in partnership with," "brought to you by," "in association with," "hosted by," or simply "with."

Takeaways

▷ Be on the lookout for ads disguised as news stories.

▷ Look for small print, generally located at the top corner of an article, with a company name or logo.

▷ Rarely will stealth ads identify themselves with the word "ad." Stay current on the slithery alternatives: "sponsored content," "brand partner," "presented with," "in partnership with," "brought to you by," "in association with," "hosted by," or simply "with." (Remember, more weasel words are being added all the time).

▷ Foreign governments engage in stealth advertising. Look for markers (often in the tiniest print on the screen) that identify a story as paid for by a foreign power.

▷ Even when a story is labeled as an ad, it might shed that label once it moves to social media. Resist the impulse to forward a social media post until you've pressed on the link and traced it back to where it originally appeared.

Once More with Feeling

USING YOUR EMOTIONS TO FIND THE TRUTH

In many popular accounts, our embrace of false information comes down to a single villain: our emotions. Emotion, we are told, bypasses our critical faculties. Our feelings make us do stupid things. That dumb thing you shared? Emotion's fault. That fake video everyone fell for? Blame your feelings. If we could be more robotic, more Spock-like, we wouldn't have such problems. Or so the story goes.

We're not here to tell you your feelings don't muck things up. They absolutely can. That said, the emotional side of this debate could use a better press agent. Your feelings aren't simply a chaos agent messing up the perfect life of the mind. Rather, it's best to think of your feelings as a partner with your slower, rational self. When you draw on the strengths of both feelings and analysis, you can make better decisions than using either one alone.

Emotion Doesn't Know the Truth,
But It Knows What You Care About

You see something online, and it's shocking. Or enraging. Or heart-warming. Or enlightening, or surprising, or hilarious. Uh-oh, say cognitive scientists, the world's biggest party poopers. Slow down. You may be about to make a mistake.[1]

And they aren't wrong. That's our advice too. That's the *stop* in SIFT. When something triggers one of the above feelings, when it is *compelling*, people tend to skip past those quick checks they should do before engaging with it or sharing it. We sometimes feel like we've just heard the *juiciest* rumor, and if we don't share it now, we will *die*. And it's tempting to think of the emotion here as just being purely downside, distorting our view of what is true, what is real, what is logical. If we could remove the feelings, problem solved, right?

Here's the thing: we've found when people try to gauge the accuracy of news that elicits *no* feeling, they often struggle *more*.

How is that possible? Let's imagine you hear a fact about a sport you know well. Glancing at your phone during what seems the world's longest lecture, you see that in a current championship soccer game, a new player, only with the club for seventeen months, scored a goal from *half field* with twenty minutes left in the game.

If you know soccer, and you like soccer, you're going to have a lot of feelings about this, trust me. But you're busy at work or school, and you don't want to share false information, so you text your trusty roommate, who couldn't care less about soccer, and ask, "Is this true?" A few minutes later, you get a text back: "Sadly, no." So, you skip the repost and go back to listening to the lecture. But, as you head home, you pass a bar and see . . . a replay of the most perfectly executed half-field shot you've ever seen, planted upper left corner, as if guided by God herself.

You get home and confront your roommate: Why did you say it wasn't true? Oh, your roommate replies, the player *did* plant it from half field. But he had been with the club two years, not seventeen months, and there were actually twenty-five minutes left in the game, not twenty. So really, 33 percent true, at best.

Sure, this is a contrived, low-stakes example. But we see the same sorts of differences in interpretation in more important matters. So, what's going on here?

On one hand, we could chalk up the misunderstanding to a difference in conscious process. You've seen a lot of games, you know half-field goals sometimes happen but are statistically rare, whereas a goal with twenty or twenty five minutes to go is exceedingly common. The important part of the story you heard was *obviously* the length of the shot. You didn't need to sit there with a list of soccer statistics to figure out which aspects of the story were probable. You knew this the moment you heard it—before you gave it a moment's thought. You knew because the idea of a half-field shot was *compelling*. It got you to say, "No way! I've got to check this out." It engaged you. It sparked a feeling.

GOING DEEPER
Man versus Machine

Some of the older research on the importance of feelings for processing information comes from an interesting source: computer scientists in the 1970s.

Back then, several linguists were trying to teach computers to understand stories. By the late 1970s, they had hit a problem. As described in Roger Schank's foundational paper "Interestingness: Controlling Inferences,"[2] their language models could read a story that involved a person walking down the street, getting a lemonade, and spotting a secret invading army in the woods, and the computer would spend as much time learning about the lemonade as the invading army. Schank proposed that something that humans do quite naturally—using the feeling of interest to direct attention—was

(continued)

not happening with the processing modules, and as a result, the computer sucked at interpretation.

Because we are interested in more than stories and events, instead of "interestingness," we use the term "compellingness," which covers not only things of interest but a mishmash of feelings regarding things like authority, relevance, and timeliness. But the underlying principle is the same. Properly conceived, our feelings can be a strength, not a weakness, and one that helps us outperform more methodical processes.

"Compellingness" Tells Us What's Important to Check

Psychologists call emotional thinking "hot" cognition. It's not a flattering term. People often think of emotions as something they are trying to turn off. But those quick emotional reactions do something that the logical brain couldn't accomplish in three hours with a stack of spreadsheets. With endless possible targets for our attention, our feelings tell us "Pay attention over here!" You don't have to decide what's interesting. It's just . . . *interesting*. When we apply a bit of conscious thought to this element of compellingness, we become more efficient at checking. By reflecting on why we find something compelling, we can understand what to look for in a source or claim, and we can separate trivial issues from dealbreakers.

Understanding *exactly* what you find compelling may take some reflection. Our feelings give us baseline information fast, but they do not file detailed reports. Consider an example from chapter 4, where we did a brief source investigation of the American College of Pediatricians. People we tested found that organization to be a compelling source—they had a positive, reassuring feeling about the website. It was ultimately the *wrong* feeling, but part of its "compellingness" was a gut feeling, or assessment, that this was some sort of large, reputable association of physicians that weighs in on lots of matters. We know this is what many people thought because if we took the same content and put it on a site named "Some Docs and a Laptop Who Post a Lot of Politically Inflammatory Content," that feeling would disappear in a flash.[3] What made the site compelling was the idea it was run by a well-known, large organization that cares about kids.

We've watched people find their way to the Wikipedia page on the organization. They read the first few lines and . . . gasp. There are the facts: the American College of Pediatricians has at most a few employees, only about five hundred members, and a budget less than a year's tuition at some colleges. It's immediately evident to these readers that the thing that made this site attractive—the idea that it was a big professional organization—is gone, and with it compellingness has sailed away.

For other people, however, it doesn't immediately click. After all, the Wikipedia page is sort of like that goal from half field. There's lots of stuff happening on the Wikipedia page, after all—what, exactly, should you pay attention to? The time on the clock or the length of the kick? The number of members in the organization or the names of its publications?

Over time, we've developed a helpful ten-second exercise to do before clicking over to Wikipedia. Ask yourself what is compelling about the source you're looking at. Free associate. Think of nouns and adjectives. Maybe it's "pediatricians," "respected," or "impartial." Then head over to Wikipedia. Once you've highlighted what made the source compelling, the way the Wikipedia page undoes everything compelling about the source becomes more pronounced. Compellingness isn't your shovel. But it tells you where to dig.

Fear not—we aren't going to make you free associate for every claim or source you find while doom scrolling on your phone. But as you practice SIFT, especially at first, we encourage you to use your sense of compellingness to help identify how the quick context you build either intensifies or diminishes your initial reaction. If you find yourself overwhelmed with detail in a search, come back to the question of what originally drew you to the news item, video, or statistic. Has additional context changed your first reaction? You started out asking "Is this what I think it is?" Now that you know, is it more compelling or less?

That feeling of compellingness, implicated in so many bad decisions of the past, can, with a bit of practice, help you in the future.

Surprise Is a Sign Our Assumptions Might Be Wrong

We encounter a mass of content each day, and we're not as likely to analyze our feelings in the moment the way we might during a guided classroom exercise. Luckily, many years of evolution have given us another signal that our initial assumptions were incorrect—the gift of surprise.

You may think that surprise is simply what you feel when something is not what you thought. That's partly right. But consider two different situations. In the first, you're invited to what you think is a cookout for about fifteen people, but when you arrive there are twenty-two there. Surprised? Not so much. In the second, you are invited to what you think is a cookout for about fifteen people, but when you get there, you realize it's a book club. Or instead of fifteen people, there are three. Or two hundred. Surprised? A bit more, right?

Surprise doesn't just indicate that something is different from what you expected. It indicates that it is different in a way or at a level that is significant. And because surprise indicates that our expectations have been violated in a nontrivial way, it can be a good sign the additional context we've found should make us rethink our initial reaction.

Let's go back to an earlier example. Remember the story about Wandrea "Shaye" Moss in chapter 8? The woman who was "caught" on video supposedly taking out "secret" containers of ballots in Fulton County, Georgia. If you saw that video framed as being about "suitcases full of ballots," you might be upset (quite understandably). A bit of context-seeking (about thirty seconds) shows you they weren't suitcases; they were security bins created to prevent ballot tampering. You feel surprised. "Wait, they weren't suitcases? They were security bins?"

When learning new context, it's so normal to be surprised in this way that it can be difficult to grasp how crucial it is. When investigating, we process a lot of information. Maybe we learn that an incident was a bit earlier than we thought or that it was in a different city than we thought. Yawn. But some things hit us differently. It's like a scene in a murder mystery where the detective is told a laundry list of items about a crime scene but suddenly stops on a particular detail—"Wait a second, you're saying the television was *on when you found her*?" The surprise indicates that some detail doesn't fit with previous assumptions. The weird thing is, you often feel the surprise even before you fully know what it means.

We encourage you to be on the lookout for your own surprise— don't run from it. When you do feel it, it's a signal to stop and go back to what you initially saw or read or calculated. If you had known this new information beforehand—that it was standard security bins, not smuggled-in suitcases—would the video have been more compelling or less? And if the answer is "less," is it possible your initial reaction was a bit off?

It takes some mental practice to cultivate a sense of surprise when context-seeking. This can be particularly true when your initial reaction was emotionally intense. Compared to the feeling of shock you might have when first encountering a video, the surprise you feel at finding out that they are called "security bins" (not suitcases) is at a distinctly lower volume. But that sense of surprise is crucial. Noticing it requires slowing down a bit. Just long enough to see if anything generates the feeling of the unexpected before you run past it. We saw that when we talked about the gestalt, or the vibe, of the results page. The first question you asked was not whether these were quality results but, rather, whether these were the sort of results you'd expect to see for these search terms. When you pause instead of clicking blindly on the blue links on the search results page, do you find that the results feel *surprising*? We're not saying you'll always have a well-developed sense of surprise whenever you need it, but often that sense is there. You just need to give it a few seconds to take in the scene: to notice the books, the chairs in the circle, and the lack of hamburgers and grilling implements, and to realize that it feels — surprisingly — more like a book club than a cookout.

Why Compellingness and Surprise Beat the Checklist

We began this book talking about the failure of checklist approaches to web credibility. Part of their failure was that they relied on cheap signals: the dot-org extension, the well-formatted page, the official-sounding "About" page. Part of their failure was that they didn't consider known markers of quality — expensive signals of quality such as professional recognition or a hard-won reputation for accuracy. But we didn't go into one of the bigger tragedies of checklists: how they dull your sense of surprise.

Let's start with a fundamental truth about checklists. When situations are standardized and routine, they work wonderfully. More than wonderfully. When you get on a plane and are about to take off, you don't want the pilot and copilot to SIFT their way to figuring out whether everything is prepared for the flight. You want them to go through the checklist, the items for that specific plane, and do the sequence of actions they do every time to make sure you end up climbing to thirty thousand feet and not, alternatively, floating in the bay.

It would be nice to imagine a world in which determining whether something was trustworthy was like preparing a plane for takeoff. Flip the right switches, in the right order, and then look at the result: "This source is 78.4 percent reputable! This claim is sufficiently correct!" Sounds ridiculous, right? But that's what checklist approaches try to do. Early information literacy checklists, like the one mentioned in chapter 2, even encouraged people to assign points for different things they found and add them up.[4] "Seven out of ten—checks out!"

Context-seeking doesn't work like that for a very simple reason— what you care about when judging a claim or source is going to vary from claim to claim, from source to source, from situation to situation. You can't use a checklist because you're never flying the same plane twice. That's because, in any given instance, what's important will change.

Take this headline and image about "mutant daisies" near a Japanese nuclear plant that had a partial meltdown. You see this and find it compelling. It seems important. It triggers emotion. Perhaps it makes you think the soil these flowers grew in is radioactive. Or perhaps the photo just produces general anger at the corporations behind such power plants.

What sort of checklist could help you check this? Let's imagine you investigate this, and you discover the following facts about these bizarrely deformed flowers found near—let us remind you—*a nuclear power plant.*

Mutant daisies spotted near Fukushima nuclear plant, photo goes viral

The photos of the mutant daisies were posted on social-networking site Twitter by a Japanese user @san_kaido.

 IndiaToday.in
New Delhi
July 23, 2015 UPDATED: July 23, 2015 23:20 IST

Daisies found near Fukushima nuclear plant (Photo: Twitter @san_kaido)

FIGURE 10.1 Story about the "Fukushima daisies" photo (https://www.indiatoday.in /world/story/daisies-fukushima-nuclear-plant-japan-photo-viral-twitter-284282-2015 -07-23)

1 The flowers were indeed found near the Fukushima power plant.

2 The photo is unaltered.

3 The person who took the photo is an ordinary resident of the area who posted the picture on Twitter.

4 Flower experts say the process resulting in this unusual appearance is called "fasciation," a naturally occurring process unrelated to radiation.

5 While the flowers look wild, they were growing in a garden near a city street.

If you initially thought the photo might be solid evidence of unsafe conditions near the plant, we're going to guess that point number four jumped out at you. You're looking at a "naturally occurring process *unrelated to radiation*." And we're not expecting jaw-dropping daytime-soap-opera levels of shock on reading that; we're guessing most of you felt a bit of a "wait, *what?*" sensation on reading that line. But notice that the photo has a lot of things going for it. It's a real photo. It's not photoshopped. It's from the area it says it is. The person who took it is a local. From a checklist perspective, it seems to be swishing baskets from the three-point line. And yet our experience of this is, quite rightly, that it's most likely junk.

Why is that?

If you found the photo compelling at first, we imagine you already believed it was real and that it was taken near a nuclear power plant. These factors would have influenced your initial reaction. You may not have guessed that the flowers were growing next to a city street—new information for sure—but that's unlikely to be what jumped out at you.

What you noticed was something (a) you didn't know, and (b) related to the compelling aspect of this photo as evidence. Not to use overly technical language here, but the flowers were interesting because they seemed *freaky*. They were weird. They demanded an explanation. And since they seemed unexplainable by normal means, the idea that their weirdness was caused by a nuclear accident seemed, well, plausible. However, once you know this process happens naturally—that its freakiness is actually normal—your reaction changed.

If you are a lover of checklists, you might think the solution is to add the flowers' compelling feature, "freakiness," to checklists. But that is a dead end. Here, the compelling bit was the freakiness. In the "suitcases of ballots" misinformation, it was the "secretiveness." For the American College of Pediatricians, the compelling aspect was, weirdly, that you thought it was a bigger and blander organization than it turned out to be. It works the opposite way as well—you may find something not particularly useful because you assume it was written by someone without knowledge, a "dude with a Twitter account," but a short investigation reveals that person to be a well-respected expert. An article you dismiss, assuming it is a non-peer-reviewed preprint, turns out to be published in a major journal.

Checklists can get at some of that. Some qualities of good sources can be defined and listed. But one of the downsides of checklists is they obscure the wonderfully quick processing a sense of surprise can bring. The problem with a checklist is that what you *care* about varies broadly depending on *what you thought something was.* No checklist captures this. And when you're going through a checklist methodically, it's easy to lose sense of what drew you to the source or claim in the first place. You should absolutely learn about what makes a good source good or a trustworthy claim trustworthy—in ways that help you develop better initial reactions. But in the moment, anything that doesn't take full advantage of the context of *you* is a liability. Paying attention to *your* context will always be more powerful than any checklist.

GOING DEEPER

Mutant Flowers

The Fukushima flowers example doesn't represent a merely hypothetical issue. Sam's research group found that only 20 percent of students using more common approaches to information literacy found the photo dubious, whereas 40 percent considered it "strong evidence" that the region around Fukushima was toxic.[5] Most of those students were not getting off the page at all; instead, they were engaging in that "look deeply at the page" sort of behavior this book warns against.

That said, in both Sam's work and work Mike did with the same example with first-year college students, many of the "correct" responses were not so great either. "It's a random picture on the internet—FAKE!" seemed to be a prominent school of thought. Point well taken. But in this case, that turned out to be wrong. The photo of mutant daisies was real. Very few people got to the heart of the matter: a real photo that wasn't nearly as compelling as it first appeared.

Feeling Overwhelmed? Rethink Your Approach

Some people interpret a sense of feeling overwhelmed as a sign that they're stupid or lack "grit." For these folks, this bad feeling represents a personal failing on their part. Other people, when they feel overwhelmed, take it as a challenge: they tell themselves to buckle down, apply the good old mental elbow grease, and plow through to a result. For these folks, this bad feeling is a sign they should apply more effort.

Sometimes that second idea is true. If you're reading that intro biology book and having trouble understanding homeostasis on the first pass, maybe you need to turn off your phone, pull out a notebook, and go through each sentence, word by word, until it starts to click. In schoolwork, pushing through frustration can be a healthy impulse.

In many other cases, however, feeling overwhelmed is a sign your information-seeking strategy needs rethinking.

What do we mean? Imagine you are looking into the safety or effectiveness of a medication. "I'll help you with that!" says a former high school friend who is somehow inexplicably still on your group chat. But, hey, you need to look into this, so what the heck. You click his link.

It leads to a YouTube video engaging in rapid-fire presentation of evidence. Dozens of documents, things circled and highlighted, and a running live line chart of something or other. Maps with unexplained percentages; lists of effect sizes. As you watch, you're understanding . . . maybe half of it? A third? It's just . . . overwhelming. You persevere, though, processing bits and pieces, following along somewhat, filling in the gaps with a vague sense of unease. At the end of this process, do you truly know more? Or would you have been better served with a more general summary?

When we get overwhelmed, we often think of it as our fault. But our emotional reaction isn't here only to make us feel bad about ourselves. Feeling overwhelmed is a sign that our current strategy isn't working. Maybe we're entering a topic at the wrong level of detail. Maybe we need to develop a bit more knowledge by reading a Wikipedia article or two before drinking from a data firehose. And maybe, just maybe, we shouldn't be drinking from the data firehose at all.

Think of the feeling of being overwhelmed while context-seeking as being like the feeling of growing increasingly tired on a long drive. Yes, you could power through. Maybe it'd be fine. But it might also be a sign of an impending accident. Pull over, look at your GPS, and rethink your journey.

Because of the many downsides of emotional processing, it's tempting to think you should ignore your emotions when seeking context. But the better route is to *notice* your emotions and ask yourself what they can tell you and what they can't. Define what is compelling to you, and see if that sense of compellingness disappears after more context. Be attentive to when you feel overwhelmed, and consider rethinking your strategy. By partnering with your emotions rather than ignoring them or being controlled by them, you'll chart a faster, more accurate, and ultimately more humane journey through the maze of the web.

Takeaways

▷ Emotional reactions can get in the way of evaluation, but they can also be powerful tools in helping you focus on what you found important.

▷ Paying attention to what surprises you when you seek additional context can help you realize the wrong assumptions you made.

▷ Feeling overwhelmed during context-building might be an indication that you need to rethink your strategy and start anew.

Conclusion

CRITICAL IGNORING

Herbert Simon, the 1978 Nobel laureate in economics, was no slacker. In addition to his Nobel Prize, he was a towering figure in computer science, winning that field's highest honor, the A. M. Turing Award. He's considered by many to be the father of artificial intelligence and one of the founders of cognitive psychology. To these many honors, we might add another: seer of the future. Years before everyone else, Simon understood how an excess of information vexes the human psyche.

In a 1971 paper, Simon told the story of how one Easter his neighbors bought their children a pair of bunnies. "Whether by intent or accident, one was male and one female. And soon the neighborhood was overrun by bunnies." Simon proposed the following law: overabundance of one thing leads to the scarcity of another. The neighborhood bunny explosion, he explained, led to a scarcity of lettuce.

You've heard our current era called the "information age," but that merely names what is abundant. What does this overabundance lead to? Simon's answer: it leads to a "scarcity of whatever it is that information consumes." And since information "consumes the attention of its recipients," Simon believed "a wealth of information creates *a poverty of attention.*"[1]

When we flash Simon's quotation on the screen in our workshops, audience members nod in agreement. "Ah, yes," they say, "we all need to pay more attention."

No, we explain. Simon was saying just the opposite.

Here's the thing. Attention is a zero-sum game. You can't give something more attention without giving something less. Telling people struggling to keep their heads above water that they should think critically about every item that streams across their screens— reading closely, scrutinizing thoroughly, vetting conscientiously— actually makes things worse. Attention is frittered away, leaving us enervated. Spent. And, too often, confused.

When we drafted this book, we tossed around a bunch of different titles. Initially, a lot of them focused on not being fooled. That's still a core strength of this book: read it and you will get fooled less often, guaranteed. But as we thought more, another goal guided us. We wanted to help you to *think less intensely so you can think more effectively.*

That line shocks many people. They hear it and mistakenly jump to the conclusion that we are against critical thinking. Nothing could be further from the truth! We *love* critical thinking. We cherish cognitive engagement. We treasure deep reading. That's the reason why we want you to treat these precious capacities with the respect they deserve. Thinking critically demands sustained, focused attention. However, thinking critically about low-quality sources is a colossal waste of time. If attention is the brain's high-octane fuel, and there's only so much of it to go around, shouldn't we be especially discerning about how and when we use it?

In a book that has been filled with analogies and metaphors— parachuting into unfamiliar terrain! bottles in lakes! sriracha on the milk shelf!—we hope you'll indulge us one more. Consider a cyclist getting ready for a big race. What does that race consume? Energy, right? Does the coach tell the cyclist, "Listen up—the key to winning the race is to not run out of energy, so pedal as fast as you can"?

No! Just the opposite.

It is certainly good for a cyclist to be fit, to have the requisite muscle mass, and, sometimes, to pedal quite fast. But effective coaching is not about teaching cyclists to expend *more* energy. It's about teaching them to expend *less*. Bow your head to reduce wind resistance. Sustain correct posture. Maximize both up and down strokes. Success is about pacing and breathing and maintaining clean aerodynamic lines. The principle governing all this? At every point, cyclists seek to *minimize* the energy they expend relative to the benefit they gain. Why? Because in the middle of the race, energy is going to get scarce—really fast. Racers need to conserve energy so that they have it when they really need it.

What energy is to a cyclist, attention is to an information seeker. A journal you've never heard of claims that smoking a hookah is no more dangerous than sipping an occasional beer, laying it on thick with strings of esoteric equations. (Recall our discussion in chapter 7.) Before spending an hour spiraling down this rabbit hole, don't you want to know the same journal published articles claiming that heeled shoes led to the occurrence of the first cases of schizophrenia and that masturbation is a cure for nasal congestion?[2]

It's not just that giving your attention to dubious sources is a waste of time. It's that attention, misapplied, can be dangerous. It would be comforting to think that when you engage deeply and earnestly with neo-Nazi literature or industry-backed climate change research that you come out more informed, provided you note all the logical traps and rhetorical fallacies along the way. In reality, whenever you give your attention to bad actors, you allow them to steal your attention from better treatments of an issue, and freely offer them the opportunity to warp your perspective.

We're not Herbert Simon. We can't see what society will need fifty years into the future. But we can see what it needs now. In a world of information abundance, attention is our most precious asset. And yet, people everywhere are working overtime to make you waste it.

It's for this reason that our final word in this book comes as a plea to add a new capacity to your intellectual tool kit. Yes, be critical thinkers. But we also want you to be savvy *critical ignorers*. By adding *critical ignoring* to your intellectual repertoire, you'll quickly be able to recognize and walk away from dubious information that leaves your mind fried and your spirit enfeebled. To do so, however, will require one other ingredient—a dose of humility. The recognition that no one of us is immune to the slippery ruses plied by today's digital rogues.

By dwelling on an unfamiliar site, thinking that we're smart enough to outsmart it, we squander attention and hand over control to the site's designers. Spending a few moments SIFTing that site by drawing on the awesome powers of the open web, we regain control—and with it, our attention.

And, as we've noted throughout these pages, it can often take as little as thirty seconds. *Seriously!*

Postscript

LARGE LANGUAGE MODELS, CHATGPT, AND THE FUTURE OF VERIFICATION

As we were signing off on the final edits to this book, ChatGPT was released. ChatGPT is an interactive application built on a large language model called GPT. If that sentence sounds as incomprehensible to you as something shouted across the starship bridge on a science fiction show, you're not alone. But this technology will have some long-term implications for how we verify claims, so much so that we thought it worth a postscript.

What Do Large Language Models Do?

A lot, actually. We won't cover everything here. But one way to think about large language models is through the predictive text on your phone. You start to write, "I'm sorry I'm . . . ," and your phone immediately prompts you. Are you "late," "not feeling well," or "just getting up"? You may have even played games with this feature, where you and friends challenge each other to write sentences using only predictive text. If Mike starts with, "The thing you need to know about me" and chooses one of three choices at the bottom of the chat box for each word, he gets, "The thing you need to know about me is I need to get a new phone." This is likely because Mike (like others) often apologizes for his battery dying. If you run all those predictions through a statistical model, you can produce a somewhat peculiar version of something Mike might say by chaining predictions together.

What if, instead of running all the things you texted into that statistical model, you ran a big portion of what people said on the internet into it? A *really* big portion—like a half a trillion words? Then you started a sentence with something like, "Three causes of rumor are as follows . . ." A sophisticated model would look at the words and phrases people tend to say around that language, such as "major causes of rumor" or "one source of false stories." It might find that people often say "Uncertainty" next, and that after "Uncertainty," people tend to say, "When people are unsure of the future."

> Three causes of rumor are as follows. Uncertainty: When people are unsure of the future.

Now we repeat the game and type that in, and we get more. The thing is that these models provide spookily human-like answers to questions, many of which are surprisingly good. When we see it in action, we can forget we're seeing a predictive text generator:

> ME: What are three causes of rumor?

> REPLY: There are many causes of rumor, but three causes of rumor are as follows. Uncertainty: When people are unsure of the future, they tend to speculate on the present. Lack of information: When good information is not available, people often turn to unreliable sources. Novelty: When rumors feel new, people often wish to be the first to share them.

The reason these answers are both useful and compelling is that they mimic how we speak and write. As we worked on this book, we often started sentences without knowing how they would end. Typing one word or phrase somehow propelled us to the next. If you've ever struggled with writer's block, you know the solution is to write *anything* on that page. Words lead to other words, and as they come together, new ideas develop. If there is one thing that LLMs seem to be making clear, it's that a lot of what we do when we write and summarize is more automatic and predictive than we might care to admit.

Of course, we humans can do something that an LLM can't: we can look at the sentence we just finished and ask whether it really captures what we *mean*. We can revise based on how we imagine the sentence might be interpreted. We can do this because beneath the activity of writing we have something we want to *convey*—a model not just of language but of the world, and a set of communicative goals that are bigger than selecting the next word or phrase. Large language models don't have goals. They don't have underlying understandings. They have models of what certain people are likely to say after saying other things.[1] But that is enough to have some giant impacts on our information environment. Here, we discuss two of them.

Cheap Signals Just Got Cheaper:
The Death of Style as Marker

We titled chapter 2 of this book "Cheap Signals: Or, How Not to Get Duped." The problem we discussed was that a lot of things that used to signal authority—or at least a certain investment of resources—no longer do. It used to be that a publication without spelling or grammatical errors signaled investment in copyediting, or at least some care in production. With the advent of spell-check and grammatical help in word processors, most people can manage to write a website without major errors. A polished-looking site used to signal, at least somewhat, that the publication had some money. However, that hasn't been true for decades: cheap website templates allow anyone to spin up a polished website in an afternoon.

But there was one last holdout, a feature that seemed tougher to game—the website's vibe, the tone and style of its writing. Writing is hard. It takes years to develop a scholarly style and an academic tone. It takes training to write a newspaper article that has that feel of solid newspaper prose. Surely those signals were still an indication of *something*.

But bad actors cracked this one too. The site minimumwage.com, which we discussed in chapter 2, convincingly adopted the tone and style of a social advocacy site, despite having ties to the restaurant industry. And our hypothetical example of Jill reading the article "N95 Masks Don't Work" in chapter 5 was not purely hypothetical; many promoters of dubious treatments have learned to mimic the language and tone of science. Still, while those signals were fakeable, the skills involved were not nearly as cheap as running a spell-check or buying a twenty-five-dollar web template.

No longer. In a world with large language models, writing a professional "About" page is as easy as asking ChatGPT to write it. And while there are currently some guardrails on the use of LLM technology to produce fake news and fake scientific articles, we should expect those protections to be circumvented. One of the last expensive surface features—style—is about to get the basic spell-check treatment.

What can we do to protect ourselves? We're a bit repetitive here, but the solution is the same: use the internet to check the internet. A website's credibility shouldn't be judged by the tone or style of its pages, which can now be faked with the press of a button. Instead, the most expensive signal—online reputation—remains your best guide. What do other reputable people say about the site, the organization, or the claim? Is the organization what it first appears to be? Have people even heard of it? LLMs will be used in the future to cook up sweet, professional websites overnight that feel like they have been around for thirty years, but they can't generate thirty years of external coverage. The next time we see a Keanu Reeves death hoax, it may have a sheen of crisp prose that feels like it came from the *New York Times* rather than the clunky fake we saw in chapter 1. But if a search of Google News shows the most recent story about Reeves is about his new video game launch, he's unlikely to be dead.

Large Language Models and Lateral Reading: Easier but Trickier

A more difficult question is whether LLM-based products could aid lateral reading. Should you skip a traditional search and have an AI tool answer your question? Should you forgo Wikipedia and turn first to an LLM-based chat engine instead? If you choose the LLM, what should you watch for? How should you formulate queries? How should you verify the results?

LLM technology is already being taken up by search engines, and searches will likely look different in the future. Over time, an LLM-informed topic summary might be just what's needed when a Wikipedia article is too dense and a web snippet too brief. Three things remain unchanged, however. First, as the technology evolves, it will continue the trend that we discussed at the beginning of this book—information will become more ubiquitous and accessible. Our informational instincts are still rooted in a world where answers are rare. As with the playground rumor of Mikey and the Pop Rocks in chapter 1, we still rely too much on our own faulty intuitions when better information is readily available. As LLMs make even more information accessible in the forms that we need it, it becomes easier to practice lateral reading—and more inexcusable not to.

Second—and this may be a hard pill to swallow—for any question of importance, you are going to have to laterally verify the information you get back from an LLM. These products are so uncannily human that it's easy to forget that they don't know the subject—they just know the sort of things people say *about* the subject, whether they're true or not. The problems with this are many. For one, a lot of people say a lot of incorrect things about a lot of subjects, and these LLMs are only as reliable as the information they're fed to build their statistical models. Worse, the fact that ChatGPT doesn't understand what it's saying produces some very weird errors. These errors—programmers refer to them as "hallucinations"—are likely to be costly to you as a student, employee, or citizen.

Finally, for those of you who are students, there's the temptation to use LLMs to do your writing for you. Putting aside the ethical issues (which are many), you may find that using an LLM to write a draft of something that needs to be verified may be more time consuming than doing your own research and writing it yourself. That's because when you do the research yourself and write it up, you arrive at your draft with the knowledge and insights necessary to edit it. You know what ideas you're trying to express. Your research prepares you to evaluate, revise, extend. Asked to defend a particular point, you know where you found the evidence to support your claims. ChatGPT severs that linkage; claims arrive naked of footnotes. The result? Free-floating information—whether true or downright false.

We have tried to present a process in this book that not only allows you to resolve simple questions quickly but sets you up for more successful and productive deeper investigations. SIFT, lateral reading, reading the room—these are all processes meant not only to help you verify information and context but to put you on solid ground suitable for deeper investigation. The skills are simple but active. It is your *active* engagement that builds understanding over time. LLM-based technology is still young and has a lot of promise. But as you engage with it, we encourage you to remember that if you are not in the driver's seat, you are being taken for a ride. Approach this technology with the same skills we have detailed in this book, and use the internet to check the internet, *especially* when the prose on the other side is crafted by a convincing machine.

ACKNOWLEDGMENTS

MIKE'S ACKNOWLEDGMENTS

It was Howard Rheingold who first introduced me to fundamental concepts around web-based literacy and Jon Udell and Ward Cunningham who taught me to "think like the web." Nicole Caulfield, an amazing teacher in her own right, has been a constant sounding board for the ideas in this book as they have developed over many years.

Thanks go to Rachel Toor, who provided feedback to us in the early stages of this work, and Elise Capron, our agent, who not only made the process easy but also validated our tone and approach at a crucial moment. Elizabeth Branch Dyson at the University of Chicago Press engaged with the vision we had for the book in a way that made us feel we had a true partner in bringing it to life.

This book builds on research and practice that was only made possible through the support of my former provost and chancellor, Mel Netzhammer, who saw the value of these skills and this approach long before anyone else, and who provided me space to pursue their application at Keene State College and later at Washington State University Vancouver. Without the commitment to public engagement and education of Mel Netzhammer and those institutions more generally, this book and the larger body of work that underlies it would not exist.

SAM'S ACKNOWLEDGMENTS

It was my doctoral adviser and unpaid life coach, Lee Shulman, who planted the idea in me that historical thinking was a subcategory of something much broader—an orientation to the world that refuses to take information at face value. Even though Lee's words took several years to sink in, they eventually prompted me to consider the role of the internet in how modern citizens become informed—or don't. Elizabeth Branch Dyson at the University of Chicago Press recognized the value of this book from the first tentative email we sent and jumped on it. After many attempts to arrive at the right title for this book, it was my brilliant nephew, Zachary Wineburg, who came up with the winning entry. As this book took form, a discussion with Jerry Graff and Cathy Birkenstein proved pivotal. We received invaluable feedback on early drafts from a group of dedicated readers, including Michelle Amazeen, Joel Breakstone, Robyn Chapel, Eli Gottlieb, Jason Hu, Jake Orlowitz, Sarah McGrew, Dan Russell, Ava Sirrah, Abby Reisman, Bob Wineburg, Shoshana Wineburg, Michael Wineburg, and Raffi Wineburg. Tamara Lantze Lau, a superb graphic designer, helped enormously with our illustrations. Carrie Love copyedited this manuscript with a precision that can only be described as otherworldly, and the incomparable Mary Ryan caught errors that escaped the eyes of mere mortals. A special shout out goes to Nadav Ziv, who saved readers from countless infelicities. Even when we thought our manuscript was complete, Rachel Toor convinced us that important changes were still needed. Phil Halperin and Julie Kidd have been rocks of support through this journey. A special thanks goes to

Susan Monas, who read every word of this book—*multiple* times—and never held back when she detected a discordant note.

This book builds on the research of the Stanford History Education Group (SHEG). For twenty-three years, Stanford University has provided a home that cultivates creativity and supports risk taking. Without the intellectual fellowship of Joel Breakstone, Sarah Mc-Grew, Teresa Ortega, and Mark Smith, my trusted SHEG colleagues, none of the research on which this book rests would have been possible. I thank them all.

NOTES

INTRODUCTION

1. Damien Gayle (@damiengayle), "Activists with @JustStop_Oil have thrown tomato soup on Van Gogh's Sunflowers at the National Gallery and glued themselves to the wall," Twitter, October 14, 2022, 6:12 a.m., https://twitter.com/damiengayle/status/158086 4210741133312.

2. Andrew Doyle (@andrewdoyle_com), "Activists vandalise Vincent van Gogh's Sunflowers at the National Gallery. The vandalism or destruction of art is always an authoritarian act. But more than that - it represents a repudiation of civilisation and the achievements of humanity," Twitter, October 14, 2022, 6:46 a.m., https://twitter.com/andrewdoyle_com/status/1580872772590239746.

3. Harris, "Van Gogh's Sunflowers Covered in Tomato Soup by Eco Activists."

4. Sam Wineburg's study, "Lateral Reading and the Nature of Expertise: Reading Less and Learning More When Evaluating Digital Information," was conducted by and cowritten with Sarah McGrew, then a doctoral student at Stanford and now an assistant professor at the University of Maryland. It was summarized in *Time* magazine by Katy Steinmetz, "How Your Brain Tricks You into Believing Fake News." Prior to observing fact-checkers, Sam's research team had conducted a large-scale survey of how nearly eight thousand students evaluated digital material. The findings were less than encouraging: Wineburg et al., "Evaluating Information: The Cornerstone of Civic Online Reasoning"; Sarah Mc-Grew et al., "Can Students Evaluate Online Sources?" The survey gained wide press coverage, including a feature by Sue Shellenbarger in the *Wall Street Journal*, "Most Students Don't Know When News Is Fake, Stanford Study Finds."

5. See Axelsson, Guath, and Nygren, "Learning How to Separate Fake from Real News: Scalable Digital Tutorials Promoting Students' Civic Online Reasoning"; Brodsky et al.,

"Associations between Online Instruction in Lateral Reading Strategies and Fact-Checking COVID-19 News among College Students"; Brodsky et al., "Fact-Checking Instruction Strengthens the Association between Attitudes and the Use of Lateral Reading Strategies in College Students"; Brodsky et al., "Improving College Students' Fact-Checking Strategies through Lateral Reading Instruction in a General Education Civics Course"; Breakstone et al., "Lateral Reading: College Students Learn to Critically Evaluate Internet Sources in an Online Course"; Kohnen, Mertens, and Boehm, "Can Middle Schoolers Learn to Read the Web like Experts? Possibilities and Limits of a Strategy-Based Intervention"; McGrew, "Learning to Evaluate: An Intervention in Civic Online Reasoning"; McGrew et al., "Improving University Students' Web Savvy: An Intervention Study"; Panizza et al., "Lateral Reading and Monetary Incentives to Spot Disinformation about Science"; Pavlounis et al., *The Digital Media Literacy Gap*; Weisberg, Kohnen, and Dawson, "Impacts of a Digital Literacy Intervention on Preservice Teachers' Civic Online Reasoning Abilities, Strategies and Perceptions"; Wineburg et al., "Lateral Reading on the Open Internet: A District-Wide Field Study in High School Government Classes"; McGrew and Breakstone, "Civic Online Reasoning Across the Curriculum: Developing and Testing the Efficacy of Digital Literacy Lessons."

6.   Pavlounis et al., *Digital Media Literacy Gap*.
7.   Caulfield, *Web Literacy for Student Fact-Checkers*; Breakstone et al., "Students' Civic Online Reasoning: A National Portrait"; McGrew et al., "The Challenge That's Bigger than Fake News: Civic Reasoning in a Social Media Environment."

CHAPTER ONE

1.   Contrera, "Jack Black Will Actually Die One Day, but the Celebrity Death Hoax Is Here to Stay."
2.   "Britney Death Hoax Fools Fans," *BBC News*, June 14, 2001.
3.   Dewey, "The Internet's Perfect Death."
4.   Rozenblit and Keil, "The Misunderstood Limits of Folk Science: An Illusion of Explanatory Depth."
5.   If you wanted to take this further, you could. If a celebrity just died, maybe there really would be no reporting, at least for a small window of time. So, in this case, the source of who made the claim might matter: if the celebrity's sister or costar passed on the news, that might be reliable enough.
6.   Here's one of many examples: Between 2019 and 2020, Sam's research group surveyed 3,446 high school students who had a live internet connection and who evaluated a series of websites. When asked to investigate a site claiming to "disseminate factual reports" on climate science, 96 percent of the students never learned about the organization's ties

to the fossil fuel industry. Two-thirds were unable to distinguish news stories from ads on a popular website's home page. More than half believed that an anonymously posted Facebook video, shot in Russia, provided "strong evidence" of US voter fraud. See Breakstone et al., "Students' Civic Online Reasoning: A National Portrait."

7. This discussion of context is an amalgam of separate work Mike and Sam have done over the years. It corresponds most closely to *stop* in SIFT and the concept of "footing" in Civic Online Reasoning. See Caulfield, *Web Literacy for Student Fact-Checkers*, and Wineburg et al., *Lateral Reading on the Open Internet*.

8. Screenshots in this book are current as of July 2022, or, where the original has been deleted, they are a snapshot of a contemporaneous capture by the Internet Archive (https://archive.org). In certain cases, to provide a high-resolution version suitable for publication, we have had to reconstruct the original from lower-quality archived versions, either from archive.org or the authors' personal screenshot archive. In cases where a screenshot has been reconstructed, the month and year of the original capture is noted in the caption. Screenshots of search results are dealt with similarly—unless otherwise noted, the searches and search results were current as of July 2022.

9. Throughout this book we use the term "google" and show examples of using Google search processes. However, with some exceptions, most techniques we describe are designed to be of general use and can be used on any other search platform, such as Bing or DuckDuckGo. The choice of Google is meant to provide readers with a familiar starting point. Mike's previous works experimented with presenting techniques in a variety of search engines, but he found that the variety tended to focus students too much on the technology and not enough on the method. Both authors have provided feedback to Google on search features in the past. Additionally, Sam's research group received funding from Google.org for a digital literacy project (cor.stanford.edu). However, no part of this book should be taken as an endorsement of Google over other search products.

10. To simulate results available at the time, we have used a Google search feature to limit by date. To see an exact capture of results from that day, see Mike's post on the issue: https://hapgood.us/2018/03/07/how-to-read-laterally-a-lesson-for-new-york-times -columnists-including-but-not-limited-to-bari-weiss/.

11. Hover card reconstructed with bio current at the time.

12. This was one of the big findings of Sam's research with his colleague Sarah McGrew. Sam and Sarah observed professional fact-checkers at some of the nation's most prestigious news outlets as they went about their work. See Wineburg and McGrew, "Lateral Reading and the Nature of Expertise." For a short summary, see Brilee Weaver, "From Digital Native to Digital Expert."

13. To respect image licensing, the original card was redone with an equivalent photo from Wikimedia Commons. Photo by Christine Butler, licensed under Creative Commons At-

tribution 2.0, https://commons.wikimedia.org/wiki/File:Joro_Spider_-_Trichonephila
clavata(50564813031).jpg.

14. Turner, "Millions of Palm-Sized Flying Spiders Could Invade the East Coast."

15. This is the importance of the "context of you": by keeping in mind why we care about the information in the first place, we better comprehend how each additional layer of context should inform our reactions. Most claims are neither wholly true nor completely false, and no source is perfect. The question we ask ourselves is whether our naive reaction to a source changes as we discover more about it.

CHAPTER TWO

1. Blakeslee, "The CRAAP Test"; California State University, "Evaluating Information—Applying the CRAAP Test."

2. Jacobs, "A Shadowy Industry Group Shapes Food Policy around the World"; Nestle, "The International Life Sciences Institute: True Colors Revealed"; Schillinger and Kearns, "Guidelines to Limit Added Sugar Intake: Junk Science or Junk Food?"

3. Jacobs, "A Shadowy Industry Group Shapes Food Policy around the World."

4. Steel et al., "Are Industry-Funded Charities Promoting 'Advocacy-Led Studies' or 'Evidence-Based Science'?: A Case Study of the International Life Sciences Institute."

5. In other work, Mike has referred to this as "narrative alignment"—as we discover more context, does the signal "line up" with the story we had in mind?

6. O'Connor, "Study Tied to Food Industry Tries to Discredit Sugar Guidelines."

7. Iacobucci, "Food and Drink Industry Sought to Influence Scientists and Academics, Emails Show."

8. Terry, "Why Mars Inc. Is Telling Its Story after Decades of Avoiding the Spotlight."

9. Public Interest Registry, *Public Interest Registry Dashboard: January through June 2013.*

10. Wineburg and Ziv, "Why Can't a Generation that Grew up Online Spot Misinformation Right in Front of Them?" See also Wineburg et al., "Educating for Misunderstanding: How Approaches to Teaching Digital Literacy Make Students Susceptible to Scammers, Rogues, Bad Actors and Hate Mongers"; Ziv and Bene, "Preparing College Students for a Digital Age: A Survey of Instructional Approaches to Spotting Misinformation."

11. Wineburg and Ziv, "The Meaninglessness of the .ORG Domain"; Stanford History Education Group, "Dot-Orgs Spreading Hate: Southern Poverty Law Center Hate Group Domain Research."

12. Impact factor is a metric for measuring the influence of a scholarly journal. It is based on the average number of times that articles appearing in the journal are cited by other scholars. An impact factor of thirty puts that publication in the highest tier of scholarly journals.

13. Breakstone et al., "Students' Civic Online Reasoning."
14. Wineburg and Ziv, "The Meaninglessness of the .ORG Domain."
15. Breakstone et al., "Civic Preparation for the Digital Age: How College Students Evaluation Online Sources about Social and Political Issues." In 2019, the percentage of approvals was 91 percent, slightly less than in 2015. See IRS, "Internal Revenue Service Data Book, 2019."
16. Reich, Dorn, and Sutton, "Anything Goes: Approval of Nonprofit Status by the IRS."
17. Belluz, "The Research Linking Autism to Vaccines Is Even More Bogus Than You Think."
18. Smith, "How a Kennedy Built an Anti-Vaccine Juggernaut amid COVID-19."
19. "Vaccine Adverse Event Reporting System (VAERS)," CDC, https://wonder.cdc.gov/wonder/help/vaers.html.
20. Selbey, "CDC Accepts All Manner of Reported Vaccination Effects—Even Symptoms of the Hulk."
21. Love and Merlan, "Anti-Vaxxers Misuse Federal Data to Falsely Claim COVID Vaccines Are Dangerous."

CHAPTER THREE

1. Warnica, "Australian Birds Have Weaponized Fire Because What We Really Need Now Is Something Else to Make Us Afraid."
2. Bonta et al., "Intentional Fire-Spreading by 'Firehawk' Raptors in Northern Australia."
3. Sullivan, "A Reintroduction to Google's Featured Snippets."
4. Sawtell, "The Nineteenth of April, 1775."
5. "The Diary of Lieutenant John Barker," 98. Studying how readers from different backgrounds analyze conflicting evidence about Lexington has been a staple of Sam's research on historical thinking. See Wineburg, *Historical Thinking and Other Unnatural Acts: Charting the Future of Teaching the Past.*
6. Note that the explanation refers to a "study from the Duke Nicholas School of the Environment." This would be the *research source* using the categories we laid out.
7. Osher, "What Does $80 Million Buy Oil and Gas Interests?"
8. A relatively major revision at Google in the past few years has reduced the influence of exact keywords on search. It does this by looking at terms that are often searched in sequence. For example, if a lot of people follow a search for "best cell phone" with "best mobile phone," Google's algorithms start looking for "mobile phone" as well when people search for "cell phone." If people looking for an actor's filmography often start by searching for a bio, it may pull up the filmography when a bio is searched. But note that the principle—that Google looks for keywords—still applies. It just is a bit less rigid about it.
9. We've simplified things quite a bit here. Google increasingly focuses on the broader

context of the search to formulate its results. See Nayak, "Understanding Searches Better than Ever Before."

10. Grind et al., "How Google Interferes with Its Search Algorithms and Changes Your Results."

11. Simonite, "What Really Happened When Google Ousted Timnit Gebru."

12. See Willingham, "Does Tailoring Instruction to 'Learning Styles' Help Students Learn?"

13. D'Onfro, "Meet the Man Whose Job It Is to Reassure People That Google Search Isn't Evil."

14. *Stifling Free Speech: Technological Censorship and the Public Discourse, before the Committee on the Judiciary: Subcommittee on the Constitution*, April 10, 2019 (testimony of Dr. Francesca Tripodi, Assistant Professor of Sociology, James Madison University).

15. Lynch, "Googling Is Believing: Trumping the Informed Citizen."

CHAPTER FOUR

1. Southern Poverty Law Center, "American College of Pediatricians."

2. Hausner, "Canada Bans 'Conversion Therapy.'"

3. The page has since been deleted from the site, but an Internet Archive version can be found here: https://web.archive.org/web/20191208213100/https://www.acpeds.org/p-for-pedophile.

4. Collins wrote that the group "pulled language out of context from a book I wrote in 2006 to support an ideology that can cause unnecessary anguish and encourage prejudice." This statement is no longer online but can be found here: https://web.archive.org/web/20110727115017/http://www.nih.gov/about/director/04152010_statement_ACP.htm.

5. See Espelage, "Bullying & the Lesbian, Gay, Bisexual, Transgender, Questioning (LGBTQ) Community." Also see US Department of Health and Human Services Office of the Surgeon General, "National Strategy for Suicide Prevention: Goals and Objectives for Action."

6. Lenz, "American College of Pediatricians Defames Gays and Lesbians in the Name of Protecting Children."

7. Earnshaw et al., "LGBTQ Bullying: Translating Research to Action in Pediatrics."

8. Wineburg and McGrew, "Lateral Reading and the Nature of Expertise"; Steinmetz, "How Your Brain Tricks You."

9. Wineburg and McGrew, "Lateral Reading and the Nature of Expertise."

10. In arraying these seven tabs, the fact-checker right-clicked to open a new tab, rather than opening a new link in the current tab. You probably know how to do this, but your parents and grandparents might not. Teach them—it makes lateral reading infinitely easier.

11. Lipton, "Fight Over the Minimum Wage Illustrates Web of Industry Ties."

12. When Rick Berman spoke to an audience of oil magnates, one secretly recorded the talk

and leaked the tape to the press. Berman explained his tactics: "People always ask me one question all the time, 'How do I know that I won't be found out as a supporter of what you're doing?' We run all of this stuff through nonprofit organizations that are insulated from having to disclose donors. There is total anonymity. People don't know who supports us." The full transcript is available on the Internet Archive: https://web.archive.org/save /https://s3.amazonaws.com/s3.documentcloud.org/documents/1349204/berman-at -western-energy-alliance-june-2014-doc.pdf.

13. Daly, "Q: Are Fact Checkers the Only Credible Source for 'Lateral Reading'?"
14. See, for example, Dean, "Here's What We Learned about Organic Click through Rate."
15. "What Site Owners Should Know about Google's August 2019 Core Update," *Google Search Central Blog.*
16. The site is now defunct.
17. This section draws on the insights from McGrew, "Internet or Archive: Expertise in Searching for Digital Sources on a Contentious Historical Question."

CHAPTER FIVE

1. Caulfield, "Recalibrating Our Approach to Misinformation."
2. A fictional entity
3. Here we are drawing on Pomerantsev and Weiss, "The Menace of Unreality: How the Kremlin Weaponizes Information, Culture and Money." The authors explain that the chief goal of Soviet "dezinformatsia" was less to persuade than to sow "muddled thinking," so that citizens become more malleable and willing to follow strongmen who say, "Follow me, only *I* can be trusted."
4. This process is detailed in brief in Allan M. Brandt's "Inventing Conflicts of Interest: A History of Tobacco Industry Tactics" and at length in Naomi Oreskes and Erik Conway's *Merchants of Doubt: How a Handful of Scientists Obscured the Truth on Issues from Tobacco Smoke to Climate Change* and Robert N. Proctor's *Golden Holocaust: Origins of the Cigarette Catastrophe and the Case for Abolition.*
5. CDC, "Fast Facts and Fact Sheets: Smoking & Tobacco Use."
6. Occupational Safety and Health Administration, "COVID-19 Frequently Asked Questions: Respirators and Particle Size."
7. Even as Sam and Mike were putting together their first published alternatives to checklist approaches in 2016 and 2017, the American Library Association was promoting checklists as a valid response to the "fake news" problem (see Julian, "Libraries Transform: A Progress Report"). Recent years have brought substantial adoption of our approach. Ironically, LOEX—the publisher of the quarterly in which the CRAAP checklist approach was first introduced to the world—invited Mike to keynote its conference in 2022. When

Mike asked whether he should present the basics of his method, he was told no, but for an interesting reason—many conference attendees had likely already transitioned to using SIFT.

8. In addition to positive results in the scholarly literature, Mike and Sam's work has attracted attention from major press outlets. A small sample includes Warzel, "Don't Go Down the Rabbit Hole"; Steinmetz, "How Your Brain Tricks You"; Jargon, "How to Tell Fact from Fiction, Even during a War"; Mathews, "You Can't Believe Everything You Read Online: Many Students Don't Seem to Know That"; Moyer, "Schoolkids are Falling Victim to Disinformation and Conspiracy Fantasies"; Supiano, "Students Fall for Misinformation Online."

9. Newton, "How the Plandemic Video Hoax Went Viral."

10. Enserink and Cohen, "Fact Checking Judy Mikovits."

11. Enserink and Cohen, "Fact Checking Judy Mikovits."

12. Enserink and Cohen, "Fact Checking Judy Mikovits."

CHAPTER SIX

1. McDonald, *The Benefits of Chess in Education*.

2. Wineburg et al., "Lateral Reading on the Open Internet."

3. https://shitmyreviewerssay.tumblr.com/.

4. This number comes from a blog post, "Peer Review Is F***ed Up—Let's Fix It," by Michael Eisen, a professor of molecular biology at University of California, Berkeley. This blog was written in 2011; the number of journals has increased substantially since then.

5. Carroll, "Peer Review: The Worst Way to Judge Research, Except for All the Others."

6. Altbach and de Wit, "Too Much Academic Research Is Being Published."

7. Kazemi, Yektayar, and Abad, "Investigation of the Impact of Chess Play on Developing Metacognitive Ability."

8. Sala and Gobet "Does Far Transfer Exist?," 519.

9. "About," Google Scholar, accessed January 6, 2023, https://scholar.google.com/intl/en/scholar/about.html.

10. Ghiasi, "Abject Objects and V-Effect."

11. Ghiasi, "Abject Objects and V-Effect," 8.

12. Like many exaggerated historical claims, this one begins with a shred of historical fact. There was indeed a camp for formerly enslaved people who flooded into Natchez, Mississippi, when the port was captured by Union soldiers in May 1862. (The camp, however, was nowhere near the area today known as the Devil's Punchbowl.) The camp housed refugees who sought shelter in the middle of a war. Like makeshift refugee camps everywhere, this one suffered from crowded and unsanitary conditions. Historians estimate that around

two thousand people died, including many Union soldiers, not from starvation but from various forms of disease. (See Davis, *The Black Experience in Natchez, 1720–1880*.) Ironically, the myth of Natchez "concentration camps" also appears on "Lost Cause" white supremacist websites. (For an overview, see Young, "When Lost Causers Drink from the Devil's Punchbowl.")

13. Citation rates tend to vary by discipline: typically higher in the sciences; a bit lower in the social sciences and humanities. As you become familiar with your discipline, you'll start to develop a sense for what constitutes high and low citation rates.

CHAPTER SEVEN

1. Connors State College, "Should You Use Wikipedia as a Credible Resource?"
2. Seigenthaler, "A False Wikipedia 'Biography' Sparks Reflection."
3. Bernstein, "Culture War Has Finally Come for Wikipedia."
4. Heilman and West, "Wikipedia and Medicine."
5. Maher, "Making History, Building the Future Together."
6. Barnett, "Can We Trust Wikipedia?"
7. Thorndike-Breeze, Musselman, and Carleton, "Three Links: Be Bold, Assume Good Faith, and There Are No Firm Rules."
8. "Britannica Attacks," *Nature*.
9. Not all drive-by edits are malicious. Some—even if they have a fleeting half-life—are downright hilarious. See Šarūnė Bar, "64 of the Funniest Wikipedia Edits by Internet Vandals," Bored Panda, accessed January 8, 2023, https://www.boredpanda.com/funny-wikipedia-edits/.
10. Orlowitz, "How Wikipedia Almost Saved the Internet."
11. Lockett, "The Politics of User Agency and Participation on Wikipedia"; Vrana, Sengupta, and Bouterse, "Toward a Wikipedia for and from Us All"; Blakemore, "Wikipedia Wants You to Improve Its Coverage of Indigenous Peoples."
12. Maher, "Wikipedia Mirrors the World's Gender Biases, It Doesn't Cause Them."
13. Benkler, "Extracting Signal from Noisy Spin."
14. "Research Help: Should I Cite Wikipedia?," Wikimedia Foundation, last modified March 26, 2022, 23:47, https://en.wikipedia.org/wiki/Wikipedia:Research_help#CiteWiki; "Wikipedia Is Not a Reliable Source," Wikimedia Foundation, last modified December 5, 2022, 17:21, https://en.wikipedia.org/wiki/Wikipedia:Wikipedia_is_not_a_reliable_source.
15. Alfre Woodard, "Alfre Woodard Reads Sojourner Truth," Voices of a People's History of the United States, May 10, 2008, YouTube video, 3:43, https://www.youtube.com/watch?v=4vr_vKsk_h8&t=4s.

16. Wikipedia, s.v. "Dental Floss," last modified December 12, 2022, 01:42, https://en .wikipedia.org/wiki/Dental_floss.

17. Kuzmarov and Peace, "The Japanese Surrender in 1945 Is Still Poorly Understood."

18. Wikipedia, s.v. "Atomic Bombings of Hiroshima and Nagasaki," last modified August 11, 2021, https://en.wikipedia.org/wiki/Atomic_bombings_of_Hiroshima_and_Nagasaki.

19. Graff and Birkenstein, *They Say, I Say: The Moves That Matter in Academic Writing.*

20. Current as of August 11, 2021.

21. Note that Walker's article was published in 2005. A great way to see how other historians and political scientists have since responded to him is to use Google Scholar, a tool we discussed in chapter 6.

CHAPTER EIGHT

1. Jogalekar, "Nuclear Power May Have Saved 1.8 Million Lives Otherwise Lost to Fossil Fuels, May Save up to 7 Million More."

2. Kolbert, "Why Facts Don't Change Our Minds."

3. Bernays, *Crystallizing Public Opinion*, 170.

4. Bernays, *Crystallizing Public Opinion*, 52.

5. Szep and So, "Inside Trump's Campaign to Demonize Two Georgia Election Workers."

6. "Video Shows Suitcases Filled with Ballots Pulled AFTER Supervisors Told Poll Workers to Leave—YouTube," Donald J Trump, December 10, 2020, YouTube video, 2:38, https:// www.youtube.com/watch?v=aCenojrUwVM.

7. "Suitcases Filled with Ballots; Hidden under Table; Counted without Oversight," Facts Matter, December 3, 2020, YouTube video, 12:50, https://www.youtube.com/watch?v= wB7jhXvFl0k [video no longer available].

8. Rep. Jody Hice (@CongressmanHice), "Caught on candid camera . . . Fulton County supervisors in Georgia tell poll workers, press and observers to leave the room . . . And then pull out SUITCASES of ballots. Say it with me . . . F R A U D. WHERE IS THE DEPARTMENT OF JUSTICE?," Twitter, December 3, 2020, 4:24 p.m., https://twitter .com/CongressmanHice/status/1334609467703521283.

9. Haberman, "Three Mile Island, and Nuclear Hopes and Fears."

10. Here we simulate what was available on a past date by doing a date-constrained search. This is not an ideal way to simulate the results available at the time, but it is close enough to ground the explanation. In several other places, we have chosen to reconstruct historical results.

11. Kennedy et al., "Repeat Spreaders and Election Delegitimization."

12. Altay, Hacquin, and Mercier, "Why Do So Few People Share Fake News?"

13. We would note that this is just one lesson, particularly chosen for the reader of this book.

Other lessons about such fakery include the way it radicalizes a small number of people, its tendency to pull a subset of readers down the rabbit hole in life-destroying ways, and the leakage of such ideas from social media to more influential outlets and leaders, who then push those ideas to much larger populations.

14. Caulfield, "Control-F and Building Resilient Information Networks."
15. For certain low-follower accounts that we use as examples, we make small alterations and redactions to protect the privacy of the individual if the poster's identity is not central to the interpretation of the item.
16. Krever and Bell, "Ukrainians Prepare for War at the Site of the World's Worst Nuclear Disaster."
17. Binder, "A Conspiracy Theory about a Party Supply Store Went Viral on TikTok: Then the Police Showed Up."
18. Wagner, "Fact Check: Deceptive Edit of Interview with CDC Director Misleads on COVID-19 Deaths."
19. "CDC Director Responds to Criticisms on COVID-19 Guidance," *Good Morning America*, January 10, 2022, video, 3:44, https://www.goodmorningamerica.com/news/video/cdc-director-responds-criticisms-covid-19-guidance-82131389.
20. Molloy, "The Tighter a Video Is Clipped, the Less Inclined You Should Be to Share It."

CHAPTER NINE

1. Abrams and Kang, "The Mystery of *Teen Vogue*'s Disappearing Facebook Article."
2. For a comprehensive account of Facebook's woes, see the site https://www.facebookpapers.com, a collaboration among the Associated Press, the *Wall Street Journal*, the *New York Times*, *Vice*, *The Atlantic*, and many other publications.
3. Abrams and Kang, "The Mystery of *Teen Vogue*'s Disappearing Facebook Article."
4. Garfield, "Native Advertising Is Not Merely a Deception: It Is a Conspiracy of Deception."
5. Sirrah, "Guide to Native Advertising."
6. Forte, "Civic Online Reading in First-Year Composition." Forte's research replicates a study conducted by Sam's team at Stanford. See Sarah McGrew et al., "Can Students Evaluate Online Sources?"
7. Lazer, "The Problems Facing Native Advertising, in 5 Charts."
8. Amazeen and Wojdynski, "Reducing Native Advertising Deception." The Bank of America advertisement was one of the prompts used in Amazeen and Wojdynski's research study.
9. A small sampling includes Hyman et al., "Going Native: Can Consumers Recognize Native Advertising? Does It Matter?"; Hoofnagle and Meleshinsky, "Native Advertising and Endorsement: Schema, Source-Based Misleadingness, and Omission of Material Facts"; Ah, Kang, and Koo, "Sponsorship Disclosures of Native Advertising: Clarity and Prominence";

and Wojdynski and Evans, "Going Native: Effects of Disclosure Position and Language on the Recognition and Evaluation of Online Native Advertising."

10. Nichols, "Can This Advertising Innovation at '*The New York Times*' Save Sinking Ad Revenue?"

11. Cited in Einstein, *Black Ops Advertising*.

12. Gupta, "Four Big Threats Native Advertising Faces in 2015." Researchers at the University of Colorado and Baylor University interviewed thirty professional journalists. Guaranteed confidentiality, the journalists spoke freely about their qualms about ads disguised as news. One journalist explained why native ads corrupt the principles of journalism: "There's nothing ethical about a practice that literally goes against the foundation of journalism. [Interviewer: What's the foundation?] Truth, of course. We need to always be attempting to publish truth that will help people make important decisions. Sometimes, everything we do isn't truth[ful], but we're trying. It's about intention. If we mess up, we tell people we messed up and why. Native ads, well, there's nothing truthful about them. By their very nature they're a lie and that's the antithesis of journalism." See Schauster, Ferrucci, and Neill, "Native Advertising Is the New Journalism."

13. Sirrah, "Guide to Native Advertising."

14. Moses, "The *Wall Street Journal*'s Native Approach: 'If It Looks like a Puff Piece, Nobody's Going to Read It.'"

15. "BBC News Appoints Krystal Bowden Director, BBC StoryWorks–the Americas," BBC, September 6, 2018, https://www.bbc.com/mediacentre/latestnews/worldnews/2018/krystal-bowden.

16. See https://www.courageousstudios.com/.

17. Quoted in Einstein, *Black Ops Advertising*, 81.

18. Quoted in Einstein, *Black Ops Advertising*, 82.

19. According to a report by the nonpartisan International Energy Agency; see IEA, *World Energy Investment 2021*.

20. Supran and Oreskes, "Assessing ExxonMobil's Climate Change Communication (1977–2014)."

21. Oreskes, *Why Trust Science*, 65.

22. Federal Trade Commission, "Native Advertising: A Guide for Businesses."

23. FTC cited in Bartosz and Evans, "Going Native: Effects of Disclosure Position and Language on the Recognition and Evaluation of Online Native Advertising."

24. Dotson, "Xinhua Infiltrates Western Electronic Media, Part One: Online 'Advertorial' Content."

25. Dotson, "Xinhua Infiltrates Western Electronic Media, Part Two: Relationships with News Agencies and Distribution Services."

26. Dai and Luqiu, "Camouflaged Propaganda: A Survey Experiment on Political Native Advertising."
27. The wording on AT&T's card has since been changed. The original ad is gratefully reproduced from Amazeen and Vargo, "Sharing Native Advertising on Twitter," 927.
28. Amazeen and Vargo, "Sharing Native Advertising on Twitter," 927.
29. Ah, Kang, and Koo, "Sponsorship Disclosures of Native Advertising: Clarity and Prominence."

CHAPTER TEN

1. This may be a bit unfair, but not by much. One prevailing view has been that those intuitive first reactions benefit from speed but lack accuracy. That is, we make do with fast thinking for the sake of efficiency, but in an ideal world, we would have time for deeper reflection. For example, see Kahneman, *Thinking, Fast and Slow*. Fast thinking has flaws, but we believe that fast and slow thinking are best seen not as alternatives but partners. Call it thinking fast *with* slow.
2. Schank, "Interestingness: Controlling Inferences."
3. To be as clear as possible, we are not asserting that the American College of Pediatricians is a few doctors and a laptop; we are merely engaging in a traditional thought experiment to divine what was compelling about the source on the students' first read.
4. Caulfield, "A Short History of CRAAP."
5. Wineburg et al., "Evaluating Information."

CHAPTER ELEVEN

1. Simon, "Designing Organizations for an Information-Rich World" (emphasis added).
2. Flensmark, "Is There an Association between the Use of Heeled Footwear and Schizophrenia?"; Zarrintan, "Ejaculation as a Potential Treatment of Nasal Congestion in Mature Males."

POSTSCRIPT

1. Technically, they have models that can look forward, backward, and more holistically than a simple forward-looking sequential model, but we simplify here for readability.

BIBLIOGRAPHY

Abrams, Rachel, and Cecilia Kang. "The Mystery of *Teen Vogue*'s Disappearing Facebook Article." *New York Times*, January 8, 2020. https://www.nytimes.com/2020/01/08/business/media/teen-vogue-facebook.html.

Ah, Soontae, Hannah Kang, and Sra Koo. "Sponsorship Disclosures of Native Advertising: Clarity and Prominence." *Journal of Consumer Affairs* 53 (2018): 998–1024.

Altay, Sacha, Anne-Sophie Hacquin, and Hugo Mercier. "Why Do So Few People Share Fake News? It Hurts Their Reputation." *New Media & Society* 24, no. 6 (June 2022): 1303–24. https://doi.org/10.1177/1461444820969893.

Altbach, Phillip G., and Hans de Wit. "Too Much Academic Research Is Being Published." *University World News*, September 8, 2018. https://www.universityworldnews.com/post.php?story=20180905095203579.

Amazeen, Michelle A., and Chris J. Vargo. "Sharing Native Advertising on Twitter: Content Analyses Examining Disclosure Practices and Their Inoculating Influence." *Journalism Studies* 22, no. 7 (2021): 916–33. https://doi.org/10.1080/1461670X.2021.1906298.

Amazeen, Michelle A., and Bartosz W. Wojdynski. "The Effects of Disclosure Format on Native Advertising Recognition and Audience Perceptions of Legacy and Online News Publishers." *Journalism* 21, no. 12 (December 2020): 1965–84. https://doi.org/10.1177/1464884918754829.

———. "Reducing Native Advertising Deception: Revisiting the Antecedents and Consequences of Persuasion Knowledge in Digital News Contexts." *Mass Communication and Society* 22, no. 2 (2019): 222–47. https://doi.org/10.1080/15205436.2018.1530792.

Axelsson, Carl-Anton Werner, Mona Guath, and Thomas Nygren. "Learning How to Separate Fake from Real News: Scalable Digital Tutorials Promoting Students' Civic Online Reasoning." *Future Internet* 13, no. 3 (2021): 60–78. http://doi.org/10.3390/fi13030060.

Barnett, David. "Can We Trust Wikipedia? 1.4 Billion People Can't Be Wrong." *The Independent*, February 17, 2018. https://www.independent.co.uk/news/long_reads/wikipedia -explained-what-it-trustworthy-how-work-wikimedia-2030-a8213446.html.

Belluz, Julia. "The Research Linking Autism to Vaccines Is Even More Bogus Than You Think." *Vox*, January 10, 2017. https://www.vox.com/2015/2/2/7965885/vaccine -autism-link-false-evidence-wakefield.

Benkler, Yochai. "Extracting Signal from Noisy Spin." Edge: The Reality Club. Response to "Digital Maoism: The Hazards of the New Online Collectivism" by Jaron Lanier. *The Edge*, May 29, 2006. https://www.edge.org/conversation/jaron_lanier-digital-maoism -the-hazards-of-the-new-online-collectivism.

Bernays, Edward. *Crystallizing Public Opinion*. New York: Ig Publishing, 2011. First published 1923.

Bernstein, Joseph. "Culture War Has Finally Come for Wikipedia." BuzzFeed News, June 27, 2019. https://www.buzzfeednews.com/article/josephbernstein/wikipedia-ban-editor -culture-war.

Binder, Matt. "A Conspiracy Theory about a Party Supply Store Went Viral on TikTok: Then the Police Showed Up." Mashable, June 2, 2021. https://mashable.com/article /lumistick-party-hat-amazon-tiktok-conspiracy-theory.

Blakemore, Erin. "Wikipedia Wants You to Improve Its Coverage of Indigenous Peoples." *Smithsonian*, September 30, 2016. https://www.smithsonianmag.com/smart-news /wikipedia-wants-you-improve-its-coverage-indigenous-peoples-180960605/.

Blakeslee, Sarah. "The CRAAP Test." *LOEX Quarterly* 31, no. 3 (2004). https://commons .emich.edu/loexquarterly/vol31/iss3/4/.

Bonta, Mark, Robert Gosford, Dick Eussen, Nathan Ferguson, Erana Loveless, and Maxwell Witwer. "Intentional Fire-Spreading by 'Firehawk' Raptors in Northern Australia." *Journal of Ethnobiology* 37, no. 4 (2017): 700–718. https://doi.org/10.2993/0278-0771 -37.4.700.

Brandt, Allan M. "Inventing Conflicts of Interest: A History of Tobacco Industry Tactics." *American Journal of Public Health* 102, no. 1 (2012): 63–71. https://doi.org/10.2105 /AJPH.2011.300292.

Breakstone, Joel, Sarah McGrew, Mark Smith, Teresa Ortega, and Sam Wineburg. "Why We Need a New Approach to Teaching Digital Literacy." *Phi Delta Kappan* 99, no. 6 (2018): 27–32. https://doi.org/10.1177/0031721718762419.

Breakstone, Joel, Mark Smith, Priscilla Connors, Teresa Ortega, Darby Kerr, and Sam Wineburg. "Lateral Reading: College Students Learn to Critically Evaluate Internet Sources in an Online Course." *Harvard Kennedy School (HKS) Misinformation Review* 2, no. 1 (2021). https://doi.org/10.37016/mr-2020-56.

Breakstone, Joel, Mark D. Smith, Sam Wineburg, Amie Rapaport, Jill Carle, Marshall

Garland, and Anna Saavedra. "Students' Civic Online Reasoning: A National Portrait." *Educational Researcher* 50, no. 8 (2021): 505–15. https://doi.org/10.3102/0013189X211 017495.

Breakstone, Joel, Mark Smith, Nadav Ziv, and Sam Wineburg. "Civic Preparation for the Digital Age: How College Students Evaluation Online Sources about Social and Political Issues." *Journal of Higher Education* 93, no. 7 (2022): 963–88. https://doi.org/10.1080 /00221546.2022.2082783.

Bright, Jonathan. "The Social News Gap: How News Reading and News Sharing Diverge." *Journal of Communication* 66 (2016): 343–65.

"Britannica Attacks," *Nature* 440 (2006): 582. https://doi.org/10.1038/440582b.

"Britney Death Hoax Fools Fans," *BBC News*, June 14, 2001, http://news.bbc.co.uk/2/hi /entertainment/1388131.stm.

Brodsky, Jessica E., Patricia J. Brooks, Donna Scimeca, Peter Galati, Ralitsa Todorova, and Michael Caulfield. "Associations between Online Instruction in Lateral Reading Strategies and Fact-Checking COVID-19 News among College Students." *AERA Open* 7, no. 1 (2021): 1–17. https://doi.org/10.1177/23328584211038937.

Brodsky, Jessica E., Patricia J. Brooks, Donna Scimeca, Ralitsa Todorova, Peter Galati, Michael Batson, Robert Grosso, Michael Matthews, Victor Miller, and Michael Caulfield. "Improving College Students' Fact-Checking Strategies through Lateral Reading Instruction in a General Education Civics Course." *Cognitive Research: Principles and Implications*, 6, no. 23 (2021): 1–18. https://doi.org/10.1186/s41235-021-00291-4.

Brodsky, Jessica E., Arshia K. Lodhi, Catherine M. Messina, and Patricia J. Brooks. "Fact-Checking Instruction Strengthens the Association between Attitudes and the Use of Lateral Reading Strategies in College Students." *Proceedings of the Annual Meeting of the Cognitive Science Society* 44 (2022). https://escholarship.org/uc/item/3882t34s.

California State University. "Evaluating Information—Applying the CRAAP Test." Meriam Library, 2010. www.csuchico.edu/lins/handouts/eval_websites.pdf.

Carroll, Aaron E. "Peer Review: The Worst Way to Judge Research, Except for All the Others." *New York Times*, November 5, 2018. https://www.nytimes.com/2018/11/05 /upshot/peer-review-the-worst-way-to-judge-research-except-for-all-the-others.html.

Caulfield, Mike. "Control-F and Building Resilient Information Networks." *Hapgood* (blog), January 26, 2020. https://hapgood.us/2020/01/26/control-f-and-building-resilient -information-networks/.

———. "Recalibrating Our Approach to Misinformation." *EdSurge*, December 19, 2018. https://www.edsurge.com/news/2018-12-19-recalibrating-our-approach-to -misinformation.

———. "A Short History of CRAAP." *Hapgood* (blog), September 15, 2018. https://hapgood .us/2018/09/14/a-short-history-of-craap/.

————. *Web Literacy for Student Fact-Checkers*. Pressbooks, 2017. https://webliteracy.press books.com/.

CDC. "Fast Facts and Fact Sheets: Smoking & Tobacco Use." Data and Statistics. Last reviewed August 22, 2022. https://www.cdc.gov/tobacco/data_statistics/fact_sheets/fast_facts/index.htm.

Connors State College. "Should You Use Wikipedia as a Credible Resource?" Accessed January 8, 2023. https://connorsstate.edu/disted/wikipedia/.

Contrera, Jessica. "Jack Black Will Actually Die One Day, but the Celebrity Death Hoax Is Here to Stay." *Washington Post*, June 5, 2016. https://www.washingtonpost.com/news/arts-and-entertainment/wp/2016/06/05/jack-black-will-actually-die-one-day-but-the-celebrity-death-hoax-is-here-to-stay/.

Dai, Yaoyao, and Luwei Luqiu. "Camouflaged Propaganda: A Survey Experiment on Political Native Advertising." *Research & Politics* 7, no. 3 (2020). https://doi.org/10.1177/205316 8020935250.

Daly, Steve. "Q: Are Fact Checkers the Only Credible Source for 'Lateral Reading'?" News Literacy Matters, October 21, 2019. https://newsliteracymatters.com/2019/10/21/q-are-fact-checkers-the-only-credible-source-for-lateral-reading/.

Davis, Ronald L. F. *The Black Experience in Natchez, 1720–1880*. Natchez National Historical Park, 1993. https://archive.org/stream/blackexperiencei00davi/blackexperiencei00 davi_djvu.txt.

Dean, Brian. "Here's What We Learned about Organic Click through Rate." Backlinco, August 2019. https://backlinko.com/google-ctr-stats.

Dewey, Caitlin. "The Internet's Perfect Death." *Washington Post*, November 11, 2014. https://www.washingtonpost.com/news/the-intersect/wp/2014/11/11/the-internets-perfect-death/.

"The Diary of Lieutenant John Barker, Fourth (or The King's Own) Regiment of Foot, From November, 1774, to May, 1776." *Journal of the Society for Army Historical Research* 7, no. 28 (1928): 81–109. http://www.jstor.org/stable/44232571.

D'Onfro, Jillian. "Meet the Man Whose Job It Is to Reassure People That Google Search Isn't Evil." CNBC, June 25, 2018. https://www.cnbc.com/2018/06/22/danny-sullivan-on-being-google-new-search-liaison.html.

Dotson, John. "Xinhua Infiltrates Western Electronic Media, Part One: Online 'Advertorial Content.'" *China Brief* 21, no. 7 (2021). The Jamestown Foundation. https://jamestown.org/program/xinhua-infiltrates-western-electronic-media-part-one-online-advertorial-content/.

Dotson, John. "Xinhua Infiltrates Western Electronic Media, Part Two: Relationships with News Agencies and Distribution Services." China Brief 21, no. 16 (2021). The Jamestown

Foundation. https://jamestown.org/program/xinhua-infiltrates-western-electronic -media-part-2-relationships-with-news-agencies-and-distribution-services/.

Earnshaw, Valerie A., Sari L. Reisner, Jaana Juvonen, Mark L. Hatzenbuehler, Jeff Perrotti, and Mark A. Schuster. "LGBTQ Bullying: Translating Research to Action in Pediatrics." *Pediatrics* 140, no. 4: (2017): 1–10. https://doi.org/10.1542/peds.2017-0432.

Einstein, Mara. *Black Ops Advertising: Native Ads, Content Marketing, and the Covert World of the Digital Sell.* New York: Or Books, 2016.

Eisen, Michael. "Peer Review Is F***ed Up—Let's Fix It." *It Is NOT Junk* (blog), October 28, 2011. https://www.michaeleisen.org/blog/?p=694.

Enserink, Martin, and Jon Cohen. "Fact Checking Judy Mikovits, the Controversial Virologist Attacking Anthony Fauci in a Viral Conspiracy Video." *Science*, May 8, 2020. https://www.sciencemag.org/news/2020/05/fact-checking-judy-mikovits-controversial -virologist-attacking-anthony-fauci-viral.

Espelage, Dorothy L. "Bullying & the Lesbian, Gay, Bisexual, Transgender, Questioning (LGBTQ) Community." Stopbullying.gov. Accessed August 12, 2021. https://www .stopbullying.gov/sites/default/files/2017-09/white_house_conference_materials .pdf.

Federal Trade Commission. "Native Advertising: A Guide for Businesses." Business Guidance Resources. Updated December 2015. https://www.ftc.gov/business-guidance/resources /native-advertising-guide-businesses.

Flensmark, Jarl. "Is There an Association between the Use of Heeled Footwear and Schizophrenia?" *Medical Hypotheses* 63, no. 4 (2004): 740–47. https://doi.org/10.1016/j.mehy .2004.05.014.

Forte, Joseph. "Civic Online Reading in First-Year Composition: The Outcomes of Learning Outcomes." PhD diss., Purdue University, 2021.

Garfield, Bob. "Native Advertising Is Not Merely a Deception: It Is a Conspiracy of Deception." Media Marketing, October 2, 2016. https://www.media-marketing.com/en /theme-of-the-day-bob-garfield-native-advertising-it-is-not-merely-a-deception-it-is -a-conspiracy-of-deception-a-hustle-a-racket-a-grift/.

Ghiasi, Erfan. "Abject Objects and V-Effect." Master's thesis, Louisiana State University, 2019. https://www.academia.edu/42397753/ABJECT_OBJECTS_AND_V_EFFECT.

Gigerenzer, Gerd, and Wolfgang Gaissmaier. "Heuristic Decision Making." *Annual Review of Psychology* 62, no. 1 (2011): 451–82. https://doi.org/10.1146/annurev-psych-120709 -145346.

Graff, Gerald, and Cathy Birkenstein. *They Say, I Say: The Moves That Matter in Academic Writing.* 2nd ed. New York: Norton, 2009.

Grind, Kirsten, Sam Schechner, Robert McMillan, and John West. "How Google Interferes with Its Search Algorithms and Changes Your Results." *Wall Street Journal*, November 15, 2019. https://www.wsj.com/articles/how-google-interferes-with-its-search -algorithms-and-changes-your-results-11573823753.

Gupta, Kunal. "Four Big Threats Native Advertising Faces in 2015." VentureBeat, October 24, 2014. https://venturebeat.com/media/4-big-threats-native-advertising-faces-in -2015/.

Gupta, Kuhika, Matthew C. Nowlin, Joseph T. Ripberger, Hank C. Jenkins-Smith, and Carol L. Silva. "Tracking the Nuclear 'Mood' in the United States: Introducing a Long Term Measure of Public Opinion about Nuclear Energy Using Aggregate Survey Data." *Energy Policy* 133 (October 2019). https://doi.org/10.1016/j.enpol.2019.110888.

Haberman, Clyde. "Three Mile Island, and Nuclear Hopes and Fears." *New York Times*, April 28, 2014. https://www.nytimes.com/2014/04/29/us/three-mile-island-and-nuclear -hopes-and-fears.html.

Harris, Gareth. "Van Gogh's Sunflowers Covered in Tomato Soup by Eco Activists." *The Art Newspaper*, October 14, 2022. https://www.theartnewspaper.com/2022/10/14/van -goghs-sunflowers-covered-in-tomato-soup-by-eco-activists.

Hausner, Christine. "Canada Bans 'Conversion Therapy.'" *New York Times*, January 6, 2022. https://www.nytimes.com/2022/01/06/world/canada/canada-conversion-therapy-law .html.

Heilman, James M., and Andrew G. West. "Wikipedia and Medicine: Quantifying Readership, Editors, and the Significance of Natural Language." *Journal of Medical Internet Research* 17, no. 3 (2015), https://doi.org/10.2196/jmir.4069.

Hoofnagle, Chris Jay, and Eduard Meleshinsky. "Native Advertising and Endorsement: Schema, Source-Based Misleadingness, and Omission of Material Facts." *Technology Science*, December 15, 2015. https://ssrn.com/abstract=2703824.

Hyman, David A., David Franklyn, Calla Yee, and Mohammad Rahmati. "Going Native: Can Consumers Recognize Native Advertising? Does It Matter?" *Yale Journal of Law & Technology* 19 (2017).

Iacobucci, Gareth. "Food and Drink Industry Sought to Influence Scientists and Academics, Emails Show." *British Medical Journal* 369 (2020). https://doi.org/10.1136/bmj.m2078.

IEA. *World Energy Investment 2021*. Paris: IEA, 2021. https://www.iea.org/reports/world -energy-investment-2021.

IRS. *Internal Revenue Service Data Book, 2019*. Internal Revenue Service, 2019. https://www .irs.gov/pub/irs-prior/p55b--2020.pdf.

Jacobs, Andrew. "A Shadowy Industry Group Shapes Food Policy around the World." *New York Times*, September 16, 2019. https://www.nytimes.com/2019/09/16/health/ilsi -food-policy-india-brazil-china.html.

Jargon, Julie. "How to Tell Fact from Fiction, Even during a War." *The Wall Street Journal*,

March 5, 2022. https://www.wsj.com/articles/how-to-spot-fake-news-even-during-a
-war-11646434626.

Jogalekar, Ashutosh. "Nuclear Power May Have Saved 1.8 Million Lives Otherwise Lost to
Fossil Fuels, May Save up to 7 Million More." Scientific American Blog Network. *Scientific American*, April 2, 2013. https://blogs.scientificamerican.com/the-curious-wave
function/nuclear-power-may-have-saved-1-8-million-lives-otherwise-lost-to-fossil
-fuels-may-save-up-to-7-million-more/.

Julian, Jeff. "Libraries Transform: A Progress Report." *American Libraries*, June 1,
2017. https://americanlibrariesmagazine.org/2017/06/01/libraries-transform
-progress-report/.

Kahneman, Daniel. *Thinking, Fast and Slow*. New York: Macmillan, 2011.

Kazemi, Farhad Mozafar Yektayar, and Ali Mohammadi Bolban Abad. "Investigation of the
Impact of Chess Play on Developing Metacognitive Ability and Math Problem-Solving
Power of Students at Different Levels of Education." *Procedia-Social and Behavioral Sci-
ences* 32 (2012): 372–79. https://doi.org/10.1016/j.sbspro.2012.01.056.

Kennedy, Ian, Morgan Wack, Andrew Beers, Joseph S. Schafer, Isabella Garcia-Camargo,
Emma S. Spiro, and Kate Starbird. "Repeat Spreaders and Election Delegitimization:
A Comprehensive Dataset of Misinformation Tweets from the 2020 U.S. Election." *Journal of Quantitative Description: Digital Media* 2 (June 2022). https://doi.org/10.51685
/jqd.2022.013.

Kohnen, Angela M., Gillian E. Mertens, and Shelby M. Boehm. "Can Middle Schoolers Learn
to Read the Web like Experts? Possibilities and Limits of a Strategy-Based Intervention,"
Journal of Media Literacy Education 12, no. 2 (2020): 64–79. https://doi.org/10.23860
/JMLE-2020-12-2-6.

Kolbert, Elizabeth. "Why Facts Don't Change Our Minds." *The New Yorker*, February 19,
2017. http://www.newyorker.com/magazine/2017/02/27/why-facts-dont-change-our
-minds.

Krever, Mick, and Melissa Bell. "Ukrainians Prepare for War at the Site of the World's Worst
Nuclear Disaster." CNN, February 8, 2022. https://www.cnn.com/2022/02/07/europe
/ukraine-chernobyl-belarus-intl-cmd/index.html.

Kuzmarov, Jeremy, and Roger Peace. "The Japanese Surrender in 1945 Is Still Poorly Understood." History News Network, September 26, 2021. https://historynewsnetwork.org
/article/181372.

Lazer, Joe. "The Problems Facing Native Advertising, in 5 Charts." *The Content Strate-
gist*, September 24, 2015. https://contently.com/strategist/2015/09/16/the-problems
-facing-native-advertising-in-5-charts/.

Lenz, Ryan. "American College of Pediatricians Defames Gays and Lesbians in the Name
of Protecting Children." *Intelligence Report*, March 1, 2012. https://www.splcenter.org

/fighting-hate/intelligence-report/2012/american-college-pediatricians-defames-gays
-and-lesbians-name-protecting-children.

Lipton, Eric. "Fight over the Minimum Wage Illustrates Web of Industry Ties," *New York Times*, February 9, 2014. https://www.nytimes.com/2014/02/10/us/politics/fight-over
-minimum-wage-illustrates-web-of-industry-ties.html.

Lockett, Alexandria. "The Politics of User Agency and Participation on Wikipedia." In *Wikipedia @ 30: Stories of an Incomplete Revolution*, edited by Joseph Reagle and Jackie Koerner, 205–20. Cambridge, MA: MIT Press, 2020.

Love, Shayla, and Ana Merlan. "Anti-Vaxxers Misuse Federal Data to Falsely Claim COVID Vaccines Are Dangerous," *Vice*, February 3, 2021. https://www.vice.com/en/article
/qjpmp7/anti-vaxxers-misuse-federal-data-to-falsely-claim-covid-vaccines-are
-dangerous.

Lynch, Michael P. "Googling Is Believing: Trumping the Informed Citizen," *New York Times*, March 9, 2016. https://opinionator.blogs.nytimes.com/2016/03/09/googling-is
-believing-trumping-the-informed-citizen/.

Maher, Katherine. "Making History, Building the Future Together." In *Wikipedia @ 30: Stories of an Incomplete Revolution*, edited by Joseph Reagle and Jackie Koerner, 325. Cambridge, MA: MIT Press, 2020.

———. "Wikipedia Mirrors the World's Gender Biases, It Doesn't Cause Them," *Los Angeles Times*, October 18, 2018. https://www.latimes.com/opinion/op-ed/la-oe-maher
-wikipedia-gender-bias-20181018-story.html.

Mathews, Jay. "You Can't Believe Everything You Read Online: Many Students Don't Seem to Know That." *The Washington Post*, November 17, 2019. https://www.washingtonpost
.com/local/education/you-cant-believe-everything-you-read-online-many-students
-dont-seem-to-know-that/2019/11/17/06a171f2-0670-11ea-ac12-3325d49eacaa_story
.html.

McDonald, Patrick S., comp. *The Benefits of Chess in Education*. Accessed January 22, 2023. http://www.chessedu.org/wp-content/uploads/BenefitsOfChessInEd-1.pdf.

McGrew, Sarah. "Internet or Archive: Expertise in Searching for Digital Sources on a Contentious Historical Question." *Cognition and Instruction* (2021). https://doi.org/10.1080
/07370008.2021.1908288.

———. "Learning to Evaluate: An Intervention in Civic Online Reasoning." *Computers & Education* 145 (2020): 1–13. https://doi.org/10.1016/j.compedu.2019.103711.

McGrew, Sarah, and Joel Breakstone. "Civic Online Reasoning across the Curriculum: Developing and Testing the Efficacy of Digital Literacy Lessons." Working Paper 2022-1. Stanford History Education Group. Stanford, CA: Stanford University, 2022. https://doi.org
/10.25740/dd707pp9195. (*AERA Open*, forthcoming.)

McGrew, Sarah, Joel Breakstone, Teresa Ortega, Mark Smith, and Sam Wineburg. "Can Students Evaluate Online Sources? Learning from Assessments of Civic Online Reasoning." *Theory & Research in Social Education* 46 (2018): 165–93.

McGrew, Sarah, Joel Breakstone, Mark D. Smith, Teresa Ortega, and Sam Wineburg. "Improving University Students' Web Savvy: An Intervention Study." *British Journal of Educational Psychology*, 89 (2019): 485–500. https://doi.org/10.1111/bjep.12279.

McGrew, Sarah, Teresa Ortega, Joel Breakstone, and Sam Wineburg. "The Challenge That's Bigger than Fake News: Civic Reasoning in a Social Media Environment." *American Educator* (Fall 2017). https://www.aft.org/sites/default/files/ae_fall2017_mcgrew.pdf.

Meola, Marc. "Chucking the Checklist: A Contextual Approach to Teaching Undergraduates Website Evaluation." *Libraries and the Academy* 4 (2004): 331–44.

Molloy, Parker. "The Tighter a Video Is Clipped, the Less Inclined You Should Be to Share It." *The Present Age*, January 12, 2022. https://www.readtpa.com/p/video-clip-context-molloys-law.

Moses, Lucia. "The *Wall Street Journal*'s Native Approach: 'If It Looks like a Puff Piece, Nobody's Going to Read It.'" *Digiday*, April 9, 2015. https://digiday.com/media/wall-street-journals-native-approach-looks-like-puff-piece-nobodys-going-read/.

Moyer, Melinda Wenner. "Schoolkids Are Falling Victim to Disinformation and Conspiracy Fantasies." *Scientific American*, February 2022. https://www.scientificamerican.com/article/schoolkids-are-falling-victim-to-disinformation-and-conspiracy-fantasies/.

Mueller, John E. "Presidential Popularity from Truman to Johnson." *American Political Science Review* 64, no. 1 (March 1970): 18–34. https://doi.org/10.2307/1955610.

Nayak, Pandu. "Understanding Searches Better than Ever Before." Google company blog, October 25, 2019. https://blog.google/products/search/search-language-understanding-bert/.

Nestle, Marion. "The International Life Sciences Institute: True Colors Revealed." *Food Politics* (blog), October 3, 2019. https://www.foodpolitics.com/2019/10/the-international-life-sciences-institute-ilsi-true-colors-revealed/.

Newton, Carey. "How the Plandemic Video Hoax Went Viral." *The Verge*, May 12, 2020. https://www.theverge.com/2020/5/12/21254184/how-plandemic-went-viral-facebook-youtube.

Nichols, Beth. "Can This Advertising Innovation at '*The New York Times*' Save Sinking Ad Revenue?" The Motley Fool, September 20, 2014. https://www.fool.com/investing/general/2014/09/20/can-this-advertising-innovation-at-the-new-york-ti.aspx.

Occupational Safety and Health Administration. "COVID-19 Frequently Asked Questions: Respirators and Particle Size." United States Department of Labor. Accessed January 6, 2023. https://www.osha.gov/coronavirus/faqs#respirator.

O'Connor, Anahad. "Study Tied to Food Industry Tries to Discredit Sugar Guidelines." *New York Times*, December 19, 2016. https://www.nytimes.com/2016/12/19/well/eat/a-food -industry-study-tries-to-discredit-advice-about-sugar.html.

Oreskes, Naomi. *Why Trust Science*. Princeton, NJ: Princeton University Press, 2019.

Oreskes, Naomi, and Erik Conway. *Merchants of Doubt: How a Handful of Scientists Obscured the Truth on Issues from Tobacco Smoke to Climate Change*. New York: Bloomsbury Press, 2010.

Orlowitz, Jake. "How Wikipedia Almost Saved the Internet." In *Wikipedia @ 30: Stories of an Incomplete Revolution*, edited by Joseph Reagle and Jackie Koerner, 130. Cambridge, MA: MIT Press, 2020.

Osher, Christopher N. "What Does $80 Million Buy Oil and Gas Interests? Voter Profiles, Door Knocking, and Influence at Local and Statewide Levels." *Denver Post*, July 16, 2017. https://www.denverpost.com/2017/07/16/oil-gas-industry-public-influence -campaigns/.

Panizza, Folco, Piero Ronzani, Carlo Martini, Simone Mattavelli, Tiffany Morisseau, and Matteo Motterlini. "Lateral Reading and Monetary Incentives to Spot Disinformation about Science." *Scientific Reports* 12 (2022): 5678. https://doi.org/10.1038/s41598-022 -09168-y.

Pavlounis, Dimitrios, Jessica Johnston, Jessica Brodsky, and Patricia Brooks. *The Digital Media Literacy Gap: How to Build Widespread Resilience to False and Misleading Information Using Evidence-Based Classroom Tools*. Toronto: CIVIX Canada, November 2021. https:// ctrl-f.ca/en/the-evidence/.

Pomerantsev, Peter, and Michael Weiss. "The Menace of Unreality: How the Kremlin Weaponizes Information, Culture and Money." *The Interpreter* and *Institute of Modern Russia*, November 24, 2014. https://www.interpretermag.com/the-menace-of-unreality-how -the-kremlin-weaponizes-information-culture-and-money/.

Proctor, Robert N. *Golden Holocaust: Origins of the Cigarette Catastrophe and the Case for Abolition*. Oakland: University of California Press, 2012.

Public Interest Registry. *Public Interest Registry Dashboard: January through June 2013*. Report. Accessed October 15, 2019. https://docplayer.net/13026868-Public-interest -registry-dashboard.html.

Reich, Rob, Lacey Dorn, and Stephanie Sutton. "Anything Goes: Approval of Nonprofit Status by the IRS." Stanford University Center on Philanthropy and Civil Society, October 2009. https://pacscenter.stanford.edu/wp-content/uploads/2015/08/Anything-Goes -PACS-11-09.pdf.

Rozenblit, Leonid, and Frank Keil. "The Misunderstood Limits of Folk Science: An Illusion of Explanatory Depth." *Cognitive Science* 26 (2002): 521–62. https://doi.org/10.1207/s15 516709cog2605.

Sala, Giovanni, and Fernand Gobet. "Does Far Transfer Exist? Negative Evidence from Chess, Music, and Working Memory Training." *Current Directions in Psychological Science* 26, no. 6 (2017): 515–20. https://doi.org/10.1177/0963721417712760.

Sawtell, Clement C., ed. *The Nineteenth of April, 1775: A Collection of First Hand Accounts.* Lincoln, MA: Sawtells of Somerset, 1968.

Schank, Roger C. "Interestingness: Controlling Inferences." *Artificial Intelligence* 12, no. 3 (November 1979): 273–97. https://doi.org/10.1016/0004-3702(79)90009-2.

Schauster, Erin E., Patrick Ferrucci, and Marlene S. Neill. "Native Advertising Is the New Journalism: How Deception Affects Social Responsibility." *American Behavioral Scientist* 60, no. 12 (November 2016): 1408–24. https://doi.org/10.1177/0002764216660135.

Schillinger, Dean, and Cristin Kearns. "Guidelines to Limit Added Sugar Intake: Junk Science or Junk Food?" *Annals of Internal Medicine* 166 (2017): 305–6, https://doi.org/10.7326/M16-2754.

Scholz-Crane, Anne. "Evaluating the Future: A Preliminary Study of the Process of How Undergraduate Students Evaluate Web Sources," *Reference Services Review* 26, no. 3/4 (1998): 53–60.

Seigenthaler, John. "A False Wikipedia 'Biography' Sparks Reflection." *USA Today*, December 12, 2005.

Selbey, W. Gardner. "CDC Accepts All Manner of Reported Vaccination Effects, Even Symptoms of the Hulk." *Politifact*, May 11, 2017. https://www.politifact.com/factchecks/2017/may/11/bill-zedler/bill-zedler-insists-program-doesnt-collect-wide-ra/.

Shellenbarger, Sue. "Most Students Don't Know When News Is Fake, Stanford Study Finds." *Wall Street Journal*, November 21, 2016. https://www.wsj.com/articles/most-students-dont-know-when-news-is-fake-stanford-study-finds-1479752576.

Simon, Herbert. "Designing Organizations for an Information-Rich World." In *Computers, Communications, and the Public Interest*, edited by Martin Greenberger, 40–41. Baltimore: Johns Hopkins Press, 1971.

Simonite, Tim. "What Really Happened When Google Ousted Timnit Gebru," *Wired*, June 8, 2021. https://www.wired.com/story/google-timnit-gebru-ai-what-really-happened/.

Sirrah, Ava. "Guide to Native Advertising." *Columbia Journalism Review*, September 6, 2019. https://www.cjr.org/tow_center_reports/native-ads.php.

Smith, Michelle R. "How a Kennedy Built an Anti-Vaccine Juggernaut amid COVID-19." *Associated Press*, December 15 2021. https://apnews.com/article/how-rfk-jr-built-anti-vaccine-juggernaut-amid-covid-4997be1bcf591fe8b7f1f90d16c9321e.

Southern Poverty Law Center. "American College of Pediatricians." Extremist Files. Accessed January 21, 2023. https://www.splcenter.org/fighting-hate/extremist-files/group/american-college-pediatricians.

Stanford History Education Group. "Dot-Orgs Spreading Hate: Southern Poverty Law

Center Hate Group Domain Research." Research Note B-2019.12. Stanford History Education Group, Stanford University, November 23, 2019. https://stacks.stanford.edu/file/druid:vt471sv7857/SHEG%20Research%20Note-%20Dot-Orgs%20and%20Hate%20Groups.pdf.

Steel, Sarah, Gary Ruskin, Lejla Sarcevic, Martin McKee, and David Stuckler. "Are Industry-Funded Charities Promoting Advocacy-Led Studies or Evidence-Based Science? A Case Study of the International Life Sciences Institute." *Globalization and Health* 15 (2019): 36. https://doi.org/10.1186/s12992-019-0478-6.

Steinmetz, Katy. "How Your Brain Tricks You into Believing Fake News." *Time*, August 9, 2018. https://time.com/5362183/the-real-fake-news-crisis/.

Stifling Free Speech: Technological Censorship and the Public Discourse, before the Committee on the Judiciary, Subcommittee on the Constitution. April 19, 2019. Testimony of Dr. Francesca Tripodi, Assistant Professor of Sociology, James Madison University. https://www.judiciary.senate.gov/meetings/stifling-free-speech-technological-censorship-and-the-public-discourse.

"Suitcases Filled with Ballots; Hidden under Table; Counted without Oversight." Facts Matter. December 3, 2020. YouTube video, 12:50. Accessed March 26, 2022. https://www.youtube.com/watch?v=wB7jhXvFl0k. Video no longer available.

Sullivan, Danny. "A Reintroduction to Google's Featured Snippets." Google company blog, January 30, 2018. https://blog.google/products/search/reintroduction-googles-featured-snippets/.

Sullivan, M. Connor. "Why Librarians Can't Fight Fake News." *Journal of Librarianship and Information Science* 51, no. 4 (2019): 1146–56. https://doi.org/10.1177/0961000618764258.

Supiano, Beckie. "Students Fall for Misinformation Online: Is Teaching Them to Read Like Fact Checkers the Solution?" *Chronicle of Higher Education*, April 25, 2019. https://www.chronicle.com/article/students-fall-for-misinformation-online-is-teaching-them-to-read-like-fact-checkers-the-solution/.

Supran, Geoffrey, and Naomi Oreskes. "Assessing ExxonMobil's Climate Change Communication (1977–2014)." *Environmental Research Letters*, 12 (2017).

Szep, Jason, and Linda So. "Inside Trump's Campaign to Demonize Two Georgia Election Workers." Reuters, December 1, 2021. https://www.reuters.com/investigates/special-report/usa-election-threats-georgia/.

Terry, Robert J. "Why Mars Inc. Is Telling Its Story after Decades of Avoiding the Spotlight." *Washington Business Journal*, March 4, 2018. https://www.bizjournals.com/washington/news/2018/03/01/why-mars-inc-is-telling-its-story-after-decades-of.html.

Thorndike-Breeze, Rebecca, Cecelia A. Musselman, and Amy Carleton. "Three Links: Be Bold, Assume Good Faith, and There Are No Firm Rules." In *Wikipedia @ 30: Stories of an*

Incomplete Revolution, edited by Joseph Reagle and Jackie Koerner, 117. Cambridge, MA: MIT Press, 2020.

Turner, Ben. "Millions of Palm-Sized Flying Spiders Could Invade the East Coast." *Scientific American*, March 7, 2022. https://www.scientificamerican.com/article/millions-of -palm-sized-flying-spiders-could-invade-the-east-coast/.

US Department of Health and Human Services Office of the Surgeon General. "National Strategy for Suicide Prevention: Goals and Objectives for Action." National Action Alliance for Suicide Prevention. Washington, DC: US Department of Health and Human Services, 2012. http://www.surgeongeneral.gov/library/reports/national-strategy -suicide-prevention/overview.pdf.

"Video Shows Suitcases Filled with Ballots Pulled AFTER Supervisors Told Poll Workers to Leave." Donald J Trump. December 10, 2020. YouTube video, 2:38. https://www.you tube.com/watch?v=aCenojrUwVM.

Vrana, Adele Godoy, Ansuya Sengupta, and Siko Bouterse. "Toward a Wikipedia for and from Us All." In *Wikipedia @ 30: Stories of an Incomplete Revolution*, edited by Joseph Reagle and Jackie Koerner, 239–57. Cambridge, MA: MIT Press, 2020.

Wagner, Bayliss. "Fact Check: Deceptive Edit of Interview with CDC Director Misleads on COVID-19 Deaths." *USA Today*, February 2, 2022. https://www.usatoday.com/story /news/factcheck/2022/02/02/fact-check-deceptive-edit-cdc directors-interview-goes -viral/9169511002/.

Warnica, Richard. "Australian Birds Have Weaponized Fire Because What We Really Need Now Is Something Else to Make Us Afraid." *National Post*, January 9, 2018. https:// nationalpost.com/news/world/australian-birds-have-weaponized-fire.

Warzel, Charlie. "Don't Go Down the Rabbit Hole." *New York Times*, February 18, 2021. https://www.nytimes.com/2021/02/18/opinion/fake-news-media-attention.html.

Weaver, Brilee. "From Digital Native to Digital Expert." Harvard Graduate School of Education. *Usable Knowledge*, June 7, 2018. https://www.gse.harvard.edu/news/uk/18/06 /digital-native-digital-expert.

Weisberg, Lauren, Angela Kohnen, and Kara Dawson. "Impacts of a Digital Literacy Intervention on Preservice Teachers' Civic Online Reasoning Abilities, Strategies and Perceptions." *Journal of Technology and Teacher Education* 30, no. 1 (2022): 73–98. https://www .learntechlib.org/primary/p/220255/.

"What Site Owners Should Know about Google's August 2019 Core Update." *Google Search Central Blog*, August 1, 2019. https://developers.google.com/search/blog/2019/08/core -updates.

Willingham, Daniel T. "Does Tailoring Instruction to 'Learning Styles' Help Students Learn?" *American Educator*, Summer 2018. https://www.aft.org/ae/summer2018 /willingham.

Wineburg, Sam. *Historical Thinking and Other Unnatural Acts: Charting the Future of Teaching the Past*. Philadelphia: Temple, 2001.

————. "To Navigate the Web You Need Critical Thinking, But Also Critical Ignoring." *The Conversation*, 13 May 2021.

————. *Why Learn History (When It's Already on Your Phone)*. Chicago: University of Chicago Press, 2018.

Wineburg, Sam, Joel Breakstone, Nadav Ziv, and Mark D. Smith. "Educating for Misunderstanding: How Approaches to Teaching Digital Literacy Make Students Susceptible to Scammers, Rogues, Bad Actors & Hate Mongers." Working Paper A-21322. Stanford History Education Group. Stanford, CA: Stanford University, 2020. https://purl.stanford.edu/mf412bt5333.

Wineburg, Sam, Joel Breakstone, Sarah McGrew, Mark Smith, and Teresa Ortega. "Lateral Reading on the Open Internet: A District-Wide Field Study in High School Government Classes." *Journal of Educational Psychology* 114, no. 5 (2022): 893–909. https://doi.org/10.1037/edu0000740.

Wineburg, Sam, and Sarah McGrew. "Lateral Reading and the Nature of Expertise: Reading Less and Learning More When Evaluating Digital Information." *Teachers College Record* 121 (November 2019):1–40. https://doi.org/10.1177/016146811912101102.

Wineburg, Sam, Sarah McGrew, Joel Breakstone, and Teresa Ortega. "Evaluating Information: The Cornerstone of Civic Online Reasoning." Stanford History Education Group, November 22, 2016. https://stacks.stanford.edu/file/druid:fv751yt5934/SHEG%20Evaluating%20Information%20Online.pdf.

Wineburg, Sam, and Nadav Ziv. "Why Can't a Generation That Grew Up Online Spot the Misinformation in Front of Them?" *Los Angeles Times*, November 6, 2020. https://www.latimes.com/opinion/story/2020-11-06/colleges-students-recognize-misinformation.

————. "The Meaninglessness of the .ORG Domain." *New York Times*, December 1, 2020. https://www.nytimes.com/2019/12/05/opinion/dot-org-domain.html.

Wojdynski, Bartosz W., and Nathaniel J. Evans. "Going Native: Effects of Disclosure Position and Language on the Recognition and Evaluation of Online Native Advertising." *Journal of Advertising* 45 (2016): 157–68.

Woodard, Alfre. "Alfre Woodard Reads Sojourner Truth." Voices of a People's History of the United States. May 10, 2008. YouTube video, 3:43. https://www.youtube.com/watch?v=4vr_vKsk_h8&t=4s.

Young, Patrick. "When Lost Causers Drink from the Devil's Punchbowl They Are All Wet." *The Reconstruction Era* (blog), March 10, 2020. https://thereconstructionera.com/when-lost-causers-drink-from-the-devils-punchbowl-they-are-all-wet/.

Zarrintan, Sina. "Ejaculation as a Potential Treatment of Nasal Congestion in Mature

Males." *Medical Hypotheses* 71, no. 2 (2008). https://doi.org/10.1016/j.mehy.2008.03
.010.

Ziv, Nadav, and Emma Bene. "Preparing College Students for a Digital Age: A Survey of Instructional Approaches to Spotting Misinformation." *College & Research Libraries* 83, no.
6 (2022), https://doi.org/10.5860/crl.83.6.905.

INDEX